S0-AGL-632

TRANSFORMING THE PEACE PROCESS IN NORTHERN IRELAND

TRANSFORMING THE PEACE PROCESS IN NORTHERN IRELAND

From Terrorism to Democratic Politics

Editors

AARON EDWARDS
STEPHEN BLOOMER

Foreword by
RICHARD ENGLISH

IRISH ACADEMIC PRESS
DUBLIN • PORTLAND, OR

First published in 2008 by Irish Academic Press

44 Northumberland Road,
Ballsbridge,
Dublin 4, Ireland

920 NE 58th Avenue, Suite 300
Portland, Oregon,
97213-3786

www.iap.ie

copyright © 2008 This edition Irish Academic Press
Chapters copyright © 2008 individual contributors

British Library Cataloguing in Publication Data
An entry can be found on request

ISBN 978 0 7165 2955 2 (cloth)
ISBN 978 0 7165 2956 9 (paper)

Library of Congress Cataloging-in-Publication Data
An entry can be found on request

All rights reserved. Without limiting the rights under copyright reserved alone,
no part of this publication may be reproduced, stored in or introduced into a
retrieval system, or transmitted, in any form or by any means (electronic,
mechanical, photocopying, recording or otherwise) without the prior written
permission of both the copyright owner and the above publisher of this book.

Printed by Biddles Ltd., King's Lynn, Norfolk

For Jim, Barbara, Ryan and Stephanie Edwards;
and for Fiona, Georgia and Martha Bloomer and
Harry and Yvonne Bloomer

Contents

PART I POLITICAL IDENTITIES AND IDEOLOGIES
AFTER THE BELFAST AGREEMENT

PART II   PARAMILITARIES AND POLITICIANS

PART III   NGOs, STATE STRATEGIES AND
CONFLICT TRANSFORMATION

PART IV   POST-CONFLICT NORTHERN IRELAND AND
THE INTERNATIONAL DIMENSION

Foreword

According to some accounts, the Northern Ireland peace process has lasted longer than the war process which preceded it. And just as the Ulster conflict generated a strikingly vast literature, so too the Peace Process has now prompted shelves of analysis and commentary.

This current book – *Transforming the Peace Process in Northern Ireland: From Terrorism to Democratic Politics* – makes an important contribution to that latter literature, and offers rich insight into the decade that has elapsed since Northern Ireland's 1998 Belfast Agreement. The editors have assembled an impressively expert team, and their coverage is far-reaching and balanced. James McAuley, Claire Mitchell, Lyndsey Harris and Stephen Bloomer offer valuable reflections on Ulster loyalism, while Christopher Farrington develops his already significant body of writing on Ulster unionist politics. Catherine O'Donnell and Kevin Bean write sharply on Irish republicanism, and Jonathan Tonge casts a wise eye over nationalist political realities. Neil Jarman and Anthony McIntyre comment very thoughtfully on paramilitary politics, Paul Dixon analyses the important subject of British governmental policy, and the international dynamics of peace processes are usefully assessed by Aaron Edwards, Michael Kerr and Eamonn O'Kane.

In addition to this strong team of authors, the book seems to me to possess four main strengths.

First, it focuses attention on all levels of political change, from the high-political to the particular realities of the back alley. From international context to the most localised of exigencies, the story is carefully told, and this means that the book avoids either myopic parochialism or overly schematic and bland generalisation.

Second, the book draws on the expertise of scholars from a wide variety of disciplines, and this is vital if we are truly to learn collective lessons about such episodes as those of the past decade in a fluid Northern Ireland.

Third, the book pays more attention than most to what will surely emerge as the most pressing group for study in Northern Ireland in the coming generation: the loyalist population in Ulster. As the editors note, Irish republicanism has attracted attention from 'countless academic and non-specialist commentators' since the birth of the Provisional IRA in 1969. Despite the excellent pioneering work of scholars and writers such as Steve Bruce, Sarah Nelson, James McAuley, Henry McDonald and Jim Cusack, it is only comparatively recently that loyalism has become an appropriately fashionable and seriously-regarded subject for study by significant numbers of people. Quite rightly, Edwards and Bloomer have placed loyalism firmly at the centre of their discussions, and this is important.

Fourth, the Northern Ireland transformation is also now, of course, of international interest to those preoccupied with other conflicts. In a post-9/11 setting, the Northern Irish sea change is increasingly examined by many who want – perhaps rather naively – to learn the lessons of how terrorism ends. In truth, there are no easily applied lessons to be transported around the globe. But there are aspects of what has (and what has not) changed in Northern Ireland which might valuably be reflected on, in hard-headed fashion, by those who are keen to avoid the unnecessary prolonging of futile political violence. Within that ongoing debate, this book will take its deserving place.

Professor Richard English
Queen's University Belfast

Preface and Acknowledgements

This book evolved out of a desire on the part of the editors to examine the Northern Ireland peace process from a variety of empirical and theoretical perspectives across a number of academic disciplines. Initially, we sought to bridge the gap between academics and practitioners in the study of Ulster loyalist politics and ideology in detail, but very quickly realised that we needed a more holistic and rounded analysis of the peace process in general, which included an appreciation of the ways that loyalism related to unionism and how republicanism related to nationalism and, importantly, how they interacted with one another at the 'top level', 'middle range' and 'grass-roots' levels. For those of us working on peace-building initiatives in the community/voluntary sector in Northern Ireland the disconnection between these spheres in the academic literature on the conflict seemed rather odd, especially when one considers that the political forces in the province today emerged from – and were shaped by – the street politics which took root in the late 1960s and early 1970s.

Living and working at the 'middle-range' and 'grassroots' levels, we have observed at first hand the destructive effects of the long war. That political violence and sectarian antagonism have taken their toll on the everyday lives of ordinary people – particularly along the interfaces – is the great tragedy of 'the troubles'. The paramilitary ceasefires of 1994 (and the Provisional IRA's reinstatement of theirs in 1997) and the resulting Belfast Agreement of 1998 saw the de-escalation of the military dimension of the conflict. However, it was to be almost a decade of 'stop–start' negotiations before the political process finally bedded down. The establishment of a devolved power-sharing administration on 8 May 2007, although by no means a perfect compromise between ethno-political rivals in the DUP and Sinn Féin, gives us much hope for the future.

Both of us have been fortunate to work alongside people who recognise the value of community development, peace-building and conflict transformation across the ethno-political divide. One such person who merits a brief mention here is the former UVF prisoner and senior PUP strategist, Billy Mitchell, who died suddenly in July 2006. Billy came to peace-building following his incarceration for his prior involvement in paramilitarism, although he soon came to recognise better than anybody the futility of political violence. Following fourteen years in prison for his part in the conflict, Billy dedicated his remaining fourteen years to redressing the legacy of the violent past. In the wake of the ceasefires, Billy – together with Liam Maskey – established Intercomm, a conflict mediation and social justice NGO dedicated to eradicating the root causes of political violence in Northern Ireland. During his oration at Billy's funeral Liam said:

> Billy was a man before his time. He was a visionary and passionately longed for peace between our two communities. But he wasn't just a visionary. He was a doer. Billy was a true leader in every sense of the word and a man who people found it easy to follow but hard to live up to. Not only did he walk the talk he demanded that everyone walk with him. While in that lonely position of leadership he was always at the forefront of guiding and directing people and events.

The journeys both of these men took away from violent conflict and towards the path of peace-building and conflict transformation is remarkable and something that should serve as a stark reminder to those who believe that the Northern Ireland peace process transpired only because political elites eventually struck a deal. Furthermore, while it is true to say that endogenous and exogenous factors undoubtedly played a key role in ending the long war, too essentialist a view denies the capacity of rational actors to transform their identities and ideological outlook in what remains a fluid socio-political environment. Many former combatants have learned the value of dialogue and how to resolve their differences non-violently only by 'walking the talk'. Moreover, it could be argued that civil society filled the vacuum left by years of political stalemate, when elites proved incapable of brokering a deal; it is only appropriate that these 'grassroots' and 'middle-range' actors (to paraphrase the scholar and conflict transformation practitioner, John Paul Lederach) are juxtaposed alongside 'top-level' elites in a volume such as this.

There are a number of people we wish to thank here. We would first and foremost like to pay tribute to our contributors for staying the course with the project. Our joint thanks must go to Professor Richard English, who has been a consistent supporter of the idea for this book from concept to completion and who generously took time to write the Foreword. Aaron Edwards would also like to thank Professor Graham Walker, Professor Lord Bew of Donegore, Dr Margaret O'Callaghan and Professor Adrian Guelke, who provided much support and advice during his postgraduate studies, as well as the Head of School, Professor Shane O'Neill, and other members of staff in the School of Politics, International Studies and Philosophy at Queen's University Belfast who were continually supportive of research seminars and conferences he organised over the years. Stephen Bloomer would like to thank Professor Adrian Guelke for his encouragement and guidance on academic matters and Stevie Nolan, Joe Law and the late Billy Mitchell for their inspiration over very many years. He would also like to pay tribute to his family: his parents, Harry and Yvonne, for their support, and his wife and daughters, Fiona, Georgia and Martha Bloomer, for the inspiration and confidence they give to him and their boundless good humour. Aaron Edwards thanks his parents, Jim and Barbara, for their continued support and encouragement and also his brother and sister, Ryan and Stephanie, for being there when they were needed most. We dedicate this book to our families as a small token of our appreciation.

Aaron Edwards and Stephen Bloomer

List of Contributors

Kevin Bean is a Lecturer in the Institute of Irish Studies at the University of Liverpool. His recent publications include: 'Defining Republicanism: Shifting Discourses of New Nationalism and Post-Republicanism', in Elliott, M. (ed.), *The Long Road to Peace* (Liverpool University Press, 2002), and *Republican Voices*, co-edited with Mark Hayes (Seesyu Press, 2001). He has contributed articles on Irish republicanism and the peace process to various newspapers, magazines and journals.

Stephen Bloomer, BA (Hons), MSSc, is Project Co-ordinator of *The Other View*, an inter-community, cross-border quarterly periodical. He was previously Policy Officer at Interaction Belfast, Policy and Research Communications Officer at the Community Foundation for Northern Ireland, and a researcher with Counteract (1999–2002), where he conducted an in-depth ethnographic study of the effects of the Shankill Feud of 2000–01. Also at Counteract he completed empirical research on the Non-Violent Social Change Initiative (later the Duncrun Cultural Initiative), which was designed to politicise loyalist ex-combatants. He has written numerous policy-orientated research reports for a range of community organisations and sits on the Board of Directors of Community Evaluation Northern Ireland.

Paul Dixon is a Senior Lecturer in Politics and International Studies at the University of Kingston, London. He is author of *Northern Ireland: The Politics of War and Peace* (Palgrave, 2001, second edition, 2008) and *The Northern Ireland Peace Process: Choreography and Theatrical Politics* (Routledge, 2008). He has published numerous articles and chapters on Northern Ireland (British policy, counterinsurgency, the peace process and the international dimension), conflict resolution theory and Kosovo in the journals *Political Studies, Political Science Quarterly, Political Quarterly, Civil Wars* and the *Journal of Peace Research.*

Aaron Edwards is the Co-ordinator of the 'Journeys Out: From Conflict to Participation' project at INCORE, a University of Ulster/United Nations University centre for excellence in conflict and peace studies. He completed his PhD in the School of Politics, International Studies and Philosophy at Queen's University Belfast in 2006. His publications include: 'Democratic Socialism and Sectarianism: The Northern Ireland Labour Party and Progressive Unionist Party Compared', *Politics*, 27, 1 (2007), pp. 24–31 and 'Social Democracy and Partition: The British Labour Party and Northern Ireland, 1951–64', *Journal of Contemporary History*, 42, 4 (2007), pp. 595–612. His monograph, *Democratic Socialism and Sectarianism: A History of the Northern Ireland Labour Party*, is forthcoming from Manchester University Press.

Christopher Farrington is a Research Fellow in the School of Politics and International Relations at University College Dublin. He was previously a Lecturer in Politics and a Government of Ireland Postdoctoral Fellow in the same department. In 2003 he was awarded a PhD from Queen's University Belfast, and he has worked as a Research Fellow at the same institution. He has contributed several articles in the journals *Irish Political Studies, Irish Studies Review*, the *Journal of Contemporary European History* and *Political Studies*. His book *Ulster Unionism and the Peace Process in Northern Ireland* was published by Palgrave Macmillan in 2006.

Lyndsey Harris graduated from King's College, London, with a BA (Hons) in War Studies and History in 2003. She is currently completing her PhD in the School of Economics and Politics at the University of Ulster at Jordanstown on the project 'A Strategic Analysis of Loyalist Paramilitaries in Northern Ireland'. Her recent publications include 'Introducing the Strategic Approach: An Examination of Loyalist Paramilitaries in Northern Ireland', *British Journal of Politics and International Relations*, 8, 4 (2005), pp. 539–49.

Neil Jarman is the Director of the Institute for Conflict Research, an independent social policy research organisation based in Belfast. He holds a PhD from Trinity College Dublin. His recent publications include: *Material Conflicts* (Berg, 1997) and *Displaying Faith* (Institute of Irish Studies, QUB, 1999), in addition to numerous papers published in journals such as *Terrorism and Political Violence*, the *Journal of Material Culture*, *Critical Anthropology*, *Peace Review*, *Folklore*, *Fordham International Law Review*, *Youth and Policy*, *Children and Society* and *Child Care in Practice*. He has published numerous reports and papers on issues related to the management of public order, and is currently completing a study of community-based policing activity in Belfast funded by the Royal Irish Academy.

Michael Kerr is a Leverhulme Research Fellow in the Department of International History at the London School of Economics, where he completed his PhD in 2003. He specialises in ethnic conflict regulation and power-sharing in divided societies. His present research interests focus on conflict in the Middle East and Northern Ireland. His books *Imposing Power-Sharing: Conflict and Coexistence in Northern Ireland and Lebanon* and *Transforming Unionism: David Trimble and the 2005 General Election* were published by Irish Academic Press in 2005. His most recent publications include 'Approaches to Power-sharing in Northern Ireland and Lebanon', in Miller, Rory (ed.), *Ireland and the Middle East: Trade, Society and Peace* (Irish Academic Press, 2007) and 'The Philosophy of Lebanese Power-sharing', in Choueiri, Y. (ed.), *Breaking the Cycle: Civil Wars in Lebanon* (Centre for Lebanese Studies, 2007).

James W. McAuley is Professor of Political Sociology and Irish Studies at the University of Huddersfield. His recent publications include: *An Introduction to Politics, State and Society* (Sage Publications, 2003) and *(Re) Constructing Ulster Loyalism* (Pluto, 2007). He has contributed several chapters to edited collections and academic journals, including the *Journal of Social Issues*, the *Global Review of Ethnopolitics* (now *Ethnopolitics*), *Irish Political Studies*, *Political Psychology*, *Terrorism and Political Violence* and *Etudes Irlandaises*.

Anthony McIntyre is a former IRA volunteer and ex-republican prisoner. He completed his doctoral thesis, a study of the provisional Irish republican movement, between 1969 and 1973, at Queen's University Belfast in 1999. His recent publications include 'Provisional Republicanism – Internal Politics, Inequities and Modes of Repression', in McGarry, Fearghal (ed.), *Republicanism in Modern Ireland* (UCD Press, 2003) and 'Modern Irish Republicanism and the Belfast Agreement: Chickens Coming Home to Roost, or Turkeys Celebrating Christmas?', in Wilford, Rick (ed.), *Aspects of the Belfast Agreement* (Oxford University Press, 2001). At present he is co-editor of the online journal *The Blanket* and a frequent contributor to the broadcast and print media.

Claire Mitchell is a Lecturer in the School of Sociology and Social Policy at Queen's University Belfast. Her previous research focused on religion and politics in Northern Ireland and her book, *Religion, Identity and Politics in Northern Ireland: Boundaries of Belonging and Belief*, was published by Ashgate in 2005. She has published numerous articles on religion and politics in *Sociology*, *Irish Political Studies*, *Ethnic and Racial Studies*, *Political Studies* and *Sociology of Religion*. Her current research projects focus on evangelicalism in Britain and Ireland, religion and ethnicity, Ulster loyalism and moral values and voting behaviour.

Catherine O'Donnell received her PhD from the School of Politics, International Studies and Philosophy at Queen's University Belfast in 2004. She was a Research Fellow at the same institution in 2004–05. She is the author of articles in the journals *Irish Political Studies* and *Contemporary British History*. Her book, *Fianna Fáil, Irish Republicanism and the Northern Ireland Troubles, 1968–2005*, was published by Irish Academic Press in 2007. Dr O'Donnell was latterly a Government of Ireland Postdoctoral Fellow at the Humanities Institute of Ireland at University College Dublin in 2005–07.

Eamonn O'Kane is a Senior Lecturer in Politics at the University of Wolverhampton. He has published on the Northern Ireland conflict, British–Irish relations and aspects of conflict resolution theory in the journals *International Politics*, *Contemporary British History*, *Civil Wars*, *Irish Political Studies* and *Irish Studies in International Affairs*. His monograph, *The Totality of Relationships: Britain, Ireland and the Northern Ireland Conflict since 1980*, was published by Routledge in 2007.

Jonathan Tonge is Professor of Politics at the University of Liverpool and Chair of the Political Studies Association of the United Kingdom. His recent books include *Northern Ireland* (Polity, 2006); *The New Northern Irish Politics* (Palgrave, 2005); *Sinn Féin and the SDLP* (Hurst/O'Brien, 2005; with Gerard Murray) and *Northern Ireland: Conflict and Change* (Pearson, 2002). He has also published a wide range of journal articles and book chapters on Northern Ireland.

List of Abbreviations

APNI Alliance Party of Northern Ireland
CRC Community Relations Council
DFA Department of Foreign Affairs (Ireland)
DUP Democratic Unionist Party
EACTF East Antrim Conflict Transformation Forum
INLA Irish National Liberation Army
IRA Irish Republican Army
IRSP Irish Republican Socialist Party
MLA Member of the Legislative Assembly
NGO Non-governmental Organisation
NIO Northern Ireland Office
OIRA Official IRA
PIRA Provisional Irish Republican Army
PSNI Police Service of Northern Ireland
PUP Progressive Unionist Party (provides political analysis to UVF/RHC)
RHC Red Hand Commando (satellite of UVF)
RUC Royal Ulster Constabulary
SDLP Social Democratic and Labour Party
SF Sinn Féin
UDA Ulster Defence Association
UDP Ulster Democratic Party (now defunct political wing of the UDA/UFF)
UDR Ulster Defence Regiment
UFF Ulster Freedom Fighters (military wing of the UDA)
UPRG Ulster Political Research Group (provides political analysis to UDA/UFF)
UUP Ulster Unionist Party
UVF Ulster Volunteer Force

Introduction
Transforming the Peace Process:
From Terrorism to Democratic Politics?

Aaron Edwards and Stephen Bloomer

The transition from long war to long peace in Northern Ireland has exposed inherent contradictions and tensions within, first, Ulster loyalism and between loyalism and unionism; and, second, within Irish republicanism and between republicanism and nationalism. There now appears to be a clear demarcation between those prepared to take risks for peace and those 'spoilers' (in the main tiny republican ultra groupings) poised and ready to thwart attempts to find peaceful co-existence in this deeply divided society. This book focuses on the transitional period between the Belfast Agreement of 1998 and the return of a devolved power-sharing administration on 8 May 2007, as paramilitary groups and their political confidents adjusted to the rigours of democratic participation. It delineates the key stumbling-blocks in the 'peace' and 'political' processes and examines in detail just how the transformation from paramilitarism to democratic politics is being managed by the key actors in the conflict. That communities traditionally sympathetic to paramilitarism are now making moves towards abandoning the option of 'armed struggle' in the 'new' Northern Ireland is a phenomenon hitherto under-explored by academics.

This volume aims to fill a gap in the literature by juxtaposing 'top-level' political party and inter-governmental politics alongside 'middle-range' civil society interventions and 'grassroots' community-level politics, which has developed – in its latent phase – since the paramilitary ceasefires of 1994. It addresses the central political ideologies, parties and identities in conflict as well as the methodologies by which paramilitary actors have sought to transform their organisations beyond violence in post-conflict Northern Ireland. It draws its contributors from across the disciplinary boundaries of political science, history, anthropology, sociology and political sociology. The book is placed within a broad and diverse analytical and theoretical framework, and several of its chapters engage with the contemporary debate on terrorism and political violence. Each contributor to the volume is a distinguished or emerging scholar, chosen specifically for the breadth of their conceptual insights and scholarly analysis of the Northern Ireland conflict.

FROM TERRORISM TO DEMOCRATIC POLITICS

Recent political developments in Northern Ireland have rekindled global interest in the politics of Ulster loyalism and Irish republican-ism. The end of the Provisional IRA's physical force campaign in 2005 signalled the closing of one bloody chapter in the bitter history of inter-communal conflict in Ireland and the heralding of new dangers, priorities and possibilities in Anglo-Irish relations. The return of devolved government and the sharing of power between two staunch rivals – the Democratic Unionist Party (DUP) and Sinn Féin – on 8 May 2007 may have surprised many, but, as some of the contrib-utors to the volume suggest, this rapprochement had been evident for some time.

To those familiar with the intricacies and complexities of the 'new' Northern Irish politics the IRA's moves to dismantle its war machine had been widely anticipated, especially in light of Al Qaeda's attacks in the United States on 11 September 2001, but the failure of loyalist paramilitaries to dump arms by entering into a symmetrical decommis-sioning process was perhaps a little more surprising. Moreover, the continuing bewilderment of outside audiences was understandably swollen by the scenes of working-class Protestants running amok in their own communities and turning their guns on the Police Service of Northern Ireland and the Home Service battalions of the Royal Irish Regiment in September 2005. Rightly or wrongly, loyalists, and indeed unionists generally, perceived their culture and tradition to be under threat, especially when the authorities re-routed a contentious Orange Order parade on the Springfield Road in West Belfast.

The self-destructive violence which continues to grip Protestant working-class housing estates has to be seen in the light of develop-ments within that community since the signing of the Belfast Agreement. One respected journalist even suggested that:

> The sight of hard-line Protestants expressing their insecurities by attacking the security forces is nothing new. It has been happen-ing for so long, a couple of hundred years, that any sense of paradox or incongruity has long since gone. It is, rather, the resort of the chronically inarticulate. The issue of the Orange march was

simply the last straw for many parts of loyalism, a brutal, ugly *cri de coeur* from people who feel friendless, leaderless and out of sorts with the world.[1]

Yet it also has to be considered in the context of the British government's peace strategy in Northern Ireland. Arguably, unionism has always been an integral component in the search for peace in Ireland but its continued alienation from that process has led many Protestants to believe that their political voice has been banished to the wilderness, forever to be refrigerated in what the former Secretary of State for Northern Ireland John Reid called 'a cold place for Protestants'.[2]

'A WATCHING BRIEF': LOYALISTS AND THE PEACE PROCESS

Loyalists have always maintained that in the event of a 'war is over' statement from the Provisional IRA their armed campaign would also cease. In 1991 the Ulster Volunteer Force (UVF), Red Hand Commando (RHC), Ulster Defence Association (UDA) and Ulster Freedom Fighters (UFF) under the auspices of the Combined Loyalist Military Command (CLMC) called a ceasefire to facilitate political dialogue between the then Secretary of State for Northern Ireland Peter Brooke and the four main parties. Arguably, the ingredients of the current peace process can be dated to this period, especially when the British government reiterated that it had no 'selfish, strategic or economic interest' in the province; thereby laying the groundwork for political engagement by republicans. The ceasefire held between 30 April and 4 July 1991 and demonstrated that the loyalist paramilitary campaign could ebb and flow in accordance with the tempo of the strategic political environment. As one senior loyalist recalled:

> The CLMC called a ceasefire during the Brooke Talks [1991] to provide the space for meaningful dialogue, with a view to a possible settlement. Loyalism had reached a point where it realised an end game was possible, but it had yet to figure out how the game would be played. A key problem during the ceasefire was that the move received no reciprocal gesture from mainstream unionism; neither the UUP [Ulster Unionist Party] nor DUP felt the need to engage with loyalism. That's when the CLMC decided that it would no longer have the mainstream unionist parties speaking on its behalf – we would have our own political representation.[3]

In many ways the genesis of the paramilitary ceasefires of 1994 can be traced to what later became known as the Brooke/Mayhew talks, a process which confirmed the importance of dialogue in resolving the conflict.

Between 2001 and 2007 the UVF maintained what it referred to as 'a watching brief' over republican and dissident loyalist activity. In the wake of IRA decommissioning it steadfastly refused to be drawn into a symmetrical process of disarmament. Reacting to IRA decommissioning in 2005 one senior UVF commander was at pains to stress how:

> Loyalism wasn't going to jump because the Provos jumped. Loyalists didn't see decommissioning on the radar screen. They did see an end to paramilitarism and they are (as we speak) trying to get to that point. They are not making anyone any promises. I would be quietly confident that at some juncture we can get to the point where there is no paramilitary action from the UVF.[4]

It was to take almost two years of 'internal consultation' before the UVF finally declared an end to its armed campaign. On 3 May 2007 it announced how:

> All recruitment has ceased, military training has ceased, targeting has ceased and all intelligence rendered obsolete, all active service units have been de-activated, all ordinance has been put beyond reach.[5]

The statement was read out by Gusty Spence, the 'alpha and omega' of violent loyalist paramilitarism, and it effectively heralded an end to the group's paramilitary activities. Unsurprisingly the UVF failed to deliver on decommissioning and – along with the UDA – seems unlikely to do so in the immediate future.

Too often commentators have displayed an inability to objectively assess the social and political environment in which loyalist politicians and paramilitants find themselves co-existing. And even fewer actually apply rigorous investigative techniques in their studies of the origins and development of paramilitarism among the Protestant community. This book aims to consider the broad range of understandings and values with which loyalists (and republicans) construct their everyday worldview. By analysing how they articulate their discourse and ideologies it is possible to apprehend a truer reflection of the socio-political reality of Northern Irish politics and society.

In many ways the complexities underpinning Northern Irish politics and society have intrigued both those scholars seeking to comprehend the conflict within narrow disciplinary strictures, and those searching for a more holistic interpretation of 'the Troubles'. Similarly, there are many questions being asked in policy-making circles about the nature and trajectory of paramilitary violence and how it might be addressed. Clearly these questions cannot be answered by focusing on only one side of this divided community, nor will they be answered by focusing too much attention on any two political actors such as the DUP and Sinn Féin, or even on the apparently symbiotic relationship between Provisional republicanism and the British state. Other key actors have been performing on the socio-political stage in Northern Ireland too – albeit with varying prominence and at different times – and their part in the conflict must also be explored. Recent events have brought into sharp focus some of the political divisions and differences within the Ulster Protestant community, but they have also shown the creative possibilities still being pursued by activists who wish to empower their beleaguered communities. Perhaps, then, it is an opportune time to shift the academic focus onto issues surrounding this sense of Protestant defeatism and growing Catholic confidence to examine positive examples of change within these marginalised communities.

ABANDONING 'ARMED STRUGGLE': REPUBLICANS AND THE PEACE PROCESS

Republicans, long the enemy in loyalist eyes, have excited the glare of countless academic and non-specialist commentators since the birth of the Provisionals in 1969–70. The boom in the terrorism literature since the 1970s can also be attributed to the proliferation of small arms across various continents during the Cold War, as well as a change in the endogenous ideological and structural positions of minority communities within states where dominant groups have ruled almost unopposed. In Ireland, the uncertainty generated by the fall of the Berlin Wall in 1989–90 seriously affected the orthodox perception of republican violence as anti-imperialist in nature and reconfigured the basis upon which the British state viewed its role in Northern Ireland since the Second World War.[6] Revisionist scholarship may have challenged the 'romantic' genre of terrorism and political violence literature in Ireland but few academics, if any, anticipated the paramilitary cease-fires of 1994 and even fewer were prepared to consider the possibility of various camps co-existing within the apparent monolith of Provisional republicanism.

The confirmation on 26 September 2005 that the Provisional IRA had finally decommissioned its weapons brought a major sigh of relief from those political actors intimately involved in the peace process. It also trumpeted Sinn Féin's move from a 'Brits out' agenda to participatory politics, the abandonment of former republican shibboleths concerning the legitimacy of violence, and the need for abstentionism and ideological purity. For many republicans the recent PIRA moves herald a new dawn for those activists wishing to embrace a purely non-violent social and political struggle. While the motivations behind IRA decommissioning are still largely unclear it seems likely that the pragmatic leadership of Gerry Adams and Martin McGuinness steered the organisation towards acceptance of a much diminished endgame.

Sinn Féin's emergence as the dominant nationalist force in Northern Ireland, at the expense of the SDLP, has had profound effects on the management of the peace process. The continuing differences between both parties in their interpretations of the Belfast Agreement have important ideological implications as both now articulate the need for a territorially defined nation-state. Moreover, the electoral and political advances of Sinn Féin in Northern Ireland have so far been limited in the Republic. The electoral battles between Sinn Féin and Fianna Fáil are far from over and will continue to have consequences for the future political dispensation of Northern Ireland, though for the moment the forward march of Sinn Féin's all-island political project has been halted.[7]

Despite the double-edged electoral successes one ought to recognise the long and winding road down which republican paramilitaries have travelled. In its thirty-five-year campaign against the British presence in Northern Ireland the Provisional IRA refused to be beaten. In the end the republican juggernaut was brought to a grinding halt by the Adams and McGuinness leadership. Although the age-old tradition of employing physical force to achieve Irish nationalist political objectives has been abandoned, the socio-political objectives of the republican movement remain.[8] This book aims to provide a critical discussion of these objectives by examining the peaceful methodology by which republicans are now seeking to realise them.

GRASSROOTS PEACE-BUILDING AND CONFLICT TRANSFORMATION INITIATIVES

Although there are countless explanations for the transformation in the Northern Ireland conflict, this book focuses on two key variables for understanding the abandonment of political violence by paramilitary groups in the region: 'the nature of the goals they seek and their relationship to the community they claim to represent'.[9] Both of these factors have been consistent since the outbreak of the Troubles and go some way in explaining the nature of the conflict and its possible solution. Moreover, since the 1994 paramilitary ceasefires many former combatants have sought to transform their communities beyond violence. Some have opted to work within conflict transformation initiatives or through involvement in organic peace and reconciliation NGOs as a means of reinvesting social capital back into their beleaguered communities. These grassroots-based groupings employ the weaponry of dialogue and legitimate lobbying as a means of communicating their political philosophy to rivals and opponents. In this more congenial post-conflict environment former opponents recognise the need to 'bury the hatchet' and settle their differences by non-violent means, which may ostensibly leave the door open to reconciliation between the two communities. As the scholar and conflict transformation practitioner John Paul Lederach has pointed out, '[t]he overall process of conflict transformation is related to our broader theme of reconciliation inasmuch as it is orientated toward changing the nature of relationships at every level of human interaction and experience.'[10] The capacity of key actors to recognise the position of the 'other' and envision a shared future is the key challenge in peace-building and conflict transformation.

Politically, however, the challenge of transforming this single-identity and inter-community work in a way that translates into electoral support for moderates and liberals is probably impossible. This relates to the fact that middle unionism is so unforgiving of past loyalist paramilitary activities, unlike their nationalist/republican counterparts, who seem to take such activities to their bosom with considerably more ease. It is obvious that the activities of some high-profile activists have tainted the public's perception of loyalism. There are undoubtedly individuals in it for the long haul who wish to do what is best for working-class communities. Consequently, the Progressive Unionist Party (PUP), aligned to the UVF, and the Ulster Political Research Group, aligned to the UDA, tend to deal with local issues while mainstream unionist parties are left to deal with the 'risky' game of high-stakes politics.

It could be argued that these grassroots-based actors are well-placed to aid in the breaking of the violent cycle of conflict. Yet it is important that all parties in conflict, in terms of Lederach's pyramidal conceptualisation of peace-building – which encompasses top-level elites and middle-range and grassroots actors – work together to maximise the transformational potential of conflict resolution and management strategies. Lederach argues that:

> Constructing a peace process in deeply divided societies and situations of internal armed conflict requires an operative frame of reference that takes into consideration the *legitimacy, uniqueness,* and *interdependency* of the needs and resources of the grass-roots, middle range, and top level. The same is true when dealing with the specific issues and broader systematic concerns in a conflict. More specifically, an integrative, comprehensive approach points toward the functional need for *recognition, inclusion,* and *coordination* across all levels and activities.[11]

The positive grassroots-driven initiatives superintended by loyalists and republicans sit somewhat uneasily in juxtaposition to the self-profiteering materialism of those criminal elements peppering paramilitary ranks. Nevertheless it seems that a new direction towards reinstating social justice and human rights has been embarked upon.

It is something of a truism that loyalists and republicans are their own worst enemies because of their tendency to split, haemorrhage and fluctuate at crucial points when the transformation process looms large on the distant horizon. Importantly, the ever-present 'sabre rattling' by dissidents remains a nuisance more than a real challenge for those wishing to transform their communities beyond sectarianism and political violence. Similarly, many commentators, prior to 8 May 2007, saw the electoral consolidation of the more 'extreme' varieties of unionism and nationalism in the 2005 elections to have stalled the prospects for a return to devolution and shared responsibility in the near future. This did not happen. Rather devolution returned and a sharing of power became a reality. However, trust has become a much more emotive issue in politics today as new cross-community roots are being laid. It necessitates recognising, in Lederach's words, that 'war – protracted armed conflict – is a system, a system that can be transformed only by taking a comprehensive approach to the people who operate it and to the setting in which it is rooted'.[12] This book is a contribution to that ongoing debate and discussion about contemporary conflict, of a violent nature, and the methodologies by which it can be transformed.

STRUCTURE OF THE BOOK

There are two principal reasons why this book is necessary. First, on the intellectual front: academia has failed to allot adequate research time to studying loyalist and republican politics at the elite, middle-range and grass-roots levels – and has only partially succeeded in its attempts to demystify the central political tenets of paramilitary activism associated with these two ideologies. Consequently an absence of dispassionate academic analysis of loyalist and republican politics and ideology has given way to the influence of journalistic sensationalism on public discourse and has hindered our understanding of the complexity of these social and political phenomena. Second, it is often forgotten how loyalists and republicans have sought to transform their respective communities from highly localised and inherently jingoistic entities into coherent social and political philosophies operating beyond traditional binary ethnic boundaries. The book's added value is that post-conflict Northern Ireland is placed within a comparative perspective by several of the authors, rather than viewed in isolation or in terms of the largely discredited perspective of 'a place apart'.[13]

In order to provide a comprehensive analysis of how the peace process is currently evolving, this edited collection is divided into four parts.

Part I focuses on the key dynamics animating loyalist and republican politics and situates these two ideologies within the broader frameworks of Ulster unionism and Irish nationalism. Issues explored in detail by the contributors include the pressures brought to bear on unionist hegemony by the development of an increasingly articulate form of class-based unionism by the PUP (McAuley; Farrington) and the evolving antagonism between the competing republicanisms of Fianna Fáil and Sinn Féin, which may dominate all-Ireland republican politics in the future (O'Donnell). A chapter on the development of Sinn Féin's republicanism is analysed in terms of its journey from a dual strategy of physical force and democratic politics, via a rejection of abstentionism, to a form of participatory politics (Tonge). Importantly, Tonge then provides an analysis of the displacement of constitutional nationalism in Northern Ireland by Sinn Féin.

Part II begins with an in-depth examination of the motivations, value systems and operational strategies of key actors in the propagation of loyalist political violence, an approach specifically employed to strip away the self-serving sensationalism of media reports and to move beyond the narrow disciplinary boundaries in much of the academic studies on political violence (Harris). This is followed by an examination of the relationship between politicians and paramilitaries (Bloomer). Probing questions are asked about the strategic nature of the PUP–UVF connection, especially in light of the fact that no serious conflict transformation strategy has been developed since the ceasefires of 1994. The strain placed on the PUP's capability to transform its military associates is highlighted, and it is suggested that the burden imposed on the party by this onerous task is the most telling factor in its recent electoral demise. A number of searching questions are also asked of the broader unionist family in relation to its complete disregard for the importance of reintegrating former combatants. McIntyre then addresses the question of dissent within loyalism and republicanism at the level of political and paramilitary leadership, perhaps one of the most under-explored aspects of the Northern Ireland peace process.

Part III examines the conflict management role of the voluntary/community sector, arguably a hitherto forgotten element of the peace process. Thus the centre of attention is not just on boardroom negotiations but also on cross-community dialogue at interface areas (Jarman). The involvement of loyalist ex-combatants in faith-based peace-building/conflict transformation schemes across Northern Ireland features prominently here (Mitchell). That loyalist and republican political ambitions appear to be rooted in community politics is something given critical consideration throughout this volume as a whole, but it is made more explicit in three of these chapters. In particular the development of the concept of community by the republican movement is charted over time, from community activism to full 'institutionalised' engagement with the British state as a partner in the peace process (Bean). The aims of the state in developing a social and economic strategy of community development to strengthen civil society are then explored. This section rounds off with a discussion of the political strategies deployed by the British state in meeting the challenge of peace-making in Northern Ireland and the perceptions of Britain's role in the conflict as held by the various key actors in the conflict (Dixon).

Part IV frames discussion of the peace process in a wider comparative perspective. Edwards considers the effects of political violence in comparative peace processes and asks how far the British state's negotiations with the IRA have been successful in neutralising the Provisionals' so-called 'armed struggle'. Many of the variables commonly associated with political violence in this case are also present in other territorially linked conflicts around the globe – for instance, strong ethnic group affiliations, the question of political legitimacy, the separatist ambitions held by a minority, and the asymmetrical relationship between a state power and an insurgent group.[14] Perhaps the most salient feature of the conflict in Northern Ireland is that it is essentially 'a quarrel involving two groups who wish to belong to different states'.[15] Thus, Protestant unionists wish to maintain their links with Great Britain, while Irish nationalists hold firm to their aspirations for a united and independent Ireland. Although both groups hold democratic views on constitutional matters, a cutting-edge response has also emerged – in the form of paramilitary organisations – in a bid to further these ethno-national goals by force of arms. The integrity of the quarrel has meant that any options tabled for a termination of the conflict have had to acknowledge the key role played by these armed non-state actors. The issue of decommissioning and strategies to address the question of arms is also highlighted here, with Kerr drawing illuminating comparisons between Northern Ireland and Lebanon. Finally, O'Kane assesses the comparisons between Northern Ireland and Sri Lanka in terms of the role of third parties in peace processes. In all three chapters Northern Ireland proves to be a useful model for conflict management.

Overall, this book delineates some of the important elements underpinning the peace process. In many ways some of the chapters raise more questions than they answer, though anyone who thinks that power-sharing has irreparably transformed the conflict beyond violence may be disappointed. Conflict transformation practitioners recognise that conflict in Northern Ireland – like quarrels elsewhere in the world – has merely entered a new phase in the development of human relationships. Although sectarianism persists and will not be eradicated until meaningful dialogue has taken place, there has been a reconfiguration of relationships within and between the two communities. The peace-building efforts of all three levels of leadership in the process must continue to work in concert if we are to begin to eradicate the dangers of deadly conflict and reconstruct our fractured society. Political elites at the top have certainly reached a deal and this has been accepted by middle-range actors, such as those from within civil society, although it will undoubtedly take another generation before this 'trickles down' to the grassroots. Thankfully, though, there are positive signs that this is beginning to happen.

NOTES

1. McKittrick, D., 'Violence in Belfast: How a Banned March Revived the Troubles', *Independent*, 14 September 2005.
2. McKittrick, D., 'Reid Calls for Move Beyond Sectarianism', *Independent*, 21 November 2001.
3. Interview with William 'Plum' Smith, 25 August 2004.
4. Interview with a senior UVF commander, 9 November 2005.
5. McKittrick, D., 'UVF "Deactivates" and Agrees to Put Weapons "Beyond Reach"', *Independent*, 4 May 2007.
6. Cox, M., 'Bringing in the "International": The IRA Ceasefire and the End of the Cold War', *International Affairs*, 73, 4 (1997), pp. 671–93.
7. McDonald, H., 'Sinn Féin's Hopes Dashed in Irish Elections' and 'United Ireland Plays No Part in the Election', *Observer*, 27 May 2007.
8. Irish Taoiseach Bertie Ahern writing in the *Irish Times*, 27 September 2005.
9. Richardson, L., *What Terrorists Want: Understanding the Terrorist Threat* (London: John Murray, 2006), p. 29.

10. Lederach, J.P., *Building Peace: Sustainable Reconciliation in Divided Societies* (Washington, DC: United States Institute of Peace, 1997), p. 84.
11. Ibid., p. 60. Emphasis in original.
12. Ibid., p. 18.
13. See McGarry, J., 'Introduction: The Comparable Northern Ireland', in McGarry, J. (ed.), *Northern Ireland and the Divided World: The Northern Ireland Conflict and the Good Friday Agreement in Comparative Perspective* (Oxford: Oxford University Press, 2001), pp. 1–33.
14. Horowitz, D.L., *Ethnic Groups in Conflict* (London: University of California Press, 2000); Zartman, I.W., 'Dynamics and Constraints in Negotiations in Internal Conflicts', in Zartman, I.W. (ed.), *Elusive Peace: Negotiating an End to Civil Wars* (Washington, DC: Brookings Institution, 1995), pp. 3–29.
15. McGarry, J., 'Political Settlements in Northern Ireland and South Africa', *Political Studies*, 46, 5 (December 1998), p. 854.

PART I

POLITICAL IDENTITIES AND IDEOLOGIES
AFTER THE BELFAST AGREEMENT

Chapter 1
Constructing Contemporary Loyalism

James W. McAuley

There is a painful process of adapting to change and the loss of dominance. There is the challenge of the due recognition of the other and of relationships of equality and mutuality. Some want to return to imagined yesterdays, to retreat from a future which looks more and more unpalatable. There is defensiveness, pain, denial and numbness. There are increasing tensions within Loyalist communities as a sense of hopelessness, abandonment and anger is turned inward ...[1]

Subjugation can play no part. Indeed, in a divided society – a zero-sum society, a 'them and us' society – subjugation must not play any part, for that would create an explosive situation, which would put us in deep trouble ... I ask Mr Adams [Sinn Féin] to take serious cognisance of the fears and difficulties of the Unionist community. Unionists feel that they are being subjugated and destabilised.[2]

INTRODUCTION

As Coakley[3] reminds us, while loyalist is now commonly used as a term to distinguish an ideology and politics in contradiction to mainstream unionism, it can also be seen to represent a strand of political action and thought (based on political radicalism, religious fundamentalism and tactical militancy) that has been present from the beginning within organised unionism. Loyalism took on its contemporary form after the outbreak of the conflict, with David Ervine of the Progressive Unionist Party (PUP) suggesting that it really began to be defined in the late 1960s as unionism fractured politically and ideologically and paramilitarism emerged.[4]

It would be wrong, however, to reduce loyalism simply to its physical force tradition.[5] Rather, loyalism has also continued to position itself around points of ideological and social difference, and has drawn on broader identifiable reference points. Loyalism generates and draws upon its own discourses and identifiable cultures and consistently promotes a distinct set of political values, transmitted through identifiable patterns of political socialisation. While to many general observers loyalism remains simply a form of unionist extremism, this is a far from adequate definition.

Loyalism has attempted to create ideological space, and to formulate independent political representation, while finding strong expression at the level of the everyday, often through strong feelings of 'belonging', which are characterised by political allegiance to Ulster[6] and strong declarations of devotion to the British crown, rather than to its government or political representatives.[7] Loyalism rests on an intense sense of socio-cultural and political difference.[8] It is the willingness to defend this sense of identity that has become central to contemporary understandings of loyalism.[9]

As has been pointed out, however, loyalism is a contradictory creed and, at times, loyalists have been far from inhibited in organising determined opposition to the political representatives of the same crown and flag to which they claim such strong allegiance.[10] Always underpinning loyalism is a relationship with the British state that is essentially contractual,[11] an idea recently repeated by one leading loyalist when he declared that the 'Loyalist community will honour its obligations and fulfil its duties to Parliament so long as Parliament acknowledges and upholds our right to equal citizenship within the United Kingdom'.[12]

Despite the key points identified above, however, loyalism remains difficult to define with precision. Perhaps the best-known starting point remains Todd's categorisation between 'British unionists' and 'Ulster loyalists', the former identifying primarily with Britain, rather than Northern Ireland, while the latter look to the six counties of Northern Ireland as their primary imagined community.[13] The strength of this dichotomy has, however, dissolved as, increasingly, both groupings display suspicion of their relationship with the British state and the political direction of the UK government.

Class remains central in defining loyalism, especially if we recognise widening class divisions within the Protestant community.[14] Indeed, it is possible to understand loyalism as the political expression of unionism filtered through the mesh of everyday Protestant working-class life. The outcome is a wide spread of social organisation and political goals, which manifest in a range of political strategies and representations.[15] All of these are invoked to frame a particular worldview and to confirm the strength of loyalism as a cultural and ethnic identity.[16] Here I will deal largely with senses of loyalism projected by those associated with paramilitary groupings.

PARAMILITARISM AND LOYALIST IDENTITY

At times throughout the contemporary period, representatives of both the Ulster Defence Association (UDA) and Ulster Volunteer Force (UVF) have displayed political thought beyond that of the established unionist leadership. This line of independent reasoning eventually gave birth to the so-called 'new loyalism' of the PUP, and to a lesser extent the Ulster Democratic Party (UDP), that emerged to reflect the direct experiences of some of those who had been centrally involved in the conflict.[17] I have dealt extensively with the politics of such groups in detail elsewhere,[18] but overall it is fair to say that the political positioning of the PUP, in particular, reflected a more socially aware, sometimes even class-based, expression of loyalist identity and open criticism of the unionist leadership.[19]

This drew a direct response and, certainly in the period immediately following the signing of the Belfast Agreement, the parameters of politics within many loyalist communities were widened to include the active participation of local people and community activists, who were 'directing their energies into a radical reappraisal of where they have come from and where they are going'.[20] The political expression of this could be seen in the PUP's promotion of a more pluralist politics, resting on a socio-economic programme not dissimilar to that of 'Old' Labour in Britain,[21] and a left-of-centre positioning on social issues.[22]

The other main political organisation whose origins lay in paramilitarism was the UDP. Its platform was never as coherent as that of the PUP, and the UDA's political momentum stuttered inconsistently throughout the 1980s. As the peace process took hold, its political position was reworked,[23] supporting the establishment of a devolved power-sharing government and taking two seats in the Forum elections of 1996.[24] This proved to be a high point, and when the first elections to the Northern Ireland Assembly eventually took place the party failed to have anyone elected (whereas the PUP secured two seats), allowing space for the growing articulation by many UDA members that, despite what was claimed by the political establishment, the Belfast Agreement had not made the union secure. Indeed, Frankie Gallagher of the Ulster Political Research Group (UPRG) was later to claim that the UDA's rank and file was never pro-Agreement, and that the direction of the UDP was always leadership-led.[25]

By the end of the 1990s, it had again become obvious that any interest in formal politics had ebbed away from the UDA leadership. The UDP was subsequently disbanded, in reality dismissed by the UDA's leadership, which sought to return the organisation to its more traditional role with an upturn of primitive sectarian violence.[26] In its place, the UDA reformed the UPRG to help determine any future political direction.[27] In the background remained faction fighting and the organisation's continuing involvement in a web of illegal activities. It was not until early 2005 that the UDA made another attempt to formulate a coherent political analysis[28] and to identify a political strategy.[29] Some of the implications of this in the construction of loyalist politics and identities will be discussed more fully later.

NEW LOYALISM CHALLENGED

Although the success and influence of the PUP and UDP have varied considerably, central to both was the attempted redefinition of political loyalism. Importantly, both made strong arguments that the political leadership of unionism was, at best, misguided in the strategies they had adopted. This gave rise to a whole series of tensions; those between the PUP and the Democratic Unionist Party (DUP) were especially obvious as the latter increasingly recognised a direct challenge to its claim to be the true representative of working-class loyalist interests.

By the time of the 2003 Assembly election the limits to the PUP's constituency had been revealed. One of its two sitting Assembly members lost his seat, while its remaining representative, the then party leader David Ervine, was elected on the sixth count (with 9.7 per cent of the first preference poll). Overall, the vote for the PUP dropped by around a half to just over 1 per cent of the overall turnout.[30] As with all political representatives before them associated with loyalist paramilitaries, the political legitimacy of the PUP was openly questioned.

Any hope that the PUP had of convincing the electorate of its credentials had begun to fade in the summer of 2000, when the first of a series of bloody feuds amongst the paramilitaries[31] in the post-ceasefire era repositioned the PUP in the public gaze, not as the representatives of some new pluralist civic loyalism, but firmly within their paramilitary past.[32] The marginal electoral position of the PUP was confirmed in the 2007 Assembly election, when only Dawn Purvis (standing in East Belfast) was elected. The electoral limitations of the PUP had, however, been apparent for some time and were made even more difficult by the untimely death of the party's charismatic leader, David Ervine, in January 2007.

THE DUP: CLAIMING LOYALISM

The period of electoral expansion for the PUP was relatively brief.[33] As the sense of crisis within loyalism surrounding the post-Agreement politics deepened, the DUP established a dominant position across unionism. Much of the support for the DUP came from agreement with their argument that the Belfast Agreement was little more than a 'surrender process' and the Union itself was exposed to risk.[34] Such ideas have, of course, been central to the political rhetoric of Ian Paisley since the late 1960s,[35] but have become increasingly central to unionist interpretations of events.

The recent success of the DUP has been its ability to present a convincing analysis to unionists, part of which suggests that the actions and beliefs of all pro-Agreement unionists (including the PUP and Ulster Unionist Party) could be directly equated with the undermining of the Northern Irish state itself. Such arguments, seen as marginal at the time of the Belfast Agreement, became central to the overall political response across unionism and loyalism.[36] At the core of the establishment of the hegemonic position of the DUP has been the perceived strength of their claim that they recognised the grand plan to destroy Northern Ireland's constitutional position, and effectively mobilised against it. The DUP has increasingly convinced unionists that they have negotiated the peace from a position of strength and it is this that 'justifies' the entry of the DUP into a working power-sharing administration with Sinn Féin.

CONSTRUCTING EVERYDAY LOYALISM

Although the PUP has had limited electoral success against the DUP, it does not mean that the key issues of contestation that provided much of their initial political momentum have abated. There remains a growing feeling within working-class loyalist areas that they have gained little in the post-Agreement period and that, if anything, they have become increasingly socially and economically marginalised. While there remains widespread support for the political accord, its 'benefits' still have not been fully established at street level, where many continue to experience high levels of deprivation[37] or fail to take advantage of educational opportunities.[38]

That some of the responses to the peace process have been convulsed and confused is, therefore, hardly surprising. Some loyalists increasingly talk, in detrimental and oppositional terms, of what they call the 'middle unionism'[39] that they see as ignoring the main concerns of working-class Protestants and as having detached themselves from traditional unionist institutions that can no longer guarantee status.[40] The broad belief that the Protestant community is in decline continues, in some degree, to determine the direction of loyalist politics,[41] while notions that they have received little in comparison to republican communities are commonplace within many working-class loyalist areas.[42] It is, of course, exactly within this faction of society that the construction of loyalism is most deeply contested and relationships with paramilitarism remain a defining factor of everyday life.[43]

TRANSFORMING CONFLICT

While it is true that in the post-ceasefire era some paramilitaries continued to be involved in a range of activities, including punishment beatings[44] and widespread criminality, certainly not everyone from a paramilitary background has played out a regressive role. Within loyalism there are a wide range of groups engaged in the social reorganisation of post-conflict society at the community level.[45] Such activities include education and training programmes, the facilitation of cross-community contacts, the reintegration of ex-prisoners into the community, and working with groupings around the areas of human rights and social justice (see Chapter 9 in this volume). Another example of this can be found in those schemes based on the concept of restorative justice, largely introduced to counter physical attacks used by paramilitaries to punish those deemed to be taking part in 'antisocial behaviour'.[46]

At the core of such projects is work conducted by ex-prisoners[47] reflecting their attempt to create a solution that recognises the sense of social solidarity within that community. Such schemes demonstrate the embedding of the idea of conflict transformation, which has increasingly become established across the political discourses of loyalism. This notion has, of course, been reflected in the political thinking of the PUP for more than two decades, manifesting in groupings such as the Ex-Prisoners Interpretative Centre (EPIC) and Local Initiatives for Needy Communities (LINC).[48] Since late 2004, however, the notion of transition has also increasingly been found in the political thinking of the UDA/UPRG.

The IRA announcement in July 2005 that their military campaign was over led to the UDA leadership undertaking a consultation process with its members to decide the way forward.[49] The results were revealing: while most UDA members conceded that the military war might be over, they also believed that the political and cultural war was not.[50] Somewhat more positively, this was taken as a signal from key sections of the UDA leadership as a green light to re-emphasise the advocacy of politics and the role of the UPRG. This solidified around the 'Loyalism in Transition' initiative, which found public expression in *A New Reality*.[51] The document contained proposals highlighting a number of key issues, including a general concern amongst the unionist community regarding the broad outcomes of the Belfast Agreement and the feeling of a lack of credible political leadership at the local level.

LOYALISM AND CIVIL SOCIETY

Given the above, it is apparent that as loyalist paramilitary politics reorganises in the post-conflict era the loyalists' strongest involvement is likely to be at the local level, involving an increasing engagement with other areas of civil society.[52] Contemporary debates around civil society have become deeply intertwined with notions of social capital, particularly as writers such as James Coleman[53] and Robert Putnam[54] have forced the concept to the fore of the international research agenda.

Social capital is a complex and contested concept and its exact form opens up a debate far beyond the confines of this chapter.[55] Central to understanding it, however, is the recognition of the extent of social connections between people and the creation of shared values and understandings that hold communities together. These social networks help develop cooperative ties and the creation of an accepted set of values and expectations. Such relationships help develop trust through a shared belief that others will also engage in communal activities. This helps create social solidarity, through bonding capital,[56] which, once established, forms the basis for the formation of 'bridging capital' that helps form linkages to other external individuals, networks and resources.[57] In turn, connections are made between powerful groups, ranging from both the highly localised to the macro, or even international, levels.[58]

As several writers have pointed out, it is now almost impossible to avoid the widespread public use of the language of civil society[59] and debates around the value of social capital have increasingly been applied to communities within Northern Ireland.[60] The picture is not straightforward. Although it has been argued that the stock of social capital is high in Northern Ireland[61] and that Protestants may have stronger patterns of bridging capital, much is still to be determined. Bonding social capital is high in lower socio-economic groups,[62] and in loyalist communities social connections between individuals and local groups remain strong. Indeed, the development and history of paramilitarism makes sense only if such links are understood. Equally clear is that bridging capital is much less fully developed.[63]

Within the Protestant community, however, civil society has been constructed in particular circumstances, whereby any criticism of social or economic conditions was seen as a direct challenge to the very existence of the Northern Ireland state.[64] Hence the years of Stormont government subdued much social protest and robbed the Protestant working class of much political skill.[65] A history of marked resistance on the part of Protestants to declare themselves in need and the reluctance of many from that background to organise collectively to secure resources from the state is increasingly recognised by many community activists.[66]

Some of these aspects remain deeply ingrained in loyalist culture. One conference in the early 1990s also noted the continued negative consequences that an established culture based on conservative social and moral values, apathy and long-term opposition to socialist politics had in such areas, underpinning a continuing perception that community activism and development remain the preserve of the nationalist community. This has led some to argue that working-class Protestant areas have a less active civil society than do equivalent Catholic districts.[67] Speakers at the Protestant, Unionist and Loyalist Communities conference, held in November 2005, reinforced many of these points.[68]

But this is not to say that working-class Protestant communities do not also have some history of self-support or welfare provision, often centred on the Church and the Orange Order, or sometimes the organised Labour movement.[69] Within loyalist communities, activity was based around economic need manifested through Tenants' Associations and housing groups, while others found collective expression through cultural groups. All of these operated effectively at the community level, below that of party politics. From their origin many of those involved in paramilitaries were also engaged in other forms of local politics.[70]

In the immediate future much of the dynamic for working-class loyalism again rests in that area where civil society and localised politics come together and where community and paramilitary activism overlap. In recent times this perspective has been most often aired by the PUP, which has also increasingly argued that the weakened social and economic positions in which many working-class Protestants now find themselves can be understood only as part of the same pattern of social deprivation that affects their counterparts in nationalist areas. More broadly, loyalism finds continued expression through popular culture (witness, for example, the widespread production of recorded loyalist music, or the 12 July celebrations), through community-based organisation and expressions of politics. Much of this discourse has clearly rejected large elements of unionism as middle-class, paternalistic, exploitative and unrepresentative.

CONCLUSION

Overall, there remains a sense within loyalism that the outcome of the political process is that they have been twice marginalised: as loyalists and as working-class. This is a far from positive outcome because, as Healy points out, unless space can be made for working-class understandings then the hegemony of middle-class worldviews is never challenged.[71] Throughout the contemporary period, loyalists have sought to create and identify ideological space and find expression for their experiences of communal conflict and sense of identity. This has found representation through a wide range of social organisations, including state agencies, family and community support networks, religious and social associations, political parties and paramilitary groupings. All have influenced how people engaged with each other and responded to the wider political situation.

The construction of loyalist identity remains complex, and formal politics represents only a small part of loyalist culture. Loyalism has sought to promote solidarity, constructed not only by its external relationships (such as those with Irish nationalism and the British state), but also through internal patterns of cultural learning and bonding. Unsurprisingly, in Northern Ireland civil society remains divided,[72] as do views concerning its future role and direction.[73] Loyalists draw on a worldview resting on experiences that recognise that while working-class communities have remained socially and physically unified, they remain polarised from other factions of Northern Irish society.

Loyalism continues to challenge the ideological space it seeks to negotiate within unionism, and to contest its expression at the everyday community level. Its future direction and political representation will be determined, in part at least, by the continuing strength of community identity, and by which of the multiple discourses available (including conflict transformation and developing social capital) are seen as offering most security to those who hold loyalism as their core point of social and political reference.

NOTES

1. Faith and Politics Group, *Transition* (Belfast: FPG, 2001), p. 15.
2. Ervine, D., 'Northern Ireland Assembly Debate, Wednesday 1 July 1998', Official Report (Hansard).
3. Coakley, J., 'Constitutional Innovation and Political Change in Twentieth-Century Ireland', in Coakley, J. (ed.), *Changing Shades of Orange and Green: Redefining the Union and the Nation in Contemporary Ireland* (Dublin: UCD Press, 2002), p. 12.
4. Ervine, D. 'Redefining Loyalism', in Coakley, *Changing Shades of Orange and Green*, pp. 57–63.
5. For detailed commentaries on the military campaigns of loyalist groupings, see, for example, Cusack, J. and McDonald, H., *UVF* (Dublin: Poolbeg, 1997); McDonald, H. and Cusack, J., *UDA: Inside the Heart of Loyalist Terror* (London: Penguin Ireland, 2004); Taylor,

P., *Loyalists* (London: Bloomsbury, 2000); Wood, I.S., *Crimes of Loyalty: A History of the UDA* (Edinburgh: Edinburgh University Press, 2006).

6. Graham, B., 'The Past in the Present: The Shaping of Identity in Loyalist Ulster', *Terrorism and Political Violence*, 16, 3 (2004), pp. 483–500.

7. Graham, B., 'Contested Images of Place among Protestants in Northern Ireland', *Political Geography*, 17, 2 (1998), pp. 129–44.

8. From a variety of perspectives see Coulter, C., 'The Character of Unionism', *Irish Political Studies*, 9 (1994), pp. 1–24; Hall, M., *Beyond the Fife and Drum* (Newtownabbey: Island Pamphlets, 1995); Hall, M., 'Ulster's Protestant Working Class: A Community Exploration', *Journal of Prisoners on Prisons*, 7, 2 (1996), pp. 31–57; Spencer, G., 'The Decline of Ulster Unionism: The Problem of Identity, Image and Change', *Contemporary Politics*, 12, 1 (2006), pp. 45–63; Taylor, *Loyalists*.

9. Cairns, D., 'Moving the Immovable: Discursive Challenge and Discursive Change in Ulster Loyalism', *European Journal of Cultural Studies*, 4, 1 (2001), pp. 85–104; Parkinson, A.F., *Ulster Loyalism and the British Media* (Dublin: Four Courts Press, 1998).

10. Shirlow, P. and McGovern, M., 'Introduction: Who are "the People"? Unionism, Protestantism and Loyalism in Northern Ireland', in P. Shirlow and M. McGovern (eds), *Who Are 'The People'?* (London: Pluto, 1997), pp. 1–15.

11. Miller, D., *Queen's Rebels: Ulster Loyalism in Historical Perspective* (Dublin: Gill and Macmillan, 1978).

12. Mitchell, B., *Principles of Loyalism: An Internal Discussion Paper* (Belfast: unknown Publisher, 2002), p. 16.

13. Todd, J., 'Two Traditions in Unionist Political Culture', *Irish Political Studies*, 2 (1987), pp. 1–26.

14. Ruane, J. and Todd, J., *The Dynamics of Conflict in Northern Ireland: Power, Conflict and Emancipation* (Cambridge: Cambridge University Press, 1996), p. 61.

15. Graham, 'The Past in the Present'.

16. See Finlayson, A., 'Loyalist Political Identity after the Peace', *Capital and Class*, 69 (1999), pp. 47–76; McAuley, J.W., 'Still "No Surrender"?: "New Loyalism" and the "Peace Process" in Ireland', in J.P. Harrington and E. Mitchell (eds), *Northern Ireland – Performance in Politics* (Amherst, MA: University of Massachusetts Press, 1999), pp. 41–56.

17. See McAuley, J.W., 'The Protestant Working Class and the State in Northern Ireland Since 1930: A Problematic Relationship', in S. Hutton and P. Stewart (eds), *Ireland's Histories* (London: Routledge, 1991); McAuley, J.W., 'From Loyal Soldiers to Political Spokespersons: A Political History of a Loyalist Paramilitary Group in Northern Ireland', *Études Irlandaises*, 21, 1 (1996); McAuley, J.W., 'Ulster Unionism after the Peace', in J. Neuheiser and S. Wolff (eds), *Peace at Last? The Impact of the Good Friday Agreement on Northern Ireland* (Oxford: Berghahn Books, 2002), pp. 76–92.

18. See McAuley, J.W., '"Not a Game of Cowboys and Indians": The Ulster Defence Association in the 1990s', in A. O'Day (ed.) *Terrorism's Laboratory: The Case of Northern Ireland* (Aldershot: Dartmouth, 1995); McAuley, J.W., '(Re) Constructing Ulster Loyalism: Political Responses to the Peace Process', *Irish Journal of Sociology*, 6 (1996), pp. 165–82; McAuley, J.W., 'Flying the One-Winged Bird': Ulster Unionism and the Peace Process', in Shirlow and McGovern, *Who Are 'The People'?*; McAuley, J.W., 'The Ulster Loyalist Political Parties: Towards a New Respectability', *Études Irlandaises*, 22, 2 (1997), pp. 117–32; McAuley, J.W., 'Redefining Loyalism: An Academic Perspective', IBIS Working Paper, No. 4 (Dublin: Institute for British–Irish Studies, 2001).

19. McAuley, J.W., 'Very British Rebels': Politics and Discourse within Contemporary Ulster Unionism', in P. Bagguley and J. Hearn (eds), *Transforming Politics: Power and Resistance* (Basingstoke: Macmillan, 1999); McAuley, J.W., 'Mobilising Ulster Unionism: New Directions or Old?', *Capital and Class*, 70 (Spring 2000), pp. 37–64; McAuley, J.W., 'Surrender? Loyalist Perceptions of Conflict Settlement', in J. Anderson and J. Goodman (eds), *(Dis)Agreeing Ireland* (London: Pluto, 1998); McAuley, J.W., 'Ulster Unionism after the Peace', in J. Neuheiser and S. Wolff (eds), *Breakthrough to Peace? The Impact of the Good Friday Agreement on Northern Irish Politics and Society* (New York and Oxford: Berghahn Books, 2002).

20. Hall, M., *Ulster's Protestant Working Class: A Community Exploration* (Newtownabbey: Island Pamphlets, 1994), p. 27.

21. Edwards, A., 'Democratic Socialism and Sectarianism: The Northern Ireland Labour Party and Progressive Unionist Party Compared', *Politics*, 27, 1 (February 2007), pp. 24–31.

22. McAuley, J.W., 'The Emergence of New Loyalism', in Coakley, *Changing Shades of Orange and Green*, pp. 106–22; McAuley, J.W., '"Just Fighting to Survive": Loyalist Paramilitary Politics and the Progressive Unionist Party', *Terrorism and Political Violence*, 16, 3 (2004), pp. 522–43.

23. At the time the UDA's politicisation resulted in the formation of the New Ulster Political Research Group and a policy document, *Beyond the Religious Divide* (Belfast: unknown publisher, 1979). This was largely republished as the *Common Sense* document (UPRG, 1987) and remained formal UDA policy throughout until around the mid-1980s. For more details, see McAuley, J.W., 'The Ideology and Politics of the Ulster Defence Association', in E. Hughes (ed.), *Culture and Politics in Northern Ireland* (Milton Keynes: Open University Press, 1991), pp. 44–68.

24. Ulster Democratic Party, *The Anglo-Irish Agreement – it hasn't gone away you know!*, press release, 19 November (Belfast: UDP, 1996).

25. Cited in Crawford, C., *Inside the UDA: Volunteers and Violence* (London: Pluto, 2003), p. 95; see also McDonald and Cusack, *UDA*, p. 304.

26. Langhammer, M., 'Cutting with the Grain. Policy and the Protestant Community: What is to be Done?', A Paper to the Secretary of State for Northern Ireland, Mr Paul Murphy and the Northern Ireland Office team (Belfast: published by author, 2003).

27. Cited in Garland, R., 'UPRG May Hold Loyalists' Key to Moving Forward', *Irish News*, 31 March 2003.

28. See interview with UDA representative, *East Belfast Observer*, 13 May 2004.

29. Breen, S., 'UPRG Influence Grows as Politics Replaces Violence', *Sunday Life*, 2 July 2006 and 'Men Bringing UDA in from Cold', *Sunday Life*, 30 July 2006.

30. CAIN Web Service 'Assembly Election (NI): Results 26 November 2003', <http://cain.ulst.ac.uk/issues/politics/election/ra2003.htm> [accessed 4 December 2003].

31. Persic, C. and Bloomer, S., *The Feud and the Fury … The Response of the Community Sector to the Shankill Feud, August 2000* (Belfast: Springfield Intercommunity Development, no date).

32. McAuley, J.W., 'Whither New Loyalism? Changing Loyalist Politics After the Belfast Agreement', *Irish Political Studies*, 20, 3 (2005), pp. 323–40; Gallaher, C. and Shirlow, P., 'The Geography of Loyalist Paramilitary Feuding in Belfast', *Space and Polity*, 10, 2 (2006), pp. 149–70.

33. See McAuley, J.W. and Tonge, J., ESRC Award L327253058 'The Role of "Extra-Constitutional" Parties in the Northern Ireland Assembly', Final Report to the ESRC, January 2001; McAuley, J. W. and Tonge, J., 'Over the Rainbow? Relationships Between Loyalists and Republicans in the Northern Ireland Assembly', *Études Irlandaises*, 28, 1 (2003), pp. 177–98.

34. Knox, C., 'Alienation: An Emerging Protestant Phenomenon in Northern Ireland', Ulster Papers in Public Policy in Management, 53 (Jordanstown: University of Ulster, 1995).

35. See Bruce, S., *God Save Ulster* (Oxford: Oxford University Press, 1986); Cooke, D., *Persecution: A Portrait of Ian Paisley's Zeal* (Dingle: Brandon, 1996); Smyth, C., *Ian Paisley: Voice of Protestant Ulster* (Edinburgh: Scottish Academic Press, 1987).

36. McAuley, J.W. and Tonge, J., '"For God and for the Crown": Contemporary Political and Social Attitudes among Orange Order Members in Northern Ireland', *Political Psychology* 28, 1 (2007), pp. 33–54; McCartney, R., *The McCartney Report on Consent* (Belfast: J C Print, no date); *The McCartney Report on the Framework Documents* (Belfast: J C Print, no date); *Reflections on Liberty, Democracy and the Union* (Dublin: Maunsel and Company, 2001); 'This is a Situation Hardly Calculated to Produce Either Clarity or Truth' (*Belfast Telegraph*, 26 October 2006); See Hanna, R. (ed.), *The Union: Essays on Ireland and the British Connection* (Newtownards: Colourpoint Books, 2001); various editions of the *Orange Standard*.

37. The Noble Index of economic deprivation in 2002, for example, suggests that more Protestant areas were suffering high levels of economic deprivation than were Catholic areas (NI Statistics and Research Agency 2006).

38. In 2006, David Hanson, the Social Development Minister, reported that of the fifteen wards performing worst in educational attainment, thirteen were in Protestant working-class parts of Belfast (cited in McGill, P., 'Spending in Protestant Areas', *Scope*, May 2006, p. 12), while throughout Northern Ireland, a greater proportion of Protestants than Catholics had no qualifications (*Census 2001: Community Background in Northern Ireland* (Belfast: Equality Commission, 2006), p. 24.

39. Faith and Politics Group (2001), p. 15.

40. Coulter, C., 'The Culture of Contentment: The Political Beliefs and Practice of the Unionist Middle Classes', in P. Shirlow and M. McGovern (eds), *Who Are 'The People'?* (London: Pluto, 1997), pp. 114–39; Shirlow, P. and Murtagh, B., *Belfast: Segregation, Violence and the City* (London: Pluto, 2006), pp. 106–7.
41. See Brown, K. and MacGinty, R., 'Public Attitudes toward Partisan and Neutral Symbols in Post-Agreement Northern Ireland', *Identities: Global Studies in Culture and Power*, 10 (2003), pp. 83–108; Dunn, S. and Morgan, V., *Protestant Alienation in Northern Ireland: A Preliminary Survey* (Coleraine: Centre for the Study of Conflict, University of Ulster, 1994); Morrow, D. 'Nothing to Fear but ...? Unionists and the Northern Ireland Peace Process', in D. Murray (ed.), *Protestant Perceptions of the Peace Process in Northern Ireland* (Coleraine: University of Ulster, 2000); Southern, N., 'Protestant Alienation in Northern Ireland: A Political, Cultural and Geographical Examination', *Journal of Ethnic and Migration Studies*, 33, 1 (2007), pp. 159–80.
42. Hall, M., *An Uncertain Future: An Exploration by Protestant Community Activists* (Belfast: Island Pamphlet, 2002); McKittrick, D., 'What Makes the Loyalists Angry is Seeing the Other Side Doing so Well', *Independent*, 17 January 2002.
43. McAuley, J.W., 'Fantasy Politics? Restructuring Unionism After the Good Friday Agreement', *Eire-Ireland*, 39, 1/2 (2004).
44. Although the number of such attacks was high for several years following the signing of the Agreement, in the period between January and the end of June 2007 the number had dropped to zero, *News Letter*, 18 July 2007.
45. Gribbin, V., Kelly, R., and Mitchell, C., *Loyalist Conflict Transformation Initiatives*, research paper presented to the Office of the First Minister and Deputy First Minister (University of Ulster: Coleraine, 2005).
46. See McEvoy, K. and Mika, H., 'Punishment, Politics and Praxis: Restorative Justice and Non-violent Alternatives to Paramilitary Punishment in Northern Ireland', *Police and Society*, 11, 3 (2001), pp. 359–82; 'Restorative Justice in Conflict: Paramilitarism, Community, and the Construction of Legitimacy in Northern Ireland', *Contemporary Justice Review* 4, 3–4 (2001), pp. 291–319.
47. The primary restorative justice initiative operating in loyalist districts is Alternatives. It largely deals with offences that do not involve violence against the person.
48. The history of the development of the idea of conflict transformation within the PUP grouping can be traced through such documents as Progressive Unionist Party, *War or Peace: Conflict or Conference*, Policy Document of the Progressive Unionist Party (Belfast, no date); *Agreeing to Differ for Progress*, (Belfast, 1985); *Sharing Responsibility* (Belfast, 1985); *War or Peace? Conflict or Conference: Policy Document of the Progressive Unionist Party* (Belfast, 1986); 'Submission to the Northern Ireland Office by the Progressive Unionist Party on the Question of Political Prisoners and Prisons', *Journal of Prisoners on Prisons*, 7, 2 (1996); LINC Resource Centre, 'Ex-Prisoners and Conflict Transformation', Conflict Transformation Papers, 4 (Belfast: LINC Resource Centre, 2003).
49. UDA internal consultation document, in author's possession.
50. Hall, M., *Loyalism in Transition 1: A New Reality?* (Newtownabbey: Island Pamphlets, 2006), p. 10.
51. For more details see Hall, M., *Loyalism in Transition 2: Learning from Others in Conflict* (Newtownabbey: Island Pamphlets, 2007).
52. The notion of civil society is contested and has produced a vast literature and a gamut of definitions.
53. Coleman, J.S., 'Social Capital in the Creation of Human Capital', *American Journal of Sociology*, 94, pp. S95–S120 (1988); *Foundations of Social Theory* (Cambridge, MA: Harvard University Press, 1990).
54. Putnam, R.D., *Making Democracy Work – Civic Traditions in Modern Italy* (Princeton, NJ: Princeton University Press, 1993).
55. For useful reviews of what is now a huge body of work on social capital see Yaojun, L., Pickles, A. and Savage, M., 'Social Capital and Social Trust in Britain', *European Sociological Review*, 21, 2 (2005), pp. 109–23; Harper, R., *Social Capital: A Review of the Literature* (Social Analysis and Reporting Division Office for National Statistics, 2001).
56. Putnam, R.D., 'Bowling Alone: America's Declining Social Capital', *Journal of Democracy*, 6, 1 (1995), pp. 65–78.
57. Beem, C., *The Necessity of Politics: Reclaiming American Public Life* (Chicago: University of Chicago Press, 1999).

58. See Cote, S. and Healy, T., *The Well-being of Nations: The Role of Human and Social Capital* (Paris: Organisation for Economic Co-Operation and Development, 2001).
59. Walters, W., 'Social Capital and Political Sociology: Re-imagining Politics?', *Sociology*, 36, 2 (2002), pp. 377–97; Foley, M.W. and Edwards, B., 'Escape from Politics? Social Theory and the Social Capital Debate', *American Behavioural Scientist*, 40 (1977), pp. 550–61; Woolcock, M., 'The Place of Social Capital in Understanding Social and Economic Outcomes', *Canadian Journal of Policy Research*, 2, 1 (2001), pp. 11–17.
60. See, for example, Morrissey, M., Harbinson, J., Healy, K., McDonnell B. and Kelly J., *Mapping Social Capital: A Model for Investment*, (Community Foundation for Northern Ireland, 2005); Cairns, E., Van Til, J. and Williamson, A., 'Social Capital, Collectivism-Individualism and Community Background in Northern Ireland,' Report to the Office of the First Minister and Deputy First Minister and Head of the Voluntary and Community Unit of the Department for Social Development (2003).
61. Murtagh, B., 'Social Activity and Interaction in Northern Ireland,' NI Life and Times Survey, *Research Update* (10 February 2002).
62. Office of the First Minister and Deputy First Minister, *Social Capital in Northern Ireland: An Analysis of the 2003/04 Continuous Household Survey* (Belfast: OFMDFM, 2006).
63. See Bacon, D., 'Revitalising Civil society in Northern Ireland: Social Capital Formation in Three Faith-based Organisations', paper presented at the 7th Researching the Voluntary Sector Conference, London, 2001.
64. Ditch, J., 'Social Policy in "Crisis"? The Case of Northern Ireland', in M. Loney, D. Boswell and J. Clarke (eds), *Social Policy and Social Welfare* (Milton Keynes: Open University Press, 1983).
65. McKittrick, D., *Endgame: The Search for Peace in Northern Ireland* (Belfast: Blackstaff Press, 1994).
66. Community Relations Information Centre, *Community Development in Protestant Areas* (Belfast: Community Development in Protestant Areas Steering Group, 1992).
67. Robson, T., 'The Community Sector and Conflict Resolution in Northern Ireland', paper presented at The Role of Civil Society in Conflict Resolution Conference, NUI Maynooth, 2001.
68. Community Convention and Development Company, *Protestant, Unionist, Loyalist Communities; Leading a Positive Transformation*, Conference Report (Belfast: CCDC, 2006).
69. See Morrow, D., 'The Protestant Churches and Social Welfare: Voluntary Action and Government Support', in N. Acheson and A. Williamson (eds), *Voluntary Action and Social Policy in Northern Ireland* (Aldershot: Avebury, 1995) and Finlay, A., 'Defeatism and Northern Protestant "Identity"', *Global Review of Ethnopolitics* 1, 2 (2001), pp. 3–20.
70. McAuley, J.W., *The Politics of Identity* (Aldershot: Avebury, 1994).
71. Healy, J., 'Locality Matters: Ethnic Segregation and Community Conflict – the Experience of Protestant Girls in Belfast', *Children and Society*, 20 (2006), pp. 105–15.
72. McCarron, J.J., 'Civil Society in Northern Ireland: A New Beginning?', CIVICUS Civil Society Index Report for Northern Ireland (Belfast: NICVA, 2006).
73. Farrington, C., 'Models of Civil Society and their Implications for the Northern Ireland Peace Process', IBIS Working Papers, 43 (Dublin: UCD Press, 2004).

Chapter 2
Loyalists and Unionists:
Explaining the Internal Dynamics of an Ethnic Group

Christopher Farrington

THE INTERNAL DYNAMICS OF ETHNIC GROUPS

We know much more about the dynamics of conflict between ethnic groups than we do about the internal dynamics of ethnic groups. How do the internal divisions of class, region, gender, and so on affect how that ethnic group reacts to political change and interacts with other ethnic groups in their particular territory? The most developed aspect of this question relates to party politics. However, even within this field we still have a limited amount of comparative data about how parties compete for votes in ethnic democracies.[1] In Northern Ireland we have seen how the competition between the DUP and UUP has affected the peace process. However, this article is concerned with an internal boundary among Northern Ireland Protestants, which is only partly a party political one, between unionists and loyalists. This division has taken on institutional and ideological significance, and how it is managed tells us something about how ethnic groups manage their own internal differences.

This chapter will outline some of the underlying differences that condition the relationship between unionists and loyalists. I begin by suggesting that existing definitions of the two groups do not adequately explain the differences between loyalists and unionists. Because the boundary between the two groups is very hazy, it is relatively easy to use institutions to ascribe some kind of content to the two groups. However, identifying distinct constituencies is much more difficult. Once we have identified, and perhaps resolved, some of these definitional problems we can then address the political effects of these differences. We therefore have two questions to address. The first one is definitional: how do we identify the internal boundaries within ethnic groups? The second one relates more to political behaviour: what effects do these internal boundaries have on the politics of ethnic conflict?

DEFINING UNIONISM AND LOYALISM

The boundary between unionism and loyalism is very hazy. For example, the Progressive Unionist Party (PUP) is clearly a loyalist political party and yet it calls itself the Progressive *Unionist* Party. However, there is frequently hostility between loyalists and unionists. One edition of the Ulster Volunteer Force (UVF) journal, *Combat*, complained about the attitude of the Orange Order towards loyalist (not necessarily paramilitary) banners:

> Obviously we expect opposition from Republicans and the like to our parades and Standards. We don't, however, appreciate criticisms and castigations from those we deem as our own people (i.e. the Loyal Orders, etc).[2]

Similarly, Jim Wells stated in the Assembly: 'I have long since stopped including Mr Ervine and Mr Hutchinson in the term "Unionism". I am talking about true Unionists with true, traditional Unionist values.'[3] Thus, while the boundary is hazy, it clearly exists. The standard method of distinguishing unionists from loyalists is by ideology. Jennifer Todd, in her 1987 article, described two traditions in unionist political culture: the Ulster loyalist tradition and the Ulster British tradition. These were primarily distinguished by their respective imagined communities, Britain or Ulster, and these, in turn, informed the preferred political options for Northern Ireland, integration, devolution or even independence.[4] Of course, many of the terms of reference have changed since Todd published her article but it still remains dominant in the general analysis of unionism. However, it is necessary to interrogate a few issues to illustrate that it may no longer be meaningful to talk about these 'two traditions' in ideological terms. First, the debate around national identity in unionism and in Britain in general has changed fundamentally. Regionalism and regional identities are in vogue again and unionists and loyalists no longer look aberrant from the perspective of Wales or Scotland. Indeed, in this changing environment there is nothing inherently contradictory in being *both* Ulster loyalist and Ulster British in terms of imagined communities. The difficulty Ulster Protestants have had is that they have looked peculiar to their fellow British citizens. Devolution has altered this. Dual identities are more common, and the definition of the United Kingdom as a state moulded by one national identity is no longer a standard analysis.

Both unionists and loyalists subscribe to an analysis of the UK as a multinational state. For example, a discussion document written by prominent loyalist Billy Mitchell, *The Principles of Loyalism*,[5] clearly sets out loyalism in terms which would be familiar to many of what would be called Ulster British. Indeed, Arthur Aughey or Robert McCartney could have written parts of it.[6] Although the similarity of ideas is striking, it is also notable that there was little or no dialogue between unionists and loyalists when either discussed these ideas. In unionist circles this happened in two phases. The first was in the aftermath of the Anglo-Irish Agreement and the second was the period between Trimble's election as UUP leader and the Agreement in 1998. In Ulster unionist circles this appeared to be the dominant debate and yet this does not seem to have filtered through into loyalist circles. This is probably because loyalists were concerned with selling and consolidating a ceasefire. Nevertheless, it is interesting to note that the debates in which loyalists participate, in journals such as *The Blanket* and *The Other View*, are with republicans and not unionists.

If loyalists and unionists were developing similar ideas about their national identity, then loyalism should be seen more as a subdivision of unionism than the other way round; loyalism is not distinguishable enough to merit a separate classification. In many ways the varieties of unionist national identity tended to obscure other important, and perhaps more salient, divisions within the unionist/loyalist community. It might therefore be more applicable to think in terms of a distinct type of community rather than in terms of ideological structures. We could use political organisations as a crude and initial guide to the relative strengths of each group; however, we come up against a significant problem: loyalist political parties receive minimal electoral support. This is a problem only if we think that there are more people who would be loyalists than express their political preferences for loyalist parties. Alternatively, this could support the argument above, in so far as it could be that the boundary between the two groups is so hazy and broad that people can vote for unionist political parties on the basis that these parties represent aspects of loyalist identity or ideology.

The clearest dividing line between unionists and loyalists is that of class. Loyalists' social situation and experience is crucial to understanding the interaction between loyalists and other political actors in Northern Ireland. It is plausible to argue that loyalists would generally describe themselves first in class terms and, second, in relation to their proximity to the conflict (although in reality there is a very close correlation between the two). This situates loyalists in a social context which shapes attitudes and political options. The relationship between the Protestant working class and the Protestant upper class has been one which has baffled nationalists and frustrated loyalists throughout the twentieth century. As James Connolly argued:

According to all Socialist theories North-East Ulster, being the most developed industrially, ought to be the quarter in which class lines of cleavage, politically and industrially, should be the most pronounced and class rebellion the most common. As a cold matter of fact, it is the happy hunting ground of the slave-driver and the home of the least rebellious slaves in the industrial world.[7]

This critique was revisited in the 1960s and 1970s by leftist activists involved with the civil rights campaign and Irish republicans. Michael Farrell, for instance, argued that the Unionist Party manipulated the national issue in order to stop the Catholic and Protestant working class from forming alliances and redefining politics.[8] It is interesting to note that this critique is similar to the loyalist critique of unionism which was developed in the late 1980s and early 1990s.

It is therefore unsurprising that a class agenda has been a key part of the policy platform of loyalist political parties. When the Ulster Democratic Party (UDP) and PUP emerged onto the political scene in 1996 as serious players, they advanced a critique of the UUP and the DUP which was based on the thesis that they had abandoned the Protestant working class. Billy Mitchell described his political position:

> I am ... trying to show ... there is another side to unionism and that it is a valid philosophy. I want the readers to know there is another unionism that is not about Protestant domination or conservative politics. My kind of unionism embraces democratic socialism and pluralism inside the UK.[9]

This is similar to how the new PUP leader Dawn Purvis described her vision for the future:

> Northern Ireland as an integral part of the UK, with links to the Republic of Ireland and Europe; a vibrant economy; strong human rights and equality; police working within the community; a stable democracy along left/right lines instead of green/orange Tory lines. I refer to the politicians in the Assembly as green Tories and orange Tories ... I want to see politicians that are prepared to work on behalf of the people.[10]

While it is untrue that there is no social democratic ideological content to the policy positions of the UUP and the DUP, this is a less prominent part of the platforms of these two parties. Indeed, in the case of the DUP, it may have a remaining rhetorical commitment to its founding purpose to be 'right wing on the constitution and left wing on social issues', but it is doubtful whether this is an ideological commitment.[11] Within the UUP, any socialist content to its policy positions is probably limited to one or two individuals.

Therefore, on an ideological level on 'normal' policy issues, there appear to be significant differences deriving from the social situation of loyalists. However, the PUP has gradually augmented these overt social democratic values with the idea of 'community politics'. This was defined as:

> The Progressive Unionist Party is committed to working for the reconstruction of our society. To achieve this goal we advocate participative community action. We encourage our members to work at local level for the development of community education and training programmes, which discover, draw out and develop the strengths and potential of the whole community. We will campaign for increased levels of core funding for community-based projects that enable capacity building and the promotion of 'good relations'.[12]

This is a logical development of its socialist agenda, as Mitchell demonstrates:

> Since those involved in the political development of that Loyalist constituency are, by and large, the same people who are involved in the community development process, it follows that for most of us there is a common thread running though both our political and community activities.[13]

There have been many studies demonstrating how the conflict affected almost all social, political and cultural life in Northern Ireland,[14] but more recent research has shown that certain areas were affected by the Troubles more than others and has even identified certain postcodes where violence was concentrated.[15]

This shows how class politics and the experience of violence are tied together. However, the lack of political support for loyalist political parties has forced them into looking for alternative avenues of political expression and relevance, and the 'community politics' avenue was the one which was part of established loyalist political practice. Billy Mitchell shows how community politics is seen as an answer to the problems which are experienced by communities with direct experience of violence:

> Whatever the faults of the paramilitary organisations may be –

and there are many – they ought not to be used as the scapegoats for society's ills or as a cover for the failure of civic society to address its own problems. In many ways, they are the physical manifestation of society's failure to resolve its differences. Social and political problems are our problems. It is time to stop passing the buck. I believe that the Loyalist Commission is saying: 'The buck stops with us, we intend to do something about what is happening to our communities'. They are to be commended for that, and I for one regard the commission and its work as a sign of hope for the future.[16]

There are related effects in terms of attitudes, such as how loyalists analyse the political positions of unionists on the question of responsibility for the conflict. For example, the following quote from David Ervine is typical of his critique:

There is a clash between superiority and inferiority in the House. There are those who are superior and those who are inferior and, before we let people pick on the poor terrorists again, I am just talking about Unionism. There are those who take superior and laudable attitudes that are founded in morality. However, there are people who take a legalistic attitude, who say that they need absolute proof and that they must be absolutely certain. Such people say that certain other people could not be honest or reasonable because in 1912 those people were bad people or their grand-dads were bad people.[17]

The Protestant areas affected by the Troubles are what we would consider loyalist Belfast, and the experience of living adjacent to republican areas and being in daily contact with republican violence has conditioned both attitudes to the conflict and attitudes to resolving the conflict. This means that, within loyalism, you can find both the most progressive activists working for conflict resolution and those wedded to a campaign of sectarian disruption.

Throughout the Troubles, loyalists criticised unionists for not doing enough for the 'cause'. In a remarkable admission during a debate on the display of Easter lilies in the Assembly, Ervine stated:

As a Unionist, I have no particular desire to appreciate or venerate the Republican dead – some of my colleagues and I might like to have added to their ranks. As members of the DUP slid about the 'Armagh desert' with rolled-up manifestos determined to destroy the Republican movement, there were those of us who tried to do exactly that, more efficiently. I am sorry to say that we did not have as much success as I would like to have been able to report.[18]

For loyalists, this had implications for how the conflict ought to be transformed, as Dawn Purvis explains:

> Up to that point you just had Ian Paisley and James Molyneaux, talking the same old claptrap. It was always the notion that if these bad people would go away this would be a wonderful place. But the so-called bad people they talk about are uncles, brothers, cousins – they're friends, part and parcel of that society, and they're not going to sail off in a wee boat into the sunset. So the question is, how do you move that community from violence to peace? The politicians we had were never going to do that because they were excluding the people that needed to sit down and resolve it. Since I was about nine or 10, that was my mentality – it's the men with the guns that need to sit down and sort this thing out.[19]

However, these positions are not readily understood by unionists for a number of reasons. First, without experience of living in working-class communities, unionists are not readily familiar with the stresses and tensions of working-class life in urban settings. When this is combined with the tensions of interaction with republican and nationalist neighbours and the intense competition for resources, the gap in understanding becomes a significant gap to bridge. Too often unionists and loyalists assume that their experiences were similar when they were not. This is of more than storytelling importance because the different experiences led to different political agendas. For example, David Ervine has argued that loyalism was a term created by unionists to describe those who were activists in the conflict in order to insulate themselves from criticism,[20] although if this was loyalism's origins it has become a term that has affirmative notions for those who would subscribe to it. Billy Mitchell also argued that the origins of the term 'loyalist' had derogatory connotations:

> Indeed, the media have been largely responsible for using the terms 'unionist' and 'loyalist' to distinguish between what they perceive to be 'respectable' law-abiding unionists and 'disreputable' law-breaking unionists. Thus, the term loyalist itself has become a term of abuse signifying all that is alleged to be bad within unionism.[21]

From the unionist side, the post-Good Friday debates over decommissioning, criminality and policing offered more examples of the tension between unionists and loyalists over the latter's relationship with violence. There were regular exchanges in the Assembly between the DUP and PUP over the issue. For example, Sammy Wilson remarked: 'In certain circles Mr Ervine is known as "the Bishop Eames of the paramilitaries"'. When I listen to his moralizing I feel that description is justified.'[22] However, the tension was most clearly seen when David Ervine came to an arrangement with the UUP to join it in an Assembly grouping (for more on this debate see below).

POLITICAL RAMIFICATIONS

Therefore, loyalists and unionists are distinguished less by identity and more by their respective experiences of the Troubles and their social situation. It is now necessary to ask what kind of political effect these different attitudes to the conflict, violence and conflict transformation have on political developments. Using evidence from the Troubles and the peace process, we can see how loyalists and unionists have interacted with each other politically. We can see that loyalists have exerted two types of influence on unionist politics: a constraining influence and an enabling influence. We can also identify two types of strategies which unionists have used in order to respond to these influences: marginalisation and enticement.

Loyalist Influences on Unionist Politics
In order to argue that loyalists have acted as a constraining influence on unionists, we need to be able to trace how loyalists prevented unionists adopting policies or positions which they might have done without the pressure from loyalists. This is precisely the logic of the ethnic conflict model of party competition, which predicts that party positions will move to the extremes through a process of ethnic outbidding. However, because loyalists did not have a significant political presence, it was not through the electoral process that loyalists could exert this kind of influence. It was, therefore, achieved through other 'extra-parliamentary' activities which mobilised the population or hardened attitudes. The use of violence as a political method is the obvious way in which loyalists acted as a constraining influence. However, we can see a couple of other specific instances where loyalist actions changed unionist policies. The clearest example is the Ulster Workers' Council strike of 1974, where loyalists took the initiative in protesting and organising against the policies of Brian Faulkner and succeeded in changing the attitudes of the general unionist population.[23]

On the other hand, loyalists could act as an enabling influence on unionist politics. One of the major ideological differences between unionists and loyalists that has been identified is the relationship with change. Todd argued that loyalism was a 'closed political ideology' not open to change, whereas the Ulster British tradition had greater scope to adapt.[24] Similarly, James McAuley ascertained the existence of a 'discourse of perpetuity' within loyalism, which was how loyalists reacted to political events by placing them within an interpretive framework that stressed sell-outs and isolation.[25] I have described this elsewhere as the tendency within unionism to use the past to interpret the present.[26] However, juxtaposed with this is the contrary strain within loyalism, which McAuley says uses discourses of transformation. This has a longer heritage than has been appreciated, as Roy Garland has demonstrated.[27] The ability of loyalism to change opens up important possibilities, if we accept that they had a constraining influence on unionist politics prior to this change.

While loyalists exerted a constraining influence through violence, there is also an argument to be made that loyalists were politically more moderate at certain times than were unionists. For example, it is frequently noted that the UDA document *Common Sense* advocated compromise and indicated movement away from some of the political positions which the UUP and DUP were holding on to. Therefore, if loyalists, as the representatives of the most closed aspects of unionist ideology, were contemplating, or even advocating, change, it could be argued that this allowed unionists to engage more fully in the political process. We can also see how loyalists acted as an enabling influence in very tangible and practical ways through the talks process leading to the Good Friday Agreement and through the operation of the first Assembly from 1998 to 2003. If the UDP, and particularly the PUP, had not occupied a pro-peace process and pro-Agreement position, then unionism as a whole would not have engaged with and operated the Agreement. The talks process was governed by a mechanism called sufficient consensus. This meant that a majority of unionists *and* a majority of nationalists needed to agree to something for it to be included in an Agreement. The UUP did not have a majority within unionism by itself and needed the two loyalist parties in order to make up that majority. Similarly, within the Assembly, Trimble had only twenty-eight UUP MLAs but needed thirty in order to pass key decisions under the concurrent majority rule. In this context, it was again crucial that the two PUP MLAs were pro-Agreement, as without their support there would not have been enough pro-Agreement unionists to elect David Trimble and Seamus Mallon First Minister and Deputy First Minister respectively.

The intersection between these two types of influence is obviously complex. The divisions within loyalism, for instance, mean that we can see both types of influence operating simultaneously. For example, while the PUP has been attempting to engage its communities in a process of conflict transformation, the UDP has been disbanded and the UDA has been engaged in numerous criminal activities and feuds. We can even see them operating simultaneously from the same branch of loyalism. So, for example, the PUP has been promoting conflict transformation but has been unable to persuade the UVF to disband or cease activities, and it has been involved in feuds with other paramilitary groups. Given these countervailing indicators, it is instructive to examine the strategies used by mainstream unionists when they interact with loyalists.

Unionist Strategies to Deal with Loyalist Influence
We can identify two very different strategies which unionists have used to deal with these influences: enticement and marginalisation. It may be tempting to see these two strategies as similar to the 'carrots and sticks' metaphor which has been used frequently to describe various strategies during the peace process. However, the idea of marginalisation is something much more punitive than simply applying sanctions in order to achieve some policy result. Marginalisation is a strategy which can be used solely to ostracise, rather than with the intention of providing an alternative route to political respectability.

It is instructive to briefly examine how nationalists interacted with republicans to illustrate some of these points. There is a general consensus that the peace process emerged only when various political actors, such as the British government, the Irish government and the SDLP, changed their strategy for dealing with republicans. It can reasonably be argued that, until the late 1980s, all three political actors attempted to marginalise republicans. The SDLP saw the Sunningdale arrangements as a method for removing support for republicans; the British government erroneously saw the criminalisation process as a way of marginalising republicans; and the Irish government consistently adopted a marginalisation strategy, such as the legislation of Section 31 censoring republicans. However, in the late 1980s these strategies began to change. The new strategies which replaced marginalisation attempted to entice republicans into a political process. This enticement strategy is now well known and included various talks and a role for the United States government, among other actions. Moreover, even after republicans were firmly established within the process, the SDLP were still reluctant to put them under pressure by adopting a marginalisation strategy. This could have been done, for instance, by supporting an exclusion motion in the Assembly to remove Sinn Féin's ministers from office. Even in the aftermath of the Northern Bank robbery and the murder of Robert McCartney, the Irish government only looked as though it was following a marginalisation strategy; in fact it was simply using the 'stick' of a 'carrot and stick' approach.

However, it seems that unionists did not adopt a comparable enticement strategy in an early stage of the peace process. This is possibly because unionists have had an ambiguous relationship with loyalist violence. We noted earlier how the relationship with paramilitaries was a clear dividing line between unionists and loyalists. However, that dividing line has been more clearly constructed since the Agreement than before it. Prior to the Agreement, and indeed since Paisley's emergence onto the political scene in the 1960s, unionists have sought to use loyalist violence in rhetorical ways to extract policy concessions. This was particularly the case during the campaign against the Anglo-Irish Agreement[28] but the following quotation from the UK Unionist party's Robert McCartney is fairly typical of this relationship:

> The British–Irish Agreement and the Downing Street Declaration are the products of a policy decision to effect a political settlement, regardless of the wishes of the majority of the people. The inevitable result is the increasing Loyalist violence: when a constitutional majority is denied political expression, the potential for anarchy is increased.[29]

Note that McCartney is not saying that he thinks this is a good thing; he is just pointing out that this is 'inevitable' but the implications from this analysis are clear. Or take this excerpt from a press conference given by Paisley:

> Q: There was an interview published in the [inaudible] on Saturday with leaders of the UDA that said – they stated that civil war is, every month, getting closer. Is that anywhere near reality? MR. PAISLEY: Well, all I can say to that is this – that the British government must act and act very speedily, or there will be serious trouble ahead. And we have already warned them of this. We warned them that there would be trouble, and we warned how they could stop that trouble. And I spoke personally to the Prime Minister on two occasion[s] about this, but he persisted in going a way that has been a way not of peace, but of anguish. The Dublin authorities have continually said that the Protestant paramilitary activity is counter-terrorism, and if the IRA stopped their bombing campaign, the Protestant paramilitaries would stop then. I think what's coming from the Protestant paramilitaries now is that

they're saying no. We are dealing now with the issue of interference in Northern Ireland's affairs by Dublin. But I can't ...

Q: Mr. Paisley, when you say 'serious trouble', what does that mean?

MR. PAISLEY: Well, we have already serious trouble. There are very, very serious killing[s] of both Roman Catholics and Protestants. Very serious.

Q: Are you saying more serious or a continuation?

MR. PAISLEY: Well, it could escalate. It could escalate very, very seriously indeed.

Q: When you say it could escalate, are you saying that the Protestant paramilitaries have the wherewithal to do this?

MR. PAISLEY: Well, I'm not saying that [;] the chief of police in Northern Ireland has said that.[30]

It was these kind of comments which led loyalists like Billy Wright to remark: 'The biggest criticism of Dr Paisley wasn't his politics, it was his methods. Any time that there was an alarm he took people to the top of the hill but he wouldn't go over it. Paisley is mild compared to what people wanted.'[31] Unionists rarely take responsibility for such rhetoric, so it was surprising for Empey to address these issues, albeit in the context of defending his Assembly alliance with the PUP: 'It is no secret. I believe Ian Paisley has a very large responsibility for that [promoting loyalist violence] [but] I would have to say even our own party in those days was less condemnatory than it ought to have been.'[32]

However, despite this ambiguous relationship with loyalist violence, unionists have been as critical of loyalists as they have been of republicans. For example, when Sinn Féin was temporarily expelled from the all-party talks in 1996, Paisley stated:

They [Sinn Féin] are not there because of their vote. They are there because they are the spokesmen for a terrorist group just the same way as the UFF spokesmen are the UDP and the UVF spokesmen are the PUP. There's no getting out of that. They are there because the Government felt that they wanted to have what was known as a 'peace' conference and not a democratic conference to decide the future of Northern Ireland ... I must say that those who took part in the talks like the Ulster Unionists, they gave credence to this. Spokesmen for gunmen should not be at these talks, full stop.[33]

In the context of unionist politics, creating this association between the loyalist political parties and Sinn Féin was damning indeed. This type of attack has continued and was particularly evident in the debates after Ervine had joined the Ulster Unionist Assembly Group. In a European Parliament debate on racial violence at the time, the then DUP MEP Jim Allister stated:

> In terms of the standards and ethics expected of democratic parties, I very much regret that in Northern Ireland the Ulster Unionist Party has seen fit to invite into its Stormont Assembly Party the political representative of the UVF, an illegal organisation which has been mired in racist, sectarian and other violence. Such a shameful association not only diminishes those who so taint themselves, but undermines what should be a united stand by all democratic parties against criminality, whether of the racist or other variety.[34]

Similarly, DUP MP and MLA Iris Robinson stated:

> A general consensus had been built upon within unionism that those who employ violence to assist in the achievement of their political ends, rule themselves out of the democratic process ... That consensus was shattered by the Ulster Unionist Party's appalling pact with the UVF. The UUP have conceded the moral high ground on this issue to Sinn Féin/IRA. Never again can an Ulster Unionist seriously state that there is no place for Sinn Féin in the government of Northern Ireland whilst the IRA persists in terror and criminality.[35]

What is interesting about this debate over Ervine's alliance with the UUP is how it was simultaneously an example of a strategy of marginalisation and a strategy of enticement. The DUP reaction has been outlined above, but the UUP rationale and reaction is also instructive. Sylvia Hermon was the most prominent UUP member who was critical of the alliance. However, she indicated that she was prepared to countenance such an alliance on 'enticement' grounds:

> Whilst I regarded our party's alignment with the PUP in the Assembly as a dangerously high-risk strategy – particularly after the UVF had issued one of its rare public statements warning that it would not decommission after November 24th – I did, nevertheless, think the link might just be worthwhile if it enabled Sir Reg Empey to hasten that decommissioning and prevent any more bloodshed. But that was three weeks ago. And what have we had since then? Any progress by the UVF towards decommis-

sioning? Definitely not. On the contrary, we've had a restatement at the weekend of the UVF's position that it's not prepared to consider decommissioning prior to November. And heaped upon that has been the murder attempt on Mark Haddock.[36]

Empey defended the alliance after the UVF had been publicly accused of the shooting of its former commander Mark Haddock by the International Monitoring Commission (IMC) by stating: 'I maintain the view that there is no government strategy for dealing with loyalist paramilitaries and somebody has to take responsibility to address the issue.'[37] Similarly, the Loyalist Commission, which was established in late 2001, does seem to represent an attempt to entice loyalists into a democratic mode of operation. It was generally reported that the UUP had been involved, if not instrumental, in its establishment.[38] However, the commission was largely made up of community and Church leaders. Nevertheless, the commission did attempt to address loyalist alienation from the peace process. For example, former Secretary of State John Reid gave his 'cold house for unionists' speech a few weeks after the announcement of the establishment of the commission. Its reaction was:

> The Loyalist Commission notes the recognition by Dr John Reid in his speech last night of the palpable sense of grievance and dangerous sense of marginalization presently being experienced within loyalist communities. The commission was established in part to address this climate of hopelessness and desperation. We look forward with interest to what steps the Secretary of State and others will now take to follow up these words with constructive actions.[39]

It was also the vehicle which other stakeholders in Northern Ireland used to provide loyalists with access to significant political figures and publicity. For example, Lord Robin Eames arranged for the commission to meet with Bertie Ahern in June 2003.[40]

CONCLUSION

Ethnic groups have a range of methods for managing their internal differences, which frequently have to be seen to be subsumed for the benefit of outside observers. They have to have ways of forcing policy changes on leaders who have conceded too much but also need ways of bringing the more extreme elements into the mainstream if circumstances change. How these changes are initiated and implemented depends on the ideology of the particular groups and the relationships between them. Throughout the Troubles, loyalists acted as a constraint on unionist policy. Their ideology was seen as being more hard-line, and their use of violence ensured that they were political players. The peace process saw this begin to change. Loyalist politicians were in the vanguard of those agitating for a peace agreement and a process of conflict transformation. However, this change in loyalism also needed a change in unionism for these policy goals to be implemented. Loyalists had to change the context for unionists to engage with the peace process and they did this primarily through their ceasefire. Unionists reacted to these changes in a variety of ways, some positive and some less than positive.

This study of the relationship between different ideological and social groups within one ethnic group shows how the interconnections between ideology, social situation and political strategy are important in explaining political outcomes. Understanding the nature of the boundary between unionists and loyalists is a necessary starting point for understanding how political competition and cooperation emerge from that boundary. It is frequently those dynamics, rather than the relationship across the ethnic boundary, which affect the success or failure of a peace process.

NOTES

1. See Chandra, K., *Why Ethnic Parties Succeed: Patronage and Ethnic Head Counts in India* (Cambridge: Cambridge University Press); Horowitz, D.L., *Ethnic Groups in Conflict* (Berkeley: University of California Press, 1985).
2. *Combat: Journal of the Ulster Volunteers*, 20 (2004).
3. Northern Ireland Assembly, Official Report, 10 April 2001, http://www.niassembly. gov.uk/record/reports/010410c.htm.
4. Todd, J., 'Two Traditions in Unionist Political Culture', *Irish Political Studies*, 2 (1987), pp. 1–26.
5. Available at http://www.pup-ni.org.uk/loyalism/principles.aspx.
6. See Farrington, C., *Ulster Unionism and the Peace Process in Northern Ireland* (Basingstoke: Palgrave Macmillan, 2006), Chapters 1 and 2.
7. *Foreword*, 23 August 1913, reprinted in James Connolly, *Socialism and Nationalism: A Selection from the Writings of James Connolly with Introduction and Notes by Desmond Ryan* (Dublin: Unknown Publisher, 1948), pp. 101–2.
8. Farrell, M. *Northern Ireland: The Orange State*, second edition (London: Pluto, 1980).
9. *Observer*, 3 October 1999.
10. *Belfast Telegraph*, 7 February 2007.
11. See the debate between Ervine and Ian Paisley Jnr in the Assembly on 16 October 2000. Northern Ireland Assembly, Official Report. Archived at: http://www.niassembly.gov. uk/record/reports/001016d.htm.
12. PUP, *How Long are You Prepared to Wait for Benefits for Our Community: Election Manifesto 2003* (Belfast: PUP, 2003), p. 4.
13. Billy Mitchell in M. Hall (ed.), *Community Development: Socialism in Practice?* (Newtownabbey: Island Pamphlets, 2003), p. 9.
14. Whyte, J., *Interpreting Northern Ireland* (Oxford: Clarendon Press, 1990).
15. Fay, M., Morrissey M., and Smyth, M. *Northern Ireland's Troubles: The Human Costs* (London: Pluto, 1999).
16. *News Letter*, 7 March 2002.
17. Northern Ireland Assembly, Official Report, 2 November 2001. Archived at: http://www.niassembly.gov.uk/record/reports/011102.htm.

18. Northern Ireland Assembly, Official Report, 10 April 2001. Archived at: http://www.niassembly.gov.uk/record/reports/010410b.htm.
19. *Irish Times*, 22 March 2006.
20. Ervine, D., 'Redefining Loyalism', in J. Coakley (ed.), *Changing Shades of Orange and Green: Redefining the Union and the Nation in Contemporary Ireland* (Dublin: UCD Press, 2003), p. 57.
21. *News Letter*, 7 March 2002.
22. Northern Ireland Assembly, Official Report, 17 Oct 2000. Archived at: http://www.niassembly.gov.uk/record/reports/001017b.htm.
23. See Fisk, R., *The Point of No Return: The Strike which Broke the British in Ulster* (London: André Deutsch, 1975).
24. Todd, J., 'Two Traditions in Unionist Political Culture', pp. 1–26.
25. McAuley, J.W., 'The Emergence of New Loyalism', in J. Coakley (ed.), *Changing Shades of Orange and Green*.
26. Farrington, C., 'Ulster Unionism and the Irish Historiography Debate', *Irish Studies Review*, 11, 3 (December 2003), pp. 251–61.
27. Garland, R., *The Ulster Volunteer Force: Negotiating History* (Belfast: Shankill Community Publications, 1997).
28. Farrington, *Ulster Unionism and the Peace Process in Northern Ireland*, pp. 59–61.
29. McCartney, R., 'Bitterness of a Community Deserted by Democracy', *Scotsman*, 1 September 1994.
30. National Press Club Morning Newsmaker, Press Conference with Ian Paisley, 11 April 1994, Federal News Service. Available on LexisNexis.
31. *Sunday Times*, 2 April 1995.
32. *Irish News*, 12 June 2006.
33. *News Letter*, 14 February 1998.
34. Press Association News File, 15 June 2006, available on LexisNexis.
35. Press Association News File, 9 June 2005, available on LexisNexis.
36. *Irish Times*, 10 June 2006.
37. *News Letter*, 31 May 2006.
38. *News Letter*, 1 November 2001.
39. *Irish News*, 23 November 2001.
40. *Sunday Life*, 15 June 2003; *Irish Times*, 12 June 2003.

Chapter 3
The Evolution of Irish Republicanism and the Peace Process in Northern Ireland

Catherine O'Donnell

INTRODUCTION

Undertaking an examination of the implications of the peace process and the 1998 Good Friday or Belfast Agreement for Irish republicanism demands a different approach from that when, for example, assessing the impact of the peace process on Ulster unionism. The reason for this relates to the nature of the relationship between the peace process and change within republicanism and its relationship with change within unionism or loyalism. For republicanism it is clear that the starting point for change preceded the peace process and indeed facilitated it. For loyalism and unionism the peace process necessitated change and reassessment.[1] So for republicanism, it is important to pose the question as to what happened within that movement to enable Sinn Féin to enter the political domain and the IRA to cease its activities. Change did not only have to occur within republicanism to allow this, but the political context in Northern Ireland, the Republic and Britain (in relation to Northern Ireland policy) also had to undergo some considerable modification. In a sense understanding the evolution of republican politics and ideas over the past twenty years also tells us much about the peace process.

This evolution has taken place through involvement with the peace process and has been pronounced for Fianna Fáil, Fine Gael and, to a much more obvious and greater degree, Sinn Féin. This was immortalised in a recent 'historic' development in the peace process when, on a day when many of us expected very little, Sinn Féin and the Democratic Unionist Party (DUP) agreed a date for power-sharing. Even someone who has observed Northern Ireland politics from a distance knows the level of mutual antipathy which has existed between Gerry Adams and Dr Ian Paisley. Yet on 26 March 2007 we were treated to the image of them sitting together in Stormont. The peace process appears to have brought the political 'extremes' to some form of reconciliation. This important juncture now offers the opportunity to assess republican discourse and politics since 1998.

This chapter examines the evolution of republicanism in a wide sense, as articulated by Sinn Féin, Fianna Fáil and Fine Gael. The chapter illustrates that one of the most significant developments, over the course of the peace process, has been the construction of a wide-ranging consensus within the broad republican family. This consensus, which has often been termed the pan-nationalist front, concerns agreement on short- as well as long-term policies (support for the peace process and unity respectively), ideology and discourse. More importantly, it has meant agreement in favour of Sinn Féin involvement in the political arena. The first section of this chapter provides a treatment of the significance and form of the development of this pan-nationalist consensus. It also demonstrates that the peace process has had significant implications for the role of the Irish government in Northern Ireland affairs and that Sinn Féin now holds a view of the Irish government (and indeed the British government) that is considerably different from that articulated by the party in the 1980s.

The second section analyses the extent to which the republican parties have undergone important ideological change over the course of the peace process. Have the peace process and the Good Friday Agreement involved significant ideological modification for Fianna Fáil, Fine Gael or Sinn Féin? Issues relating to an acceptance of the legitimacy of the Northern Ireland state, the principle of consent and self-determination are covered in this part of the chapter.

The third section also stresses the important alterations which have occurred to the way in which these parties articulate the meaning of republicanism. Here again we see the development of a consensus that republicanism relates to the ideals of democracy, equality and inclusion.

CHANGING REPUBLICAN POLITICS: INCLUSION AND CONSENSUS

A most explicit change, which has come about as a result of the peace process, the Good Friday Agreement and most recently a power-sharing agreement with the DUP, has been the core position afforded to Sinn Féin within politics in Northern Ireland and within the decision-making processes for the future of Northern Ireland. This change, which now sees Sinn Féin's Martin McGuinness as Deputy First

Minister of the Northern Ireland Executive, is easily contrasted to the severe isolation experienced by Sinn Féin throughout the 1970s and 1980s as a result of its association with the IRA's violent campaign. This feeling of isolation was articulated by Sinn Féin members. For example, at the party Ard Fheis in November 1983, Gerry Adams spoke of his perception of how the Irish government was responsible for the isolation suffered as a result of 'deliberate censorship' and also as a result of 'the massive harassment campaign by the Gardai which is aimed at republicans and their supporters and, in particular, the systematic intimidation of new members and young people to restrict organisational expansion'.[2] Adams had already claimed that 'the Labour Party, [which] is engaged with its Fine Gael partners, in a process of attempted ostracisation of Sinn Féin representatives'.[3] In 1984 Martin McGuinness also identified what he termed the government's 'deliberate intention to isolate Sinn Féin and present the SDLP as the party of the future'.[4] Clearly that isolation is no longer felt by the party, and this has been made possible by a new approach by the parties in the Republic which has centred on facilitating Sinn Féin's path to constitutional politics. Dating back to the latter part of the Charles Haughey government, 1987–1992, and more clearly the Albert Reynolds administration of 1992–94, Fianna Fáil has concentrated on securing Sinn Féin's inclusion in talks for the future of Northern Ireland. Sinn Féin policy documents and speeches by its party members highlighted the important role to be played by the Irish government in bringing about peace in Northern Ireland. Talks with Fianna Fáil were a vital part of Sinn Féin strategy from the late 1980s onwards. A Sinn Féin pamphlet, the *TUAS* document, listed the movement's 'main strategic objectives' as including the creation 'of an Irish nationalist consensus with international support on the basis of the dynamic contained in the Irish peace initiative'. Adams called for 'Irish nationalists, republicans, socialists and democrats' to unite in the cause of Irish unity, and stressed that the Irish government had 'a particular' role to play in this.[5] Sinn Féin sought the creation of a pan-nationalist position with the Irish government as lead representative for a nationalist Ireland.

Commitments to that effect were made by the Reynolds government[6] and delivered to the best of their abilities by subsequent Irish governments. Statements by members of Fianna Fáil clearly reflect the party's role as guarantor of the nationalist position. Albert Reynolds, for example, is clear that he felt his responsibility was to 'look after' republicans.[7] Tom Kitt has also described Reynolds' approach to the peace process as follows: 'The approach was certainly to facilitate and to give leadership to the pan-nationalist movement, the Hume–Adams initiative, to give recognition to that, to give substance to it. I suppose Fianna Fáil would say that we knew what we had to do based on our own party position. I would say, "look, how do we facilitate this move forward but at all times working with particularly the nationalist community in the North and then tick-tacking with the British Prime Minister of the day?"'[8] Other senior members of Fianna Fáil have emphasised the centrality of the pan-nationalist consensus to the peace process. Dermot Ahern has called it the 'major dynamic' of the peace process[9] and Conor Lenihan has stressed its importance to nationalists and republicans.[10] As a result, many politicians in the Republic now highlight the key role for Sinn Féin within the peace process and politics in Northern Ireland. Former leader of Fine Gael, Michael Noonan, has explicitly stated that 'certainly there is no peace process without Sinn Féin'.[11] Former deputy leader of Fianna Fáil, Mary O'Rourke, has also argued that 'there was going to be no process without them [Sinn Féin]'.[12]

Even at times when the peace process seemed under strain, the parties in the Republic have remained convinced of the need to continue to include Sinn Féin in the political process in Northern Ireland. Despite being critical of Sinn Féin in the aftermath of the 2004 Northern Bank robbery in Belfast and the murder of Robert McCartney in January 2005, Bertie Ahern did not divert from his view that a comprehensive deal must include republicans.[13] He also argued that 'exclusion is a hopeless exercise'.[14] Fianna Fáil has argued that Sinn Féin is not suitable for government in the Republic on the grounds that 'Northern Ireland is a different environment' and therefore 'different considerations apply'.[15] Fine Gael has articulated a similar position on the issue of Sinn Féin inclusion in government in the Republic. Senator Brian Hayes has argued that putting Sinn Féin in government in the Republic would be wrong on the basis that the 'Republic is not the North. We don't have divided allegiance in this part of the island. The Northern Ireland Assembly is a regional parliament, established with the purpose of bringing together the divided and sectarian society that is Northern Ireland.'[16] So while Sinn Féin continues to be spurned as a potential coalition partner in the Republic, the parties' insistence on their inclusion in politics in Northern Ireland has ensured just that.

In addition to the accepted inclusion of Sinn Féin in the peace process, the establishment of a strong pan-nationalist alliance has seen the role of the Irish government within the peace process develop in a way which is agreed upon by the members of that alliance. As a result, Sinn Féin's attitude towards the Irish government and towards the other parties in that alliance has altered significantly since the beginning of the peace process. During the 1970s and 1980s Sinn Féin consistently criticised both Fianna Fáil and Fine Gael for what it termed 'collaboration'.[17] The republican newspaper, *An Phoblacht/Republican News*, documented attacks on the parties in the Republic. The republican movement accused both main parties of 'constituting different brands of Free-Statism, both with the same pro-British and partitionist message'. In reality, the attitude to the North of Fianna Fáil, which makes capital out of its republican roots, differs very little from that of Fine Gael, whose roots go back to the original Free Staters. In his 1986 publication, *The Politics of Irish Freedom*, Gerry Adams criticised what he saw as Fianna Fáil's failure to 'tackle the partition issue in a meaningful way which could have led to independence'.[18] Recent statements by Sinn Féin illustrate the extent to which the party's view of the Irish government (and, in particular, Fianna Fáil) has changed as a result of the peace process.

Sinn Féin now stresses the important role assumed by Fianna Fáil within the peace process. Sinn Féin TD for Cavan-Monaghan, Caoimhghín Ó Caoláin, has reminded the Irish government of its role as 'leader of Irish nationalism and a proponent of Irish Unity as mandated by the Irish Constitution'.[19] In addition, Sinn Féin emphasises the role of both governments as having joint responsibility for the implementation of the Agreement. As a result, Sinn Féin has often claimed that the governments must work to keep the process on track[20] and have laid the blame for problems in the peace process with the governments. Gerry Adams claimed that the British government had not fulfilled commitments made under the Good Friday Agreement and that the Irish government had not done enough to prevent this.[21] He has described the role of the governments as follows:

> There is also a heavy responsibility on the two governments – and especially on the Taoiseach and the British Prime Minister – to provide the essential political leadership required to move the overall process on. As the leaders of the two governments and the joint and co-equal guarantors of the Agreement, it falls to them to marshal the pro-Agreement forces and implement a strategy to do this.[22]

Generally the Irish government has been content to adapt its role in this way. Former Fianna Fáil Minister for Foreign Affairs, Brian Cowen, described the establishment of a framework within which the two governments provide 'joint-sponsorship' of the implementation process.[23] Fine Gael TD, Brian Hayes, has also referred to the changed role of the Irish government as a 'guarantor for the Agreement'.[24] Despite the fact that Fine Gael views the role of the Irish government in the same way as Fianna Fáil, Sinn Féin has chosen to emphasise the problems it perceived to have existed in the John Bruton-led Rainbow government[25] while generally being positive about Fianna Fáil.[26]

This section has demonstrated the change that has taken place within the broad republican political domain over the course of the peace process. A number of points are key. First, Sinn Féin now enjoys a central position within Northern Ireland politics, and much of this is due to the changed approach towards Sinn Féin on the part of the British government and the main parties in the Republic of Ireland. Second, and most significantly, has been the development of an agreed approach to Northern Ireland among the parties on the island. Broad political opinion in the Republic of Ireland (as well as in Britain) is firmly in favour of continued Sinn Féin inclusion in politics in Northern Ireland. This has also meant improved relations between Sinn Féin and both governments and an agreed position with the Irish government in particular. Thus focusing on the implications for Irish republicanism concludes that the development of agreement and consensus on Northern Ireland within the wider republican filiation involving Sinn Féin, Fianna Fáil and Fine Gael is the most significant change. The level of ideological convergence between Fianna Fáil, Sinn Féin and the SDLP and Fine Gael will be assessed in the next sections, but it is clear that, in their agreed support for the peace process and the implementation of the Good Friday and St Andrews Agreements, the parties within this broad political spectrum share common short and long-term policy goals on Northern Ireland.

Third, a related development has been the altered views held by Sinn Féin towards the Irish government (and British government). Sinn Féin does not attack the Irish government as 'collaborators' with the British government but instead stresses the dual responsibility which both governments share in implementing the Good Friday Agreement and, more recently, the St Andrews Agreement. Through the creation of a broad nationalist position, Sinn Féin is no longer in opposition to the Irish government but in fact is central to, and exerts significant influence on, Irish government policy on Northern Ireland.

IDEOLOGICAL IMPLICATIONS:
SELF-DETERMINATION AND CONSENT

Different conclusions emerge as to the degree of ideological change undergone by Fianna Fáil, Fine Gael and Sinn Féin as a result of the peace process and the Good Friday Agreement. The official ideological position of the Irish state was set out in Articles 2 and 3 of the 1937 Constitution and maintained that the Irish nation extended across the entire island of Ireland and that as such the aim was to reunite the territory politically. Both Fine Gael and Fianna Fáil held unity as a core party objective. Dating back to its foundation in 1926, and inspired by founding leader, Eamon de Valera, Fianna Fáil has articulated the claim to Irish national self-determination. De Valera claimed that 'the people of Ireland constitute one distinct and separate nation, ethnically, historically and tested by every standard of political science; entitled, therefore, to self-determination'.[27] Fianna Fáil has also historically maintained that no section of the Irish nation had the right to secede from the nation. As a result, any regional assembly in Belfast would have to be devolved from the Dáil rather than from Westminster.

Fianna Fáil endorsed the reformulations contained in the 1998 Good Friday Agreement with relatively little stress, due in the main to the leadership's success in arguing that its fundamental principles remained intact. The introduction of the concept of self-determination was central to this and enabled Fianna Fáil (and Sinn Féin) to accept the principle of consent. The formula employed in the Good Friday Agreement in relation to the operation of Irish self-determination, subject to the consent of a majority in Northern Ireland, together with the changes to Articles 2 and 3 are seen to uphold the integrity of the nation, a concept vital for Fianna Fáil acceptance. As a result, the Republic has accepted the existence of two states on the island as opposed to two nations. Bertie Ahern stressed the importance of these points back in 1995.

> Maintaining the integrity of the nation as set out in Article Two is vital ... At the same time, our citizenship laws do not force anyone in the North who does not want it to accept Irish citizenship. Equally, we could not ask any nationalist, North and South, to accept the proposition that Armagh, Antrim or Down or the other counties are no longer Irish as far as we are concerned. It is another matter to claim that the whole island is or should be under the jurisdiction of Twenty Six county state institutions.[28]

While Fianna Fáil has accepted that a change to the constitutional status of Northern Ireland cannot take place without the consent of a majority there, it has pointed to the fact that nationalist consent is also required for any future Northern Ireland institutions.[29] The principle of consent has become 'a two-way process'.[30] More importantly, the acknowledgement by the British government of the right of the Irish people to self-determination, while premised on the consent of the majority of the people in the North, ensures that the Republic is also granted a say.[31] Thus the reorientation of the principle of consent, through its correlation with self-determination, shifts it onto an all-island level and this offers much consolation for Fianna Fáil.

In addition to this advance on self-determination, Fianna Fáil argued that the declaration by the British government had transferred sovereignty over Northern Ireland from the British government to the people. Bertie Ahern referred to the fact that the 1937 Constitution reflected the ideology of the leading 1916 Rising figure, P.H. Pearse, who saw the Irish people as sovereign and called for the right of the Irish people to govern themselves without external interference. Ahern argued that the principle of consent was consistent with this because 'as a result of balanced constitutional change, the ultimate sovereignty on whether to remain in the Union or join a united Ireland will also be rested in the people of the North … British territorial sovereignty over Northern Ireland will be gone. We will have helped to place sovereignty unequivocally in the hands of the people.'[32] Extending this reasoning Fianna Fáil also argued that the principle of consent amounted to 'a self-limitation on the manner in which that right [to self-determination] is to be exercised' and was in essence the Irish people's right to decide their own volition.[33]

Thus, for Fianna Fáil, the decision to give practical recognition to the state of Northern Ireland is tempered by its ability to view the constitutional reformulations contained in the Good Friday Agreement as compatible with the party's core ideology. The introduction of the concept of self-determination enabled Fianna Fáil to reconcile its fundamental ideological principles with the reality of Northern Ireland without significant compromise.

The Good Friday Agreement was a positive development also for Fine Gael. For a party that had long since advocated acceptance of the principle of consent and power-sharing[34], acceptance of the Agreement was little more than a formality and in fact represented, in its view, an endorsement of the party's policy on Northern Ireland.

On the other hand, Sinn Féin's conversion to the principle of consent, previously rejected by the party as a 'unionist veto', and acceptance of the legitimacy of the Northern Ireland state represent significant revisions to the party's original ideology. The party's abandonment of its traditional demand for a declaration on the part of the British government of its intention to withdraw and its acceptance of a devolved Assembly in Northern Ireland are also testament to this ideological change.[35] Gerry Adams has described the institutions on the island as 'partitionist',[36] yet his party is participating in both. In his contribution to this edited collection, Jonathan Tonge highlights the significant reordering of priorities for Sinn Féin as a result of its involvement in the peace process. This rearranging of ideals will also be illustrated in the next section, where the new understanding of republicanism held by Fine Gael, Fianna Fáil and Sinn Féin will be examined.

THE MEANING OF IRISH REPUBLICANISM

Clearly a pattern is emerging. Thus far, this chapter has illustrated that Fianna Fáil, Sinn Féin and Fine Gael, the main parties on the island that describe themselves as republican, have reached agreement on a number of policy and ideological points. In keeping with this, these parties have also come to agree on the meaning of Irish republicanism. For Fine Gael, for example, republicanism means the protection of the democratic state and rights. Brian Hayes has stated:

> The values that underpin our modern State with a rational legal system of government are inherently Republican values. The right of the people to determine their own government. Universal suffrage. Free speech. Rule by the majority. Respect and accommodation of minorities. Free and fair elections. The separation of powers between the executive and the courts. A written constitution. Civilian control over the army. The concept of Citizenship.[37]

The Fine Gael leader, Enda Kenny, has talked about a republic that 'upholds and practises true republican traditions – freedom, pluralism, justice, equality, brotherhood'.[38] Bertie Ahern has communicated a similar understanding of Irish republicanism: 'We value religious liberty and practice [sic] religious tolerance. Our success in Ireland is based on democratic republicanism and is inspired by the principles of equality and fraternity.'[39] Fianna Fáil has also been keen, since 1998, to reaffirm the positive values of Irish republicanism: 'The 1916 Proclamation was an explicitly democratic and egalitarian vision.'[40] Both Fianna Fáil and Fine Gael, in particular, have in the past articulated these values of central importance for the party. For example, at the 1985 Fianna Fáil Ard Fheis Haughey said:

Fianna Fáil, as the Republican party, is proud to be the political embodiment of the separatist, national tradition that is central to the freedom and independence of the Irish nation. Republicanism for us means adherence to the principles of the 1916 Proclamation, which asserted the right of the Irish people to national freedom and sovereignty, and which guaranteed religious and civil liberty, equal rights and equal opportunity to all citizens.[41]

Fine Gael has long since advocated the protection of democratic principles, equality, rights and a pluralist society.[42] But for Sinn Féin, articulating this kind of republicanism represents a significant reformulation of its ideals and restructuring of its priorities.

Like Fine Gael and Fianna Fáil, Sinn Féin now emphasises the importance of democracy and democratic values at the core of its understanding of republicanism. For example, Sinn Féin's TD for Cavan–Monaghan, Caoimhghín Ó Caoláin, has recently stated that the primary republican principle is 'the commitment to the sovereignty of the people, to democracy in its fullest sense'.[43] Sinn Féin also echoes Fianna Fáil's interpretation of the 1916 Rising and the key meanings of the 1916 Proclamation. Sinn Féin President, Gerry Adams, illustrated this when he said:

The core values of Sinn Féin are reflected in the Proclamation of the Irish republic in 1916, the founding document of modern Irish republicanism and a charter of liberty with international as well as national importance. In it, the republic guarantees religious and civil liberty; equal rights and equal opportunities to all its citizens; the Proclamation contains a commitment to cherish all the children of the nation equally. Its anti-sectarianism is evident in the words 'oblivious of the differences carefully fostered by an alien government, which have divided a minority from the majority in the past'. And at a time when women in most countries did not have the vote, the government of this new republic was to be elected by the suffrages of all her men and women ... Equality is our watchword.[44]

Adams's speech also reflects another new component of republicanism, as articulated by his party in the post-Good Friday Agreement period, the commitment to equality and the achievement of an Ireland of equals. Sinn Féin's Martin McGuinness invoked the 1798 United Irishmen leader, Wolfe Tone, as a champion of 'equality between all sections of society in Ireland, in unity between all the people of Ireland'.[45]

In addition, Sinn Féin claims that republicanism is about inclusiveness and reaching out to unionists. Martin McGuinness made this point and articulated his party's new emphasis on inclusion when he stated that Sinn Féin does not 'seek to exclude anyone' and that 'the peace process, just like the philosophy of Irish Republicanism, is founded on inclusiveness'.

Most striking in the re-branding of republicanism for Sinn Féin, in particular, is the eschewing of the historic militant component of Irish republicanism. In the 1980s, speeches by Gerry Adams and Martin McGuinness declined to reject the validity of the IRA violent campaign.[46] In contrast, Gerry Adams now maintains that Sinn Féin is about 'taking the guns out of Irish politics'.[47] Sinn Féin's rhetoric in response to the riots that resulted from protests at the planned Love Ulster parade in memory of victims of the Troubles in Northern Ireland in February 2006 is illustrative of the party's new interpretation of republicanism and its meaning. The then Sinn Féin TD, Seán Crowe, labelled the unrest that prevented the Love Ulster march from proceeding down O'Connell Street in Dublin as 'disgraceful'. He claimed that '[t]hose who took part misused the name of Irish republicanism and Irish nationalism but they were anything but Irish republicans or Irish nationalists in the real sense.' Significantly, he went on to state that for Sinn Féin the peace process 'includes outreach to the unionist community' and that '[u]nlike those who misused our National Flag last weekend, we [Sinn Féin] take seriously the message of the Tricolour – unity and equality between Orange and Green.'[48] Sinn Féin TD Aengus Ó Snodaigh made a similar point about the rioters, repeating the claim that 'they simply besmirched the national flag' and stressing that they 'must not be allowed to undermine the fundamental rights of democrats'.[49]

Clearly participation in the peace process has involved significant remodelling of Sinn Féin's core republican values, with the almost complete exclusion of the militant element from republican history. The new politics, ideology and language are justified by Sinn Féin as being responsible for bringing republicans 'to the threshold of a new beginning for Ireland and the Irish people' which contains the possibility of a new Ireland inspired by republican Wolfe Tone and based on 'equal rights and where the future of Ireland would be shaped by the people of Ireland alone'.[50]

CONCLUSION

Irish republicanism has been transformed over the course of the peace process in Northern Ireland. This transformation began in the late 1980s, when the republican movement embarked on a process of transition from a militant strategy to constitutional politics, and this facilitated the peace process. Once the two governments came on board and pursued the peace process as a policy for Northern Ireland, the transformation of republicanism was furthered over the subsequent years and development of the peace process. The first, and arguably most significant, development for Irish republicanism and nationalism has been the development of a pan-nationalist consensus in favour of Sinn Féin's inclusion in Northern Ireland politics, support for the peace process and implementation of the Good Friday Agreement. This has ensured a pivotal role for Sinn Féin in politics in Northern Ireland. It has also meant a reformed role for the Irish government in Northern Ireland politics. As a result of the Irish government's support for, and joint sponsorship of, the peace process with the British government, Sinn Féin's view of both governments has changed. While in the 1970s and 1980s Sinn Féin accused the Irish government of 'collaboration', it now highlights both governments' responsibility in working together to implement the Good Friday and St Andrews Agreements.

Participation in the peace process and endorsement of the Good Friday Agreement in 1998 involved significant ideological and discourse changes for Fianna Fáil, Fine Gael and Sinn Féin, in particular. Most important is the acceptance of the principle of consent and recognition of the legitimacy of the Northern Ireland state. This was considerably mitigated for Fianna Fáil and Sinn Féin by the introduction of the concept of self-determination which, for republicans, ensures that the principle of consent operates on an all-Ireland basis. Another important advance for republicans is that nationalist consent is required for any future administrations in Northern Ireland. Fine Gael's long advocacy of the principle of consent and power-sharing meant that the Good Friday Agreement was a positive development for the party.

In keeping with the development of consensus within the broad Irish republican filiation over the past two decades has been the formation of agreement among Fine Gael, Fianna Fáil and Sinn Féin as to the meaning of republicanism. The three parties all stress the republican values of democracy, equality, inclusion and the pursuit of political goals via constitutional rather than militant means. This understanding of republicanism is most unfamiliar to Sinn Féin, particularly since its leaders could not firmly reject the IRA violent campaign in the 1980s. These values have long since been advocated by Fine Gael and were seen in some of Fianna Fáil's utterances prior to the peace process.

Nevertheless, while Sinn Féin's transformation is most obvious, the much enhanced role for the Irish government in Northern Ireland affairs, altered Anglo-Irish relations, an altered relationship with Sinn Féin, including an agreed position on many ideological and policy points, the formation of a shared language of reconciliation and a common understanding of republicanism, ensure that the peace process has been of huge significance for all of the main republican parties.

NOTES

1. See Farrington, C., *Ulster Unionism and the Northern Ireland Peace Process* (Basingstoke: Palgrave, 2006).
2. *An Phoblacht/Republican News*, 17 November 1983.
3. *An Phoblacht/Republican News*, 21 June 1983.
4. *An Phoblacht/Republican News*, 28 June 1984.
5. Hennessey, T., *The Northern Ireland Peace Process: Ending the Troubles?* (Dublin: Gill and Macmillan, 2000), p. 41.
6. See O'Donnell, C., *Fianna Fáil, Irish Republicanism and the Northern Ireland Troubles, 1968–2005* (Dublin: Irish Academic Press, 2007) and O'Donnell, C., 'Pan-nationalism: Explaining the Irish Government's Role in the Northern Ireland Troubles, 1992–98', *Contemporary British History*, 21, 2 (June 2007), pp. 223–46.
7. Interview with Albert Reynolds, 8 August 2003.
8. Interview with Tom Kitt, 12 January 2006.
9. *Dáil Éireann Debates*, Vol. 462, Col. 968, 29 February 1996.
10. Interview with Conor Lenihan, 16 November 2005.
11. Interview with Michael Noonan, 5 October 2006.
12. Interview with Mary O'Rourke, 15 November 2005.
13. *Irish Times*, 22 February 2005.
14. *Irish Independent*, 9 February 2005.
15. Interview with Noel Treacy, 1 December 2005.
16. *Sunday Independent*, 17 October 2004.
17. Gerry Adams speaking at the 1983 Sinn Féin Árd Fheis, *An Phoblacht/Republican News*, 17 November 1983.
18. Adams, G., *The Politics of Irish Freedom* (Dingle: Brandon, 1986).
19. Caoimhghín Ó Caoláin TD, speaking at Easter ceremonies in Ballinasloe and Galway City on Easter Sunday, 2004. Archived at: http://www.sinnféin.ie/news/detail/4199. Accessed 12 June 2007.
20. For example, speech by Gerry Adams at a rally in Dublin in April 2004, *News Letter*, 12 April 2004.
21. Speech by Sinn Féin President Gerry Adams MP, MLA, St Malachy's College, North Belfast, 15 January 2004. Archived at: http://cain.ulst.ac.uk/issues/politics/docs/sf/ga150104.htm. Accessed 19 June 2007.
22. Statement by Gerry Adams, president of Sinn Féin, at the opening of the Review of the Good Friday Agreement, 3 February 2004. Archived at: http://cain.ulst.ac.uk/issues/politics/docs/sf/sf030204.htm. Accessed 12 June 2007.
23. Brian Cowen speaking on *Hearts and Minds*, BBC1 Northern Ireland, 12 June 2003.
24. Interview with Senator Brian Hayes, Fine Gael, 21 September 2006.
25. Adams has outlined his opinion of the John Bruton-led government in Adams, G., *Hope*

and History: *Making Peace in Ireland* (Dingle: Brandon, 2003), p. 197.
26. See, for example, the statement by Gerry Adams after his meeting with Bertie Ahern on 30 November 2004. Archived at: http://www.rte.ie/news/2004/1130/northpolitics. html. Accessed 19 June 2007.
27. As quoted in Fitzpatrick, D., *The Two Irelands 1912–1939* (Oxford: Oxford University Press, 1998), p. 28.
28. *Dáil Éireann Debates*, Vol. 449, Col. 1354, 22 February 1995.
29. A point made by Fianna Fáil Minister for State, Mr Noel Treacy, in an interview with the author, 1 December 2005.
30. Bertie Ahern, *Dáil Éireann Debates*, Vol. 489, Col. 1029, 21 April 1998.
31. See Coakley, J., 'Conclusion: New Strains of Unionism and Nationalism', in J. Coakley (ed.), *Changing Shades of Orange and Green: Redefining the Union and the Nation in Contemporary Ireland* (Dublin: UCD Press, 2002), p. 151 for the significance of the veto given to the Republic's electorate.
32. *Dáil Éireann Debates*, Vol. 449, Cols. 1355–6, 22 February 1995.
33. *Irish Times*, 28 February 1995.
34. Interview with Dr Garret Fitzgerald, 16 November 2006. See also 1969 Fine Gael Document on Northern Ireland reproduced in Harte, P., *Young Tigers and Mongrel Foxes: A Life in Politics* (Dublin: O'Brien Press, 2005).
35. See McGarry, J., 'Civic Nationalism and the Agreement', in J. McGarry (ed.), *Northern Ireland and the Divided World: The Northern Ireland Conflict and the Good Friday Agreement in Comparative Perspective* (Oxford: Oxford University Press, 2001), p. 112.
36. Speech by Gerry Adams, president of Sinn Féin, to the 2005 Sinn Féin Árd Fheis, 5 March 2005. Archived at: http://cain.ulst.ac.uk/issues/politics/docs/sf/ga050305.htm. Accessed 14 June 2007.
37. Speech by Senator Brian Hayes to the Ireland Institute, 10 April 2003. Archived at: www.finegael.ie/news/index.cfm/type/details/nkey/22835. Accessed 10 April 2007.
38. Speech by Fine Gael leader, Enda Kenny TD, to the Young Fine Gael 20th National Conference, 13 November 2004. Archived at: www.finegael.ie/news/index.cfm/type/details/nkey/24896. Accessed 10 April 2007.
39. Speech by the Taoiseach, Bertie Ahern, at the Wolfe Tone Commemoration, Bodenstown, County Kildare, 17 October 2004. Archived at: http://cain.ulst.ac.uk/issues/politics/docs/dott/ba171004.htm. Accessed 16 May 2007.
40. Speech by the Taoiseach, Mr Bertie Ahern TD, at the opening of the Constance Markievicz Exhibition in Lissadell, Sligo, 30 March, 2007. Archived at: http://www.taoiseach.gov.ie/index.asp?locID=558&docID=3332. Accessed 16 May 2007.
41. Presidential address by Charles J. Haughey at the Fianna Fáil Árd Fheis, 30 March 1985, Fianna Fáil Archives, P176/789.
42. See O'Donnell, C., 'Fine Gael and Republicanism: Understanding the Public Perception as a Non-republican Party', in I. Honohan (ed.), *Republicanism in Ireland: Confronting Theory and Tradition* (Manchester: Manchester University Press, forthcoming Spring 2008).
43. Sinn Féin TD Caoimhghín Ó Caoláin's address on Irish Republicanism in the New Century at the Twelfth Desmond Greaves Summer School in Dublin. Archived at: http://www.sinnféin.ie/gaelic/peace/document/139/1. Accessed 6 June 2007.
44. Sinn Féin president Gerry Adams speaking at the launch of 'The New Ireland – A Vision for the Future', Belfast, October 2005. Archived at: http://www.sinnféin.ie/gaelic/news/detail/11649. Accessed 6 June 2007.
45. Speech by Martin McGuinness at Bodenstown, 18 June 1995. Archived at: http://www.sinnféin.ie/gaelic/peace/speech/12. Accessed 14 June 2007.
46. In fact, in his presidential address to the Sinn Féin Árd Fheis in 1983, Gerry Adams said that 'Armed struggle is a necessary and morally correct form of resistance in the six counties.' As quoted in *An Phoblacht/Republican News*, 17 November 1983. Also speaking at a commemorative event in Derry in June 1984, Martin McGuinness said that 'The Irish Republican Army offers the only resolution to the present situation ... In the final analysis, it will be the combination of the Armalite and the ballot-box that will achieve freedom.' As quoted in *An Phoblacht/Republican News*, 28 June 1984.
47. Sinn Féin president Gerry Adams MP, speaking at a major rally for Irish unity in Dublin city

centre, 24 September 2005. Archived at: http://www.sinnféin.ie/gaelic/news/detail/ 11251. Accessed 6 June 2007.

48. Press release by Seán Crowe, published 28 February 2006. Archived at: http://www.sinn-féin.ie/gaelic/news/detail/13280. Accessed 19 June 2007.

49. Press release by Aengus Ó Snodaigh, published 28 February 2006. Archived at: http://www.sinnféin.ie/gaelic/news/detail/13279. Accessed 19 June 2007.

50. Speech by Martin McGuinness at Bodenstown, 18 June 1995. Archived at: http://www.sinnféin.ie/gaelic/peace/speech/12. Accessed 14 June 2007.

Chapter 4
Nationalist Convergence? The Evolution of Sinn Féin and SDLP Politics

Jonathan Tonge

INTRODUCTION

The remarkable transformation of Irish republican politics provided the largest impetus to the Northern Ireland peace process. Having pledged to enforce British withdrawal from Northern Ireland and establish an independent, thirty-two-county democratic socialist republic, republicans eventually agreed to share power in a government of Northern Ireland which remained part of the United Kingdom. The Provisional IRA, which had pledged to continue its fight indefinitely until the attainment of a united Ireland, ceased its campaign and decommissioned its weapons. Sinn Féin's new constitutionalism and pluralism was unrecognisable from the vanguardism and absolutism evident in republican violence and politics during the conflict. Political U-turns within republicanism have been portrayed by their supporters within Sinn Féin as merely tactical rather than as the abandonment of principle.[1] Moreover, they have contributed greatly to the electoral rise of Sinn Féin and the displacement of the nationalist SDLP as the principal political representative of Northern Ireland's Catholics. Sinn Féin's strength in the Assembly has made the party the second largest within Northern Ireland's governing executive. A new model of participatory republicanism has displaced old methodologies, and Northern nationalists' electoral choices lie between two parties which have seemingly converged on many political issues.

This chapter explores four areas of change in nationalist and republican politics, concentrating particularly upon ideological convergence and electoral reordering. First it examines the reasons for the emergence of a new, more moderate republicanism. Second, the chapter analyses the extent to which the changed republicanism of Sinn Féin remains divergent from the northern nationalism of the SDLP. Third, the new electoral landscape within nationalist and republican politics is assessed. Finally, there is an assessment of how nationalism and republicanism may develop within the new consociational political dispensation in Northern Ireland.

CHANGED REPUBLICAN POLITICS

Movement from republican fundamentalism towards tactical flexibility was a process which gathered pace from the mid-1980s onwards. Republicanism prior to this period was not static. Tactical debates over, for example, whether to recognise the criminal courts preceded political change. The key factor from the 1980s onwards was that electoral imperatives came to have an ever greater bearing upon the tactics of the republican movement. The decision of Sinn Féin to contest elections from 1982 is often heralded as the onset of the new departure. In terms of its ultimate impact, the decision was indeed seismic, but it was scarcely novel. Electoral politics had been part of Sinn Féin's strategy from the party's foundation, adopted with some success in the second and fifth decades of the twentieth century, but with scant reward outside those periods. In the previous significant era of electoral contestation during the 1950s, electoral politics constituted a mere support show, with no wider ambition than to demonstrate that republicanism possessed an electoral constituency.

There is no definitive starting point for modern republican change, and there remains some scepticism over whether the alterations are much deeper than a necessary response to the particular conjunction of forces which confronted republicans by the 1990s. Nevertheless, some changes have radically altered the relationships of republicans to the two states in Ireland and their electorates.[2] The decision to end abstention in respect of Dáil Éireann in 1986 marked a departure from the shibboleths which had shaped republicanism since 1918.[3] The ending of abstention did not formally convey republican legitimacy upon the 'Twenty-Six-County state', but it recognised the futility of clinging on to a republican 'mandate' provided by the usurped First Dáil of 1919. From here on, Sinn Féin would be obliged to compete as merely another actor within the Irish Republic's electoral marketplace. Henceforth, republicans spoke only for themselves, not for the Irish people.[4] The republican shift was sold to supporters as a mere complement to an increased armed struggle, with the IRA 'confident of seeing the long, hard war through to a victorious conclusion'.[5] Unconvinced, a small number of 'purist' critics, led by Ruairí Ó Brádaigh, formed Republican Sinn Féin, arguing that the new constitutional horse ridden by the Provisionals could not be ridden in the same direction as its revolutionary counterpart.[6]

Ó Brádaigh's (prescient) argument was that the end of abstention in respect of one 'partitionist parliament' ended republican distinctiveness and would be followed by an identical development in the North. The twelve years between the Dáil Éireann decision and arrival at Stormont were characterised by the increasingly rapid movement of Sinn Féin towards constitutional politics. The party's 1992 document, *Towards a Lasting Peace in Ireland*, represented a new departure towards political pluralism and deployed a new 'serviceable vocabulary of compromise'.[7] *Towards a Lasting Peace in Ireland* moved republicans beyond their 'Brits out' mantra, by removing the timetable for British withdrawal and acknowledging the need for the persuasion of unionists for a united Ireland. Those charged with the task of such persuasion were the British government, a tacit recognition that over two decades of IRA violence had failed to persuade unionists that they were simply deluded in retention of their British identity. Republican orthodoxy was also shattered in the speech by senior republican Jim Gibney at the 1992 Wolfe Tone commemoration at Bodenstown, when he cautioned republicans against being deafened by the 'deadly sound of their own gunfire', hinted strongly at an imminent ceasefire and debunked the fantasy that the Provisionals would simply seize power in Ireland, relegating the movement to merely one player in a broader peace process:

> We know and accept that the British government's departure must be preceded by a sustained period of peace and will arise out of negotiations. We know and accept that such negotiations will involve the different shades of Irish nationalism and Irish unionism engaging the British government together or separately to secure an all-embracing and durable peace process. We know and accept that this is not 1921 and that at this stage we don't represent a government in waiting.[8]

Although Gibney's reference to the oxymoron of 'Irish unionism' indicated that republican thought on the identity and politics of unionists remained underdeveloped, his Bodenstown oration suggested new flexibilities within republicanism. Sinn Féin declined to commit to a position on the following year's Downing Street Declaration, a document green in its language of Irish self-determination, but unionist in its enshrinement of the principle that constitutional change could only occur with the permission of the population of Northern Ireland. What was hitherto dismissed as a 'unionist veto' was no longer automatically rejected.

The IRA's 1994 ceasefire was predicated upon the inclusion of Sinn

Féin in talks with the British government, bereft of any preordained outcome. Although the ceasefire fractured, it was readily reinstated upon the promise of entry to such negotiations after the election of the Labour government in 1997. 'Dissident' ultras, who objected to the reinstatement of ceasefire amid assertions from the British Prime Minister that a united Ireland was unforeseeable in his lifetime, left to form the Real IRA, but hopes of significant recruitment expired with its killing of twenty-nine civilians in the 1998 Omagh bombing.[9]

Entry into a Northern Ireland Executive and Assembly had been accepted as inevitable by the Sinn Féin leadership long before the Good Friday Agreement was reached in April 1998, although grassroots members were not informed of this new reality. Clearly, prolonged power-sharing would require commitment to the state. The consequences of this were that, by 2005, the IRA had stood down and completed the decommissioning of its weapons. This was followed, eighteen months later, by Sinn Féin's declaration of support for 'civic policing', which it identified as 'representative of the community it serves, free from partisan political control and politically accountable'.[10]

This revisionist republicanism had changed sufficiently from the old model to facilitate the revival of power-sharing. Sinn Féin ministers took a pledge of office which committed them to support the institutions of a state which, under republican orthodoxy, could never be legitimate. These ministers declined to call the state by its name, yet served within its government. Upon appointment as Regional Development Minister in the Northern Ireland Executive in 2007, Sinn Féin's Conor Murphy issued a memorandum to his civil servants requesting them to use the terms the 'North' or 'here' rather than refer to the political unit of 'Northern Ireland'.[11]

The displacement of the militarism of the IRA by the politics of Sinn Féin was a logical development within republicanism, even though there is a lack of consensus over the key factors which elicited such change. Several accounts stress the problems for the IRA in maintaining its armed campaign at a level sufficient to achieve substantial movement towards historical objectives.[12] According to Alonso, the IRA's armed struggle was an 'abject failure' requiring 'categorical delegitimisation' rather than retrospective justification.[13] On this interpretation, the methodology of a campaign is judged partly by outcome, in this case clearly unsuccessful in ending partition and achieving national reconciliation, although how far Northern Ireland would have changed without violence remains difficult to answer.

The pressure for an IRA ceasefire developed through debates among republican prisoners. Discussions within jails highlighted some unease over the validity of the republican cause when conducted in its absolutist violent form.[14] Such concerns were matched by growing doubts over the effectiveness of the IRA campaign in achieving declared goals, whilst the 'regular reappearance of the same people' in prison depressed morale, highlighting the difficulty of recruiting sufficient new converts to the cause.[15]

Nevertheless, those accounts stressing the containment of the IRA require some qualification. The IRA was never more destructive than in its campaign on the British mainland during the 1990s, when, in economic terms, it wrought damage exceeding its entire campaign in Northern Ireland. The campaign could never be sustained for a long period and was heavily reliant upon the South Armagh section of the organisation. However, the requirement for the British government to create a 'ring of steel' around City of London institutions, amid spiralling insurance payments and a threat to the City's central financial position, meant that the IRA had, as a minimum, indicated its continuing capacity to veto political developments in Northern Ireland that omitted the inclusion of its political representatives. This, of course, was very different from enforcing British withdrawal, but the republican leadership had harboured few delusions about such a prospect for at least the previous decade, even if the grassroots were not always informed.[16]

The IRA's British campaign of the 1990s therefore requires reinterpretation as one orchestrated by the leadership in an attempt to allow movement from the strategic reliance upon violence and end the campaign at the optimum moment. As M.L.R. Smith argued of the IRA prior to the peace process:

> The ardent belief in the utility of physical force has often obstructed the IRA from recognizing when its strategies have been successful in fulfilling their potential, as in 1921 and 1972 when the British were pressured by republican violence to open a dialogue with the movement. The inability to think in terms of compromise made it difficult for the movement to detect the limited utility of its violence and prevented the IRA from moving ahead in stages. Instead the IRA has frequently squandered positions of temporary military advantage by persisting with a particular strategy even though it has exhausted its potential.[17]

The huge bombings of the 1990s can be seen not simply as a last fling of the IRA, although the organisation was clearly very stretched, but as a campaign designed to yield the maximum possible advantage prior to the inevitable compromises of peace negotiations.

Several other reasons for republican change also exist. Firstly, discussion of ideological departure assumes the pre-existence of a coherent ideology, an aspect of the republican movement disputed in the accounts of McIntyre and Alonso.[18] For McIntyre, the Provisionals were creatures of the street politics of 1969–70 in which oppression from loyalists and the police, soon to be followed by the British army, was what galvanised the Northern nationalist population into militant action. Loyalty to the ideals of the 1916 proclamation had always meant little in urban Belfast and Derry, and the number of 'traditional' republicans in those cities was tiny by the 1960s. The development of the Provisional IRA was thus situational rather than ideational. Any claims of ideological continuity from 1916, through 1969 and to the present day are thus fictional, as republican activity in each period has been conditioned by the activities of the British state, not shaped by republican ideology. The superficial 'tagging on' of 'true' republicanism to the circumstances of 1969 lacked depth and has allowed the Sinn Féin leadership to develop an approach in which republicanism is whatever Sinn Féin does. Alonso develops McIntyre's theme via numerous interviews with former IRA members which portray them as often confused over why they fought for the IRA, using thin and unconvincing ideological dressing as justification.

Even a sympathetic analyst, Agnes Maillot, has cautioned against the idea of Sinn Féin ever being wedded too closely to any particular set of ideological principles, allowing the party to embrace, at various intervals, a different balance of nationalism, socialism, conservatism and Catholicism while fluctuating in tactics.[19] Coakley identifies seven Sinn Féin parties, each of which has claimed to be the true standard-bearer of Irish republicanism. Each struggled over the extent to which the IRA tail wagged the Sinn Féin dog, as republicanism's military and political approaches often grappled rather than neatly dovetailed.[20]

Whilst the accounts of McIntyre and Alonso may be persuasive, they ignore the clear commitment of the original Provisional *leadership* – as markedly distinct from the grassroots – to the republican politics of 1916 and indeed 1798. The politics of founders of the Provisionals such as Ruairí Ó Brádaigh, Leo Martin, and Jimmy and Maire Drumm *was* about fidelity to an indivisible republic and about the essential unity of Catholic, Protestant and dissenter, all of whom were viewed simplistically as Irish by dint of living on the island. That the Northern Provisional leadership was often regarded as sectarian is to miss the point; in their view violence was designed to achieve the severance of any British connection, represented in modern times by the 'crown forces' of the RUC and the British army. The Provisional leadership worked hard to sour relations with these forces. The missing element from accounts which lay emphasis solely upon the politics of 1969 is *how* either the structural subordination of nationalists 'or' not 'and' the arrival of the British army became issues to arouse a hitherto docile population, which was campaigning for a civil rights agenda not that far removed from what was proposed by the unionist government of the time.

In terms of the ideological and political nationalist convergence which formed part of the peace process, Catherine O'Donnell highlights the importance of the links which developed between Fianna Fáil and Sinn Féin from the late 1980s onwards.[21] Her account is careful not to overemphasise the extent to which all-Ireland 'pan-nationalism' became a clear ideological construct. Rather, Fianna Fáil cultivated dialogue with Sinn Féin partly for the benefit of the 'Soldiers of Destiny' rather than through any conversion to the politics of militant republicanism. Furthermore, the claim of the IRA in its mid-1990s 'Totally Unarmed Strategy' (also interpreted as Tactical Use of Armed Struggle) document that, for the first time, all nationalist forces were 'rowing in the same direction' exaggerated change in the direction of republicanism. Fianna Fáil was rowing *away* from its claim to Northern Ireland, and the SDLP was formulating explicit approval of the principle of unionist consent, neither of which could be interpreted as republican advancement.

The final category of explanation of republican change is located within the international sphere. There are two elements to the international dimension: the collapse of bipolarity with the end of the Cold War and the subsequent diminution of the strategic importance of Northern Ireland. The changed international situation moved the IRA from Marxist rhetoric and allowed the British government to open negotiations with republicans.[22] The second, seemingly more important (but not unconnected) element was the influence of actors in other peace processes upon Sinn Féin, with, in particular, the African National Congress proving influential.[23] The claims of the importance of the international context are challenged by Dixon, who argues, legitimately, that it has provided a veneer for republican political change, but that the relationship between republicans and the British state is what shaped the direction of conflict and peace.[24]

MODERN DISTINCTIONS BETWEEN NATIONALISM AND REPUBLICANISM

According to Professor Richard English, much of the history of Irish nationalism has concerned a community's struggle for power.[25] Whilst such power was achieved early in the twentieth century across much of the island, the exclusion of nationalists from influence in the

'Orange' northern state ensured that a communal contest remained in place. This communal contest has resulted in the inter-communal compromise of power sharing and an intra-communal reordering of nationalist politics in favour of Sinn Féin. The partial eclipse of the SDLP and Sinn Féin's camping on its political territory of an 'agreed Ireland' has raised the question of the continued viability or utility of two nationalist parties within Northern Ireland. Do substantial ideological or political differences remain?

As English comments, despite the appearance of a seismic shift in its *modus operandi*, 'much within republican politics remained familiar and these continuities helped the movement to retain heartland support'.[26] Fidelity to an independent united Irish republic remains, but what has occurred has been a reordering of republican ideals, from, in order, liberty, equality and fraternity, to a position in which equality is frontloaded. Thus a Sinn Féin minister in the first post-Good Friday Agreement executive, Bairbre de Bruin, claimed that 'equality is the most important word in the Republican dictionary'.[27] The frontloading of equality was also emphasised by Gerry Adams, who argued in 2006 that 'two key words – concepts – of our republican future are "change" and "equality"'.[28] The new language and ordering of goals are important, given that, as late as 1995, Adams was still insisting that nationalists 'cannot be equal within the Six County state: the very nature and history of the state proves that'.[29]

Sinn Féin has been obliged to rebrand its universal republican principles in favour of being a communal standard bearer in Northern Ireland, albeit one linked to the population in the Irish Republic. The belief in the value of Irish self-determination remains, but the party adopted the SDLP position of accepting co-determination for the foreseeable future, which allows a hitherto 'illegitimate statelet' to determine whether Irish reunification can proceed. For the SDLP, the natural outworkings of its concept of an 'agreed Ireland' were the Good Friday Agreement referenda, north and south of the border, in 1998. These had great symbolic importance in permitting the entire electorate on the island of Ireland to determine the political settings on the island. A single-option referendum conducted separately within the two polities – in which the result in Northern Ireland would have dictated the outcome regardless – was none the less not a full exercise in Irish self-determination and indeed its falling short of such was admitted by Gerry Adams.[30]

Modern republicanism in its northern setting continues to retain ideological and tactical distinctiveness, even if this is fading. The nature of the republican struggle against criminalisation and the striving for legitimacy created a vitality and unity of purpose among a section of

Sinn Féin support. Cassidy may exaggerate slightly when he identifies a 'vital bond, a unique mode of understanding, between a number of voters in these [republican] communities and Sinn Féin', as such tendencies dissipate amid the demands of normal electoral politics.[31] There is also a rational choice element, as distinct from organic or historic motivation, to voting Sinn Féin, based upon the perception that the party is best placed to consolidate personal and communal interests against the competing claims of unionism. Nevertheless, there remains among Sinn Féin's core support a supportive community of former prisoners, political activists and local state workers despite the upheavals of ideological change.

The SDLP's nationalism has operated within a more diverse Catholic community. The party also engaged in a contest for legitimacy, articulating the rights of nationalists amid the loyalist backlash against the civil rights campaign. Its nationalism was novel in going beyond mere anti-partitionism towards a participatory model of nationalist politics. In representing many Catholics who had not felt the worst effects of the unionist state, but none the less felt hostility towards the polity and excluded from power, the SDLP was obliged to steer a careful course between outright support for a united Ireland, participation in the state and conciliation towards unionists. Amid the polarisation engendered by armed conflict, the SDLP greened its agenda and declared strong support for Irish unity by 1972.[32] The collapse of power-sharing in 1974 was followed by an SDLP demand two years later for immediate withdrawal of British forces. After this the party rowed back and emphasised the non-coercive nature of its nationalism. Its involvement in fostering the intergovernmental 1985 Anglo-Irish Agreement and the inter-party moves towards nationalist unity on the basis of an agreed formula for self-determination can now be seen as pieces of political altruism rather than as the means of party advancement.

Although it is tempting to see the SDLP's nationalism as merely a lighter shade of green than that espoused by Sinn Féin, this would be to oversimplify. The SDLP was certainly a communal party with an overtly denominational base. Its early aspirations of attracting Protestant support were almost entirely confounded (Protestant membership is less than 2 per cent), an unsurprising development given the party's origins and ultimate constitutional preference. Nevertheless, for the SDLP, the pursuit of Irish unity was much more concerned with process than outcome. Neo-nationalism and the need for an exercise in Irish self-determination did not require a preordained outcome; if it resulted in a divided Ireland, this did not matter provided that such division arose from explicit agreement. The SDLP thus underscored the peace process with a dynamic for change, based upon its ideas of national reconciliation: consent for change and political agreement.

Post-1998, the SDLP has faced the problem of maintaining transition. Did the exercise in national co-determination, which ratified the Good Friday Agreement, provide a final constitutional settlement and if not, why not? Sinn Féin's explicit acceptance of the Agreement as a mere staging post infused republicans with continued momentum. For the SDLP, the problem lay in finding a new basis for political advancement. For many of the party's members, over one-quarter of whom had joined at formation in 1970 and whose overall average age was 57, ending the conflict had been the primary goal. These members were satisfied that the party's main objectives had been achieved and believed that their party supported power-sharing ahead of Irish unity, which raised the obvious question: what next?[33]

THE NEW ELECTORAL LANDSCAPE

Sinn Féin's political U-turns did not have an adverse effect upon its electoral support. In contrast, the SDLP paid an electoral price for engaging in the political altruism of bringing Sinn Féin from the political wilderness. During the 1980s, the SDLP's average election poll was 20.3 per cent compared to Sinn Féin's 11.9 per cent. Over the next decade, the SDLP's role in creating a peace process appeared to have paid dividends, as the party polled an average of 25.1 per cent compared to Sinn Féin's 14.1 per cent. As Sinn Féin stole many of the SDLP's ideological clothes in backing the Good Friday Agreement, the electoral position radically altered. From 2001, the year when Sinn Féin finally overhauled its nationalist rival, until 2007, the SDLP's average vote share was 20.3 per cent – identical to that of the 1980s, despite a rise in the Catholic population – compared to Sinn Féin's 23.7 per cent.

Sinn Féin voters have maximised the return of elected representatives via the spreading of first-preference votes across the party slate. The party has also excelled at mobilising former non-voters and there is a strong positive correlation between the size of the Sinn Féin vote and turnout.[34] Nevertheless, the common belief in the exceptionalism of Sinn Féin voting discipline needs some qualification. The percentage of vote surpluses transferring to the same party's candidates is even higher for the SDLP (averaging 82.9 per cent at assembly elections since 1998) than it is for Sinn Féin (79.2 per cent). Communal solidarity is even stronger than party loyalty, with 87.2 per cent of Sinn Féin's surpluses staying within the same 'ethnic bloc' and 93 per cent of the SDLP's doing likewise. On these figures, it appears that SDLP voters are fractionally even more 'bloc tribal' than Sinn Féin's, a picture slightly tempered by analysis of terminal vote transfers, i.e. those votes cast when the voter's first-preference party candidates have all been elected or eliminated. At the first three Assembly elections, from 1998 to 2007, only 7 per cent of SDLP terminal transfers went to unionist candidates. However, this comfortably exceeds the percentage of such transfers across the bloc divide from Sinn Féin first-preference voters, a mere 0.8 per cent. Nationalist and republican voters share communal distrust of the other bloc.

There remain a sizeable percentage of SDLP supporters whose antipathy to Sinn Féin prevents a terminal vote transfer to that party; in the 2007 Assembly, for example, fewer than half of SDLP terminal transfers headed to the other bloc party, compared to two-thirds of Sinn Féin's transferring to the SDLP. Nevertheless, the pre-Good Friday Agreement picture, in which SDLP final transfers were more likely to go to the Alliance than Sinn Féin amid hostility to IRA violence, has long disappeared. The overall picture is one of reinforced communal loyalty since the Good Friday Agreement.

Sinn Féin's growth has allowed it to move from its ghetto position of the 1980s in pursuit of 'new Catholic money'. Nevertheless its polling strength remains amongst the Catholic working class. Four key variables can be identified: age, with younger nationalists tending to favour the party; education, with Sinn Féin attracting disproportionately high support from those with few qualifications; employment, with Sinn Féin garnering strong backing from the unskilled and semi-skilled in manual work; and experience of the conflict, with those most directly affected likely to back the party.[35] Electoral advances in Northern Ireland have been repeated in the Irish Republic, where the party had performed abysmally. Sinn Féin achieved its first seat in Dáil Éireann since that period in 1997 and has trebled its vote share from the 2 per cent of the 1980s, although the 2007 general election indicated that the party had reached an electoral plateau.

Confined to Northern Ireland and shorn of the 'moral' superiority over Sinn Féin with the ending of the IRA's armed campaign, the SDLP's electoral appeal has been based upon the delivery of the Good Friday Agreement. Given that the deal offered the interlinked three-stranded North, North–South (Belfast–Dublin) and East–West (Dublin–London) institutional relationships long coveted by the party, the electoral pitch of 'delivery' is natural. Nevertheless, the pitch of Sinn Féin as communal defender of the gains accruing to the nationalist community from the Agreement has been attractive to many nationalists. Sinn Féin's input to the peace process left the party and the Catholic community 'in a mutually reinforcing position' in which an 'increasingly assertive and confident Catholic population' was prepared to identify as nationalist in ever-greater numbers and turn to the perceived stouter defender of that community to continue the advancement of its position.[36]

ONWARDS, BUT NOT TO 'VICTORY'? NATIONALIST AND REPUBLICAN FUTURES

According to Gerry Adams, the 'test for this generation of republicans is how we modernize our ideology to meet the needs of our time'.[37] The modern republican discourse mirrored much of that offered by 'New' Labour in Britain during the late 1990s, emphasising the need for change and renewal, but within a context in which traditional values were retained. Sinn Féin emphasised commitments to equality and justice, but it remains unclear as to whether the party believes they are now attainable within the partitioned island which any literal interpretation of the Good Friday Agreement – with its emphasis upon Northern consent – suggests will be in place for the foreseeable future. According to Adams there are 'more republicans on this island than at any time since the 1920s', a bold claim, but one entirely dependent on how republicanism is itself interpreted.[38]

Sinn Féin's discourse of equality has become framed increasingly in terms of opportunity rather than outcome. Nevertheless, the party has maintained sufficient commitment to radical policies in key areas – notably the abolition of the 11+ education transfer test – to satisfy followers, even if there is much questioning – even derision – among the republican core over the extent to which the term 'socialist' can be used to describe party policy. The party has harnessed the new confidence of Catholics, as the distribution of power within the state has radically altered.[39] Transformation from victimhood to agents of change has brought new challenges for Sinn Féin. Having accepted that Catholic emancipation has occurred in a state the party once dismissed as impossible to reform, Sinn Féin is required to move on from language of 'struggle' towards structurally blind appeals to nationalists of various social backgrounds and aspirations.

The SDLP's mildly leftist agenda has changed little, and in terms of domestic policies there is scant distinction between its offerings and those of Sinn Féin. The Europeanism which characterised the party's outlook under John Hume has not disappeared. Sinn Féin has been obliged to follow, moving from opposition to the European Union to a policy of 'critical engagement' by the late 1990s. Neither party can be said to be post-nationalist, although the SDLP has episodically made such a claim. Both remain desirous of a sovereign Irish nation-state. Sinn Féin has moved from a conception of such a state based upon

ethno-geographic determinism, in which the British-unionist alle-
giances of northern Protestants were seen as a kind of false conscious-
ness. The party has instead been obliged to accept greater political
diversity to add to the religious tolerance of the unity of Catholic,
Protestant and dissenter of the Wolfe Tone republican tradition.

There are limits to the new liberal-cultural approach of republicanism, as, by definition, the culmination of republican aims involves
defeat for the unionist-British tradition.[40] Nevertheless, the movement
towards acceptance of the need for consent means that republicanism
is no longer concerned with a non-accommodating national aggrandis-
ement. The need for national reconciliation has replaced the vernacu-
lar of smashing Northern Ireland or ending the unionist veto. Former
republican prisoners have engaged in local cross-community reconciliation projects, particularly in sectarian interface areas, with many of
these developments funded by the British state or the European Union
peace programmes. Sinn Féin appointed a former IRA prisoner,
Martina Anderson, as the party's 'Director of Unionist Outreach'. The
need for dialogue with the 'other' community is acknowledged. An
embryonic civic republicanism is being cultivated, recognising the
legitimacy of identity within the island, but this is juxtaposed with a
continuing essentialist belief in territorial unity and the construction of
an Irish nation-state which must, ultimately, exclude Britishness.

For the SDLP, the articulation of civic nationalism was not difficult,
given that the party has always acknowledged the existence of different peoples on the island of Ireland. In so far as a tension existed, it lay
in the SDLP's apparent ambiguity over whether there were two
nations or merely two traditions on the island. The SDLP insisted that
'the Irish people do have the right to self determination. The problem
is that the Irish people are divided as to how that right should be exercised.'[41]

This implied that all the people on the island were Irish and
appeared to deny unionists a legitimacy or permanency in respect of
their British affiliation. Unionist suspicions over whether the SDLP's
formula for Irish self-determination was a vehicle to create a united
Ireland were none the less exaggerated, even if the political language
of 'Humespeak' could obfuscate the issue at times.[42] The Good Friday
Agreement reflected the SDLP's position that the consent and allegiance of both traditions on the island of Ireland was a prerequisite for
fundamental constitutional change in the position of Northern Ireland.

Concurrent with the dilution of its traditional republicanism, Sinn
Féin has moved towards the 'social democratic centre left', a position
already occupied by the SDLP.[43] The avowed revolutionary socialism of
old was never a permanent fixture, was subject to leadership denials

and was trimmed for audiences in the United States. Rhetorical or otherwise, there was, however, a commitment to tax and spend socialism which has been displaced in recent years by, as examples, the implementation of private finance initiatives when in charge of the education ministry in Northern Ireland and the dilution of proposals to increase corporation tax in the Irish Republic.

Adherence to the republican narrative of 1916–19 is now largely ghettoised within the discourse of the tiny groups of republican ultras in Republican Sinn Féin and the 32 County Sovereignty Committee, both of which left Sinn Féin alleging betrayal of republican principles. For these two groups, the 'sovereignty and unity of Ireland are inalienable and indefeasible'; only the 'Irish people as a whole acting freely and without external impediment can mandate government for the Irish people' and 'partition is illegal', as are the 'partitionist entities' of parliaments or assemblies which usurp indivisible national sovereignty.[44]

Coakley cautions that 'it would be dangerous to underestimate the potential of this [fundamentalist] strand of republicanism to destabilize current constitutional and institutional arrangements'.[45] Yet this particular strain of republicanism appears to have been marginalised to an unprecedented degree.[46] Whilst Fianna Fáil railed against partition for decades, the essential difference within the broad republican family was one of methodology to bring about Irish unity; the illegitimacy of the political division of the island was unquestioned. Since the Good Friday Agreement, the self-styled 'republican party' in the Irish Republic, Fianna Fáil, has formally accepted partition, via the downgrading of its constitutional claim to Northern Ireland. Sinn Féin has maintained a Fianna Fáil-esque critique of partition whilst entering a separate set of governing institutions in Northern Ireland, albeit with modest links to those in the Republic. The efforts of Republican Sinn Féin and assorted republican 'dissidents' from Sinn Féin's strategy to mobilise republicans against the compromises of recent years have failed, epitomised by the poor showing of the republican ultras in the 2007 Assembly elections and 'military' ineffectiveness.

Republicans, whether of mainstream or ultra orientation, are obliged to contend with a sizeable lack of interest in the national question and, where passion remains, hostility to reunification. In the run-up to the Good Friday Agreement, only 17 per cent of the electorate of the Irish Republic wanted 'Northern Ireland as part of a united Ireland' as their constitutional option, although it should be noted that the most favoured option, power-sharing within a devolved assembly within the United Kingdom, elicited only 5 per cent higher support.[47] In

Northern Ireland, Life and Times surveys since the Good Friday Agreement indicate a fairly consistent level of support for Irish unity, at around 50 per cent of Catholics.[48] This remains twice as popular as the retention of Northern Ireland's place in the United Kingdom and indicates unchanged republican-oriented desires. However, Protestant hostility to the idea of unity remains undiminished in terms of its extensiveness (although measures of intensity might be useful). The percentage of Protestants in favour of Irish unity has never reached double figures since the onset of survey research, and the overall percentage figure favouring reunification of Ireland in Northern Ireland amounts to only one-quarter of the population. Outreach to unionists in terms of post-conflict reconciliation and healing might form part of a civic republican project, but it is unlikely to yield the change in constitutional attitudes which is now enshrined, via the Good Friday Agreement, as the precursor for the fulfillment of republican aspirations.

CONCLUSION

The demands of the peace process saw much ideological and political convergence between Sinn Féin and the SDLP. Sinn Féin's new republicanism embraces respect for electoral mandates, endorses constitutional politics and accepts the need for unionist consent for change. The SDLP has long articulated these principles and oversaw their enshrinement in the Good Friday Agreement. Both parties operate within a communal political framework, in which an elite-level consociational power-sharing arrangement is grafted onto a polity in which the sectarian faultline remains a chasm.

The most important modern difference between Sinn Féin and the SDLP may be structural rather than political. Sinn Féin's status as a significant all-island party facilitates continuing growth and maintains the impression of transformation. In contrast, the SDLP's northern nationalism appears reduced in appeal, amid a political context in which all-Ireland political and economic institutions are finally becoming embedded, even if the significance of such bodies remains more symbolic than real. Sinn Féin's diminution of all that was once held to be principle to the status of mere tactic is not necessarily complete. Whilst a fevered imagination may be required to envisage Sinn Féin taking seats at Westminster, the prospect – if tactical advantage could accrue – would be no less extraordinary than the party entering a Northern Ireland Assembly once appeared.

Sinn Féin has been obliged to accept the constitutionalism it once eschewed and has been forced to acknowledge that participatory politics within the Northern state is a precursor to any longer-term constitutional changes. Such participation within the equality framework provided by the Good Friday Agreement has advanced the party's fortunes in the North and called into question the viability of the SDLP. The overall nationalist and republican balance sheet in terms of progress to the supposed supreme goal of a united Ireland, as distinct from a Northern equality agenda, is less impressive. Six new cross-border bodies, a symbolic North–South Ministerial Council and four seats in Dáil Éireann by 2007 appeared modest rewards for forty years – or, an alternative count, a century of armed struggle and political activity. The issue of a united Ireland has been kept alive, but few would predict a likely date for its realisation.

NOTES

1. Sinn Féin president Gerry Adams claimed that the changes in Sinn Féin had been achieved 'without abandoning a single republican principle'. Interview, BBC Northern Ireland, *Hearts and Minds*, 1 March 2007.
2. Ruane and Todd, J., 'The Belfast Agreement: Context, Content, Consequences', in J. Ruane and J. Todd (eds), *After the Good Friday Agreement: Analysing Political Change in Northern Ireland* (Dublin: UCD Press, 1999), pp. 1–24.
3. Tonge, J., 'The Origins of the Peace Process', in C. Gilligan and J. Tonge (eds), *Peace or War? Understanding the Peace Process in Northern Ireland* (Aldershot: Ashgate, 1997), pp. 5–18.
4. Augusteijn, J., 'Political Violence and Democracy: An Analysis of the Tensions Within Irish Republican Strategy, 1914–2002', *Irish Political Studies*, 18, 1 (2003), pp. 1–26; Ryan, M., *War and Peace in Ireland: Britain and the IRA in the New World Order* (London: Pluto,1994); Ryan, M., 'From the Centre to the Margins: The Slow Death of Irish Republicanism', in Gilligan and Tonge, *Peace or War?*, pp. 72–84.
5. *An Phoblacht/Republican News*, 16 December 1986.
6. White, R., *Ruairi Ó Brádaigh: The Life and Politics of an Irish Revolutionary* (Indiana: Indiana University Press, 2006).
7. Sinn Féin, *Towards a Lasting Peace in Ireland* (Belfast: Sinn Féin, 1992); Bean, K., 'The New Departure? Recent Developments in Republican Strategy and Ideology', *Irish Studies Review*, 10 (1995), pp. 2–6.
8. Murray, G. and Tonge, J., *Sinn Féin and the SDLP: From Alienation to Participation* (Dublin: O'Brien Press), p. 233.
9. Tonge, J., *Northern Ireland: Conflict and Change* (London: Pearson, 2002).
10. *An Phoblacht*, 4 January 2007, p. 3.
11. *News Letter*, 20 May 2007.
12. Feeney, B., *Sinn Féin: A Hundred Turbulent Years* (Dublin: O'Brien, 2002); McGladdery, G., *The Provisional IRA in England* (Dublin: Irish Academic Press, 2006); Moloney, E., *A Secret History of the IRA* (Dublin: Penguin, 2002); O'Brien, B., *The Long War: The IRA and Sinn Féin* (Dublin, O'Brien, 1999); Patterson, H., *The Politics of Illusion: A Political History of the IRA* (London: Serif, 1997).
13. Alonso, R., *The IRA and Armed Struggle* (London: Routledge, 2003).
14. English, R., *Armed Struggle: A History of the IRA* (London: Macmillan, 2003).
15. Interview with a former IRA life sentence prisoner, 24 February 2007.
16. English, *Armed Struggle*.

17. Smith, M.L.R., *Fighting for Ireland? The Military Strategy of the Irish Republican Movement* (London: Routledge, 1995), pp. 219–20.
18. Alonso, *The IRA and Armed Struggle*; McIntyre, A., 'Modern Irish Republicanism: The Product of British State Strategies', *Irish Political Studies*, 10 (1995), pp. 96–122. McIntyre, A., 'Modern Irish Republicanism and the Belfast Agreement: Chickens Coming Home to Roost or Turkeys Celebrating Christmas?', in R. Wilford (ed.), *Aspects of the Belfast Agreement* (Oxford: Oxford University Press, 2001), pp. 202–22.
19. Maillot, A., *New Sinn Féin* (London: Routledge, 2004).
20. Coakley, J., 'Constitutional Innovation and Political Change in Twentieth Century Ireland', in J. Coakley (ed.), *Changing Shades of Orange and Green: Redefining the Union and the Nation in Contemporary Ireland* (Dublin: UCD Press, 2002), p. 17.
21. O'Donnell, C., *Fianna Fáil, Irish Republicanism and the Northern Ireland Troubles, 1968–2005* (Dublin: Irish Academic Press, 2007).
22. Cox, M., 'Rethinking the International and Northern Ireland: A Defence', in M. Cox, A. Guelke and F. Stephen (eds), *A Farewell to Arms? Beyond the Good Friday Agreement* (Manchester: Manchester University Press, 2007), pp. 427–42.
23. Guelke, A., 'Political Comparisons from Johannesburg to Jerusalem', in Cox, Guelke and Stephen (eds), *A Farewell to Arms? Beyond the Good Friday Agreement*, pp. 367–76.
24. Dixon, P., 'Rethinking the International and Northern Ireland: A Critique', in Cox, Guelke and Stephen (eds), *A Farewell to Arms?*, pp. 409–26.
25. English, R., *Irish Freedom: The History of Nationalism in Ireland* (London: Macmillan, 2006), p. 415.
26. English, R., *Irish Freedom*.
27. *An Phoblacht/Republican News*, 6 November 2003; McGovern, M., 'The Old Days are Over: Irish Republicanism, the Peace Process and the Discourse of Equality', *Terrorism and Political Violence*, 16, 3 (2004), 622–45.
28. *An Phoblacht*, 5 October 2006, p. 7.
29. Adams, G., *Free Ireland: Towards a Lasting Peace* (Dingle: Brandon, 1995), p. 122.
30. Adams, G., Presidential Speech to Re-convened Sinn Féin Árd Fheis, May 1998.
31. Cassidy, K., 'Organic Intellectuals and the Committed Community: Irish Republicanism and Sinn Féin in the North', *Irish Political Studies*, 20, 3 (2005), pp. 341–56.
32. SDLP, *Towards a New Ireland* (Belfast: SDLP, 1972); McLoughlin, P., '...it's a united Ireland or Nothing? John Hume and the Idea of Irish Unity, 1969-72', *Irish Political Studies*, 21, 2 (2006), pp. 157–80.
33. Murray and Tonge, *Sinn Féin and the SDLP*.
34. Tonge, J., 'Northern Ireland: Meltdown of the Moderates or the Redistribution of Moderation' in A. Gedde and J. Tonge (eds), *Britain Decides: The UK General Election 2005* (London: Palgrave, 2005), pp. 129–48.
35. McAllister, I., '"The Armalite and the Ballot Box": Sinn Féin's Electoral Strategy in Northern Ireland', *Electoral Studies*, 23, 1 (2004), pp. 123–42.
36. MacGinty, R., 'Irish Republicanism and the Peace Process: From Revolution to Reform', in Cox, Guelke and Stephen (eds), *A Farewell to Arms?*, pp. 124–38.
37. Adams, G., 'Presidential Address, Sinn Féin Árd Fheis', *An Phoblacht/Republican News*, 13 April 2000, p. 15.
38. *An Phoblacht*, 4 January 2007.
39. Mitchell, C., 'From Victims to Equals? Catholic Responses to Political Change in Northern Ireland', *Irish Political Studies*, 18, 1 (2003), pp. 51–71.
40. See Frost, C., 'Is Post-nationalism or Liberal-culturalism Behind the Transformation of Irish Nationalism?', *Irish Political Studies*, 21, 3 (2006), pp. 277–95.
41. *Irish Times*, 13 September 1998; Ivory, G., 'Revisions in Nationalist Discourse among Irish Political Parties', *Irish Political Studies*, 14 (1999), p. 94.
42. Cunningham, M., 'The Political Language of John Hume', *Irish Political Studies*, 12 (1997), pp. 13–22.
43. McGovern, 'The Old Days are Over'.
44. 32 County Sovereignty Movement Constitution, cited in Coakley, J., 'Conclusion: New Strains of Unionism and Nationalism', in J. Coakley (ed.), *Changing Shades of Orange and Green*, p. 135.

45. Ibid., p. 135.
46. Tonge, J., 'They Haven't Gone Away You Know: Irish Republican Dissidents and Armed Struggle', *Terrorism and Political Violence*, 16, 3 (2004), pp. 671–93.
47. King, S. and Wilford, R., 'Irish Political Data 1996', *Irish Political Studies*, 12 (1997), p. 182.
48. Northern Ireland Life and Times Surveys, Political Attitudes Section, reported at www.ark.ac.uk/nilt.

PART II
PARAMILITARIES AND POLITICIANS

Chapter 5
'Exit, Voice and Loyalty': Signalling of Loyalist Paramilitaries in Northern Ireland

Lyndsey Harris

INTRODUCTION

A key element of interaction, according to strategic theory, is the use of processes or determining phases in an attempt to achieve an actor's aim. The focus of this chapter is to concentrate on loyalist paramilitary interactions through one form of determining phase – signalling. The chapter will examine how loyalists signal their own preferences, to the British government, the republican movement and each other, in the hope of influencing the value other actors will place on a specific action or philosophy. There are many forms of signalling used by loyalist paramilitaries; however, the focus of this chapter will be the political rather than explicit military action employed by the Ulster Defence Association (UDA) and the Ulster Volunteer Force (UVF).[1]

EXIT, VOICE AND LOYALTY

When evaluating the nature and efficacy of loyalist ability to signal it is useful to make comparisons of their behaviour with Albert O. Hirschman's seminal work, *Exit, Voice and Loyalty: Responses to Decline in Firms, Organizations and States*.[2] Although it was written primarily for the commercial industry, the concepts revealed in his writing can be seen to have a corresponding relevance to any situation in which there is a strategic interaction. According to Hirschman, the first option available to a member of an organisation is 'exit', which essentially means that the member may leave the organisation or stop purchasing the 'brands' that are offered. Hirschman highlights that this loss of custom may focus the minds of those in authority within the organisation.[3] The second option available to the member is to employ 'voice', which Hirschman describes as:

... any attempt at all to change, rather than to escape from, an objectionable state of affairs, whether through individual or collective petition to the management directly in charge, through appeal to a higher authority with the intention of forcing a change in management, or through various types of actions and protests, including those that are meant to mobilize public opinion.[4]

Hirschman's general rule is that 'the decision whether to exit will often be taken *in light of the prospects for the effective use of voice*' [original emphasis]. Therefore, it is stated that voice may be not only a substitute for exit but also a complement to it. Hirschman observes that 'once you have exited, you have lost the opportunity to use voice, but not vice versa; in some situations, exit will therefore be a reaction of *last resort* [original emphasis] after voice has failed.'[5] However, the overriding determining factor in the choice between the two options is said to be 'loyalty'. Therefore, Hirschman brings into the analysis cost-benefit calculations based upon the nature of loyalty.

In mapping Hirschman's theory over the signalling available to loyalists we find that it can apply both to individuals within the terrorist organisations and to the collective, UDA and UVF. If we consider the strategic environment of Northern Ireland, the overall loyalist 'brand' of the two paramilitary organisations in question differs slightly. These include: for the UVF, maintaining the Union between Great Britain and Northern Ireland; for the UDA, on the other hand, although it proclaims a wish to remain British, the primary identification includes a belief in defending Protestant culture and 'their' local communities.[6]

'EXIT' AND 'VOICE'

Applying Hirschman's thesis to the literature available on loyalism and the empirical data gathered by the author, the option of 'exit' for the UDA and UVF varies.[7] Using strategic-theory terminology to clarify the exit options available for loyalist paramilitaries has revealed that once loyalists have reached their 'fallback' or 'reservation' level in the strategic environment they are faced with the option of conceding defeat or changing their values. Hence the following exit options have been identified for loyalists: first, there is the possibility of exiting from violent means to post-conflict strategies. The second, perhaps linked with the first option, includes revisionism of loyalism as a mode of politics. The third is that the terrorist organisations cease to exist, so that in effect they exit into 'nothingness'. Historically and apparently exclusively for the UDA is the possibility of exit through the desire for an independent Northern Ireland. It appears that this latter option has not been considered in any depth by the UVF due to its core value of seeing the Union between Great Britain and Northern Ireland maintained, whereas the core values identified in this study of the UDA include defence of the loyalist communities it claims to represent and the cultural connotations surrounding these core values. That loyalists have been portrayed as having a fatalistic outlook by academics such as Steve Bruce is unsurprising when we consider the exit options available to each organisation.[8]

Considering the intensity of loyalty to the values of each organisation's preferences we can see that this may indeed obscure exit possibilities and give 'voice' the 'upper hand' in terms of signalling dissatisfaction within the strategic environment. Morrow describes three types of signals available to actors: *'"Audience Costs"; "Costly Signalling"* and *"Costless Signals"'* [original italics].[9] It is evident from the empirical data gathered by the author that all three of these types of signal manifested themselves in different forms by the UDA and UVF throughout and post-conflict. A combination of political, organisational and military initiatives have been employed to convince the republican movement, British government, their own communities and each other of their commitment to achieving and maintaining their preferences. These ranged from violent terrorist activity to peaceful political protest.

SIGNALLING THROUGH POLITICAL PARTIES AND PRESSURE GROUPS

One form of 'voice' that has been employed by loyalist paramilitaries has been the use of political parties and pressure groups to influence governmental decisions and provide political analysis to the paramilitary leadership. In the post-conflict era the line between 'voice' and 'exit' has become even more blurred than during the early stages of political input given to loyalist paramilitaries. It has become increasingly evident in recent reports that the UDA and UVF wish to receive government funding to aid them in their post-conflict transformation strategies.[10] This points us in the direction of asserting that the leadership of loyalist paramilitaries are consolidating a commitment to 'exit' the military dimension of the strategic environment.

A brief history of the political elements of signalling used by the UDA and UVF helps outline the success and failures of various attempts to exert voice within the political environment in Northern Ireland.

USE OF 'VOICE' BY THE UVF

It can be argued that the politicisation of the UVF occurred during the epoch of the May 1974 Ulster Workers' Council (UWC) strike. Gillespie and Bruce provide a convincing account of this period and conclude that there is little doubt that the intimidation and involvement of the UDA and UVF contributed to the success of the UWC strike. This is an example of loyalist paramilitaries exerting their political voice.[11]

In the jubilant aftermath of the 1974 strike prominent people within the UVF created the Volunteer Political Party (VPP). Much of the political impetus behind the VPP can be traced to the feeling amongst many loyalists that they were just as socially disadvantaged as their working-class Catholic counterparts, yet had no political party which they felt could wholly represent their needs. This was highlighted further when the United Ulster Unionist Council (UUUC), which constituted the main unionist parties who had coordinated the UWC strike, rejected an application by the VPP to become an affiliate member. The rejection served to consolidate the goals of grassroots UVF members, who were not in favour of travelling down the political route and believed the UVF were better employing the military means to which they were accustomed.

The failure of the VPP can be attributed, according to Garland and Wood, to the lack of UVF cohesion at this time; they were unable to transfer any kind of campaign into votes for the VPP. Therefore, when Ken Gibson, party chairman, stood for the Westminster election in October 1974 he managed to gain only 2,690 votes (14.2 per cent of the total unionist vote), and shortly after this the VPP was dissolved. Despite the VPP's failure to evolve into a mainstream political party it did demonstrate that there were those within the UVF who were beginning to think that political means would ultimately be far more productive. The common theme of mistrust of the unionist politicians and the belief that they were being perceived as 'common hoods' revealed in empirical research conducted by the author was clearly resonant during the earlier years of the UVF's campaign. In justifying the formation of the VPP in *Combat* the UVF explained:

> We felt that now was the opportune time to come out of the shadows into the bright sunlight and expose ourselves politically to the hostile pressures exerted by those politicians who had tried unsuccessfully to castigate us by use of lies, to prove for once and all that the Ulster Volunteer Force is a credible organisation and an organisation that can be trusted to act effectively and responsibility in any given type of situation.[12]

Bruce concludes that despite the lack of policy direction the VPP was opposed to internment and very clear in its opposition to any form of Ulster independence.

Nevertheless, the failure of the VPP to materialise resulted in the UVF continuing with its armed campaign and an increase in military activity. This was something that Gusty Spence, the commanding officer of the UVF in Long Kesh, had voiced concerns about when the formation of the VPP was first considered. It was this increase in military activity that provoked some members within the UVF to question the tactics of targeting innocent Catholics. Bruce supports Gusty Spence's analysis that these events all served to set the scene for an enduring political presence on the Shankill area of Belfast.[13]

It was not until 1977, following the failed strike initiated by Ian Paisley, that the UVF again began considering the use of political parties to influence governmental decisions and ensure that their values could be upheld. Gusty Spence, a colourful character, played a pivotal role in transforming a core group of UVF prisoners within the Maze prison – such as David Ervine, Billy Hutchinson, Plum Smith, Eddie Kinner, Tom Winstone and Billy Mitchell. These people, alongside Hugh Smyth, and a new brigade staff following the coup of October 1975, which 'was largely the old Brigade Staff of the VPP era, [which] … was regarded as a more reasonable set of men, with whom business could be done' paved the way for the UVF to once again consider a political route through obtaining political analysis from the Progressive Unionist Party (PUP) established in 1977.[14]

Spence's contribution should not be overlooked; during the early 1970s there were members of the UVF – albeit a small minority and mainly prisoners – who began to consider an 'exit' from armed conflict.[15] Basic agreements and discussions were initiated between Spence and David Morley (commanding officer of the IRA prisoners) through the formation of the 'Camp Council', which focused specifically on matters concerning prisoner welfare and conditions within the Crumlin Road Prison and later in Long Kesh; it ensured that a policy of 'no conflict' was maintained in prison between the two factions. Later Spence sought to influence the leadership of the UVF from within the confinement of prison by questioning their rationale for targeting Catholic civilians and the aims of armed conflict.[16] This stemmed from Spence's own 'rejection [of] violence as a means of solving the problems of Northern Ireland', which he described thus: 'My disillusionment was with violence, never with loyalism and never with Britishness. It was never with what I saw as a legitimate political cause but with the means being used to pursue that cause. Many republicans were going through the same turmoil and asking, "Where is the violence getting us? There has to be another way."'[17] Garland describes a further initiative of dialogue between republicans and loyalists initiated by the commanding officers of the PIRA, UDA, UVF, Irish National Liberation Army (INLA) and Official IRA prisoners. The intention was to create a series of seminars discussing issues such as 'reconciliation, political status and its phasing out, Britain and the Irish Republic, culture and art in Ireland'. Nevertheless, these cross-organisation seminars were not permitted by prison authorities, and Spence continued providing seminars for his own men on exploring the political thinking behind UVF formation and activities. The failure of the authorities to permit the proposed mixed seminars is not as important as the fact that the attempt to establish such talking forums demonstrated the willingness of those convicted of crimes committed in the name of loyalism to engage with their adversaries.

One of the most significant actions of Spence during his incarceration included the organisation of a two-day UVF seminar on 5–6 September 1977 with a stated purpose to produce 'a paper in questionnaire form for the consideration of the Brigade Staff'. The proposals discussed included whether the UVF should become more politically involved. Garland reports Spence's recollection of these discussions and states that some members believed that they should become a pressure group and others felt that the British government may try to sabotage any attempts to follow a political route. A common consensus was reached that there was a need for a 'political stance to attain "respect and recognition within the community as a progressive and constructive patriot body"'. The overall recommendation to brigade staff recorded by Spence was that if the leadership agreed with the ideas they should formulate a 'political philosophy', and if they did not they needed to provide reasons why. The recommendations also included the need for the brigade staff to ensure internal unity and for 'strict military discipline' to be adhered to alongside the 'eradication of gangsterism'. Following the increase in UVF membership during the period of non-proscription those present also recommended that the membership be 'pruned' and that 'the UVF required restructuring'. Elements of 'voice' being expressed from within an organisation are clearly evident here. The important aspect to remember is that the exertion of voice by prisoners who had proved their 'loyalty' to the organisation and brand had the potential to provide a significant impact on the leadership of the UVF.

Spence resigned as OC from the UVF and the organisation itself in 1978, and in the 1980s, following his release from prison, he was asked to become involved with the Progressive Unionist Party, under Hugh Smyth's chairmanship. Spence's attitude towards the UVF was that he would be a 'free agent' and advise in such a way. The PUP was established with the remit of wishing to 'pursue a common programme of social and economic advancement'.[18] All the issues discussed in this document were what Spence's core protégés had debated in the seminars organised during their incarceration in Long Kesh. All of these members became involved with the PUP upon release from prison and sought to provide political analysis to the leadership of the UVF.[19]

Bruce describes how the UVF saw that 'while it was still engaged in terrorism ... it had little chance of making a discrete contribution to the politics of Northern Ireland but could act to chivvy unionist politicians'.[20] Hence the ability to exert political voice and agitation within the political environment was implemented. What is also evident is that from 1977 – earlier for some UVF members incarcerated during Spence's imprisonment – the UVF had considered ways out of a conflict scenario and exit strategies that included post-conflict analysis. Nevertheless, this was not done in isolation and the IRA continued with its armed campaigns, targeting loyalists and British security forces, and therefore the impetus to commit to a ceasefire simply had no momentum. The loyalty espoused by UVF members to a union with Great Britain and Northern Ireland and defeat of the IRA obscured any possibility of exiting from military activity in the strategic environment.

The effects of PUP representation were better realised when loyalist paramilitaries, following joint UDA, UVF and RHC consultation under the banner of the Combined Loyalist Military Command (CLMC), committed to a ceasefire on 13 October 1994, shortly after the PIRA ceasefire declared on 31 August 1994. During an earlier ceasefire declared on 17 April 1991 – to allow for all-party talks with British Secretary of State for Northern Ireland, Peter Brooke – the UVF employed voice using an 'audience' (directed also at the citizens of Northern Ireland, specifically Catholics given its publication in a nationalist-orientated newspaper) and 'costly signal' (threat of continued violence towards the IRA) that very clearly conveyed the intent of the organisation to achieve its aims and the continued bargaining position with the PIRA:

> Now that they have entered the real world, the next logical step is for Sinn Féin to persuade the IRA and its acolytes to cease their primary and futile violence which, in turn, will bring a positive response from this force. Mr Gibney [Jim Gibney, a prominent member of Sinn Féin] quoted a northern Protestant as saying that republican appeals could not be heard above the gunfire. That individual's sentiments are echoed by the other one million of us. Moreover, the British withdrawal theory, propounded by Sinn Féin and the IRA, insults the ethos of one million Protestants

because they too are British. And to where do they simply withdraw? They must realise that we have no intention of withdrawing anywhere. We are here and here we will stay, whatever the
sacrifices. We say to Sinn Féin and the IRA and all republican murder gangs that, whilst they continue their campaign of genocide
against the Ulster people, they leave the UVF with no alternative
other than to continue with our campaign of counter terrorism.[21]

The statement both conveyed signals and a bargaining proposition to
the PIRA: the UVF was once again verbalising its fallback position (no
British withdrawal from Northern Ireland – implicitly understood as
the Union between Great Britain and Northern Ireland) that they
would not concede, and enticing the republicans into a bargaining
position – cease killing British citizens in Northern Ireland, accept 'our'
British identity or else 'we' will continue with a military campaign
against republicans.

The commitment of the UVF to the 1994 ceasefire indicated a further
willingness to accept the political analysis of the PUP. The PUP was able
to return two candidates, David Ervine and Hugh Smyth, in the May
1996 Forum elections, and loyalists were given a political voice in the
multi-party talks that followed in July 1996, which would eventually
become part of the designing of the Belfast Agreement (1998). The PUP
was very vocal in promoting a 'Yes' campaign for the referendum that
followed (unsurprising given their analysis of the political situation
espoused in the 1985 *Sharing Responsibility* document). In May 1998 the
PUP returned David Ervine and Billy Hutchinson as Members of the
Legislative Assembly (MLA) in Northern Ireland. In April 2002, Ervine
replaced Hugh Smyth as leader of the Progressive Unionist Party.
Significantly, it was the input of ex-UVF prisoners such as Ervine and
Hutchinson that influenced the UVF to take the analysis provided by
the PUP seriously (even if they chose not to accept it). The fact that
these PUP members had 'walked the walk' did provide a good basis for
a relationship with the UVF.

Respondents were asked to analyse the impact of political representation on loyalist paramilitaries, and the synopsis of political events
post-ceasefire is strengthened in the responses gained. Respondent A
from County Down highlights the highs and lows of political analysis
given to the UVF, particularly post-1994 ceasefire:

Over the years the UVF has had a few councillors and then the PUP,
and post-ceasefire they have had three MLAs and local councillors,
although they have just lost out in the most recent of elections. So,
the effect of that is that it has maybe had a moderating influence;

certainly, it has brought the men into the bigger world and generally kept up to date with all things. It is hard to answer that. Some activists on the ground might think that the PUP are distant a wee bit, particularly the Belfast ideas as opposed to country men; country men tend to be more conservative in their thinking. Obviously, we are not going anywhere without politics so we have to have political representation and political input at some level.[22]

Respondent A was asked to elaborate upon his answer to consider whether he could identify any period where political representation became more noticeable from a UVF perspective. The answer emphasises the period of formation of the Combined Loyalist Military Command:

I suppose that that probably goes back to when the loyalist ceasefires were declared, at that time there was a joint representation from the UVF and UDA and I think then on the back of the ceasefires there seemed to be more support for the PUP but over the last few years the way things have turned out, that support has lessened and they have lost a lot of that support. I think the problem is that most people see the Agreement [Belfast Agreement, 1998] as not having worked out for the benefit of loyalists and protestants and they probably see SF and the IRA getting away with doing what they want.[23]

Nevertheless, despite the identification of political analysis that had been provided by the PUP, respondents did relate an observation that some members of the UVF perceive themselves as a purely military force. Respondent B, from County Armagh – perhaps it is significant that there are no PUP candidates in this rural area – stated:

Speaking from the UVF, the UVF would see themselves more of a military force, whose membership would have supported various political parties – the UUP, DUP – unlike the republicans where every IRA volunteer would certainly be a SF supporter. The analogy is not there. The loyalists see themselves more as a military force; notwithstanding that they had political aspirations but they were quite content to leave their political masters to look after that at one stage.[24]

Billy Mitchell's analysis of the effects of political representation highlights a familiar concern about the marginalisation of the PUP once the

Belfast Agreement was signed. Nevertheless, he stressed that the PUP still had a good relationship with the UVF leadership and the problems of electoral politics:

> When the ceasefires were called everyone was courting the PUP. Once the agreement was signed, sealed and delivered and the referendum endorsed the Agreement the PUP was, just like the UDP, pushed to the side, as was the Alliance and other parties. It became the SDLP, UUP road show; now it's the SF, DUP road show. Political representation: the only time the government wants to engage with the PUP is when they are looking for something regarding loyalism. It probably depends on [the Secretary of State for Northern Ireland] …
>
> What I will say is that the UVF leadership does listen to the analysis of the PUP and I think, in that respect, the PUP would have a fairly good influence with the leadership within the UVF …[25]

Although loyalists have been able to voice their concerns and have a political presence in the strategic environment, the zero-sum politics that was aroused following the fourth suspension of the Northern Ireland Assembly in 2002 led to an increasingly marginalised arena for the PUP to compete in. This, coupled with the problems surrounding the Agreement's implementation, led respondents to feel that their ability to express voice during this period had been restricted and that the influence of political representation had been less effective. A PUP-aligned respondent observed:

> What we are seeing now, in some senses, [is] the void of not having a total political representation, in that what we have in the political sense – in the last five to eight years – is that we have the two main strands of unionism challenging to say that they are right so what we have is that the middle ground has been eradicated. That middle ground was taken by parties like the PUP and you saw at that time, going through that period that the parties like the PUP and UDP had influence, particularly around the 1998 Agreement to bring people along. Today, when you see less support for the likes of the PUP and the UDP are now gone, these people now look at other avenues to make their points … I think that if there was bigger political representation and more strength within loyalism, the loyalist politicians, then loyalism would be further along the road because they lack confidence. [26]

It is at this point within the strategic environment that loyalist paramilitaries had to consider additional exit strategies or alternative ways to voice their concerns. As described by Respondent N the effect of political representation for the UVF was that: 'It has given them another voice and another channel. The PUP has given them a way of achieving goals without violent means.' Nevertheless, Respondent M highlights that despite the fact that, 'I would say that at some stages they [PUP] have maybe calmed situations down once things had been pointed out to them [UVF] of the consequences', there has been very little corresponding positive effect for the PUP because 'anything they [UVF] do, the PUP is penalised for it – fined by the IMC or through the ballot box – because the people [electorate] identify that action with the PUP …'.[27] Therefore, given the political climate, the UVF had to look inwards to progress forwards.

THE ULSTER DEFENCE ASSOCIATION AND POLITICAL VOICE

Being numerically larger and bearing in mind the vigilante origins of the organisation, the UDA had an entirely different structure from the UVF. The fact that the UDA was not proscribed by the British government until 10 August 1992 points towards the community action that the UDA were legitimately involved in via the Ulster Community Action Group (UCAG). A UDA Prisoner's Aid Group document discusses the first community development initiated by the UDA in Glencairn, which was followed by community centres 'in most loyalist working class areas of Belfast and beyond'.[28] There was also said to be an establishment of 'co-operatives' with the aim 'to reduce prices and put the profits back into the community'. Nevertheless, despite these community initiatives, Bruce, maintains that there was no cross-over between the men involved in community politics and military activity: 'There were men who were only one thing or the other.'[29]

The UDA produced a number of 'costless' (with Republicans the intended recipients) and 'audience' signals (aimed at their own communities and the British government) in the early 1970s, with the erection of barricades and 'no go areas' in many loyalist districts. The purpose of this was said to be 'in order to secure loyalist areas against the IRA's murderous attacks'. It was also aimed at putting pressure on the government to bring an end to republican 'no go' areas.[30] As early as 1972 (30 June) the UDA was involved in a stand-off with the British army over the erection of a barricade adjacent to the Springfield Road on March Street.

The UDA's ability to influence British government policies through the use of political protest, such as the 1974 UWC strike, was short-lived.

Despite Andy Tyrie's (former supreme commander of the UDA) analysis in the early 1970s that the tactical use of non-violence would achieve the greatest impact on the strategic environment, the more military ori-entated members of the UDA sought to use violence to counteract an increase in republican activity, and with the creation of the specific mil-itary wing of the Ulster Freedom Fighters (UFF) in 1973 the separation between politics and military matters was consolidated.

Following the failed 1977 strike the UDA lost faith in the mainstream political parties and Tyrie, Glenn Barr, Harry Chicken, Tommy Lyttle and Bill Snoddy formed the New Ulster Political Research Group (NUPRG) in January 1978. The NUPRG's remit, according to Bruce, was to sell the political ideas to the UDA rank-and-file membership and thrash out ideas of negotiated independence.[31] Whilst the NUPRG was consulting with the rank-and-file membership a request to restrain the UDA killings was upheld, and Bruce highlights that by the end of the consultation period it could claim to have the full support of the UDA as killings decreased from 114 in 1977 to eight in 1978.[32] In November 1978 the NUPRG released its policy document, *Beyond the Religious Divide*, which advocated negotiated independence with an emphasis on promoting an 'Ulster' identity first and foremost through an inde-pendent Ulster state (the six counties of Northern Ireland), which would remain a part of the British Commonwealth, a detailed bill of rights and a constitution modelled on that of the United States.[33] It is clear that the proposals for an independent Ulster state were an exam-ple of the politically minded members within the UDA looking towards some form of 'exit' from the strategic environment.

However, if we delve deeper into the rationale of the proposals for negotiated independence it is possible to view the *Beyond the Religious Divide* document as an 'audience signal'. First, negotiated independ-ence was rejected almost outright by the community the UDA claimed to represent, and this threat must have already been in the back of Tyrie's mind because Barr's initial idea of voluntary coalition was unanimously rejected by Sammy Smyth, a key political thinker in the UDA, and by Tyrie himself back in 1975. Second, it was also signalling to the republicans that it would be more prepared than ever to give up the Union with Great Britain – though a link with the Commonwealth was still proposed – to become a part of a united Ireland. Third, it was also rather elementary signalling to the British government and unionist politicians that it was capable of providing a solution and should be taken seriously as a political player. Furthermore, it was signalling that loyalism could be self-sufficient.

The failure of *Beyond the Religious Divide* was sealed particularly by the lack of support from military members within the UDA and the failure to convince any of the major political parties in Northern Ireland. In 1981, John McMichael (UDA brigadier of South Belfast) was instrumental in the formation of the Ulster Loyalist Democratic Party (ULDP). McMichael took over as chief political spokesperson and Barr and Chicken exited the UDA stage. In 1981, McMichael stood for election in his brigade area but failed to get elected with a return of less than 2 per cent of the 43,000 votes. The ULDP remained quiet and so too did the UDA political voice until the 1985 Anglo-Irish Agreement. *Common Sense* was published in 1987 and began by stating:

> At the time of writing we are suffering yet another Ulster consti-
> tutional crisis, this time provoked by the Anglo-Irish Agreement.
> Violence, intercommunity strife, polarisation and uncertainty are
> all at a higher level than at anytime for almost a decade. The
> 'accord' will not bring peace, stability nor reconciliation to
> Northern Ireland because it is a contract between two govern-
> ments and not an agreement between those in the cockpit of the
> conflict — Ulster Protestants and Ulster Catholics.

Fundamentally, *Common Sense* proposed a power-sharing institution in exchange for Catholic commitment to a Northern Irish state and suggested that a written constitution be devised that could be amended only by a two-thirds majority. Although this document showed great depth of imagination for the time, it received no recognition from the main political parties and yet again the impetus to carry these proposals forward in the political environment stagnated. McMichael was assas-sinated by the PIRA in 1988 and Tyrie resigned as overall commander of the UDA shortly afterwards. In 1989 the ULDP was reincarnated under the auspices of the Ulster Democratic Party (UDP) and, in 1990, Gary McMichael (John's son) took over as leader of the party. Bruce reports that during this period Gary and the work of the UDP were overshadowed by the charisma of David Ervine of the PUP. However, as discussed above, the 1994 loyalist ceasefires did change the outlook of the loyalist paramilitary-associated parties to gain political ground.

In 1996 Gary McMichael and John White were returned in the Forum elections and took part in the negotiations over the Belfast Agreement (1998). The electoral success for the UDP was very limited and received very little support from the loyalist communities it was hoping to repre-sent. It failed to return any member of the party in the 1998 Assembly election, receiving only 1.45 per cent (11,760) of the votes. Following the disastrous election results, a combination of inter-and intra-organisation-al feuds and a rethink of the political voice needed for the UDA, the UDP was disbanded and the Ulster Political Research Group served to provide political analysis only (rather than run for election as a collective political body) to the UDA Inner Council. In unison with interviews conducted with UVF respondents for this study, UDA respondents were asked to identify what they believed were the effects of political representation for the paramilitary organisation.

Respondent F from County Antrim observed the following reasons behind his belief that the UDA had been unsuccessful in the political party sphere in Northern Ireland, which concentrate on the UDA's primary rationale to use military force:

> I think basically in the first instance it comes from the movement itself; the UDA does not perceive itself to be a political entity; it perceives itself now to be a military entity protecting the democratic rights of the people who it purports to represent. It has left the politics in 1974 with the DUP and UUP and allowed them to take the leadership role to try and get political development in N.I. It has taken those political parties and the annihilation of Trimble at the most recent Westminster elections to enforce the belief within the UDA itself ... With every generation, and we have watched republican history, they have come back with a rearmed campaign to take on unionism to force the IRA agenda. Loyalism will always be prepared for that strategy, to counter-strategise ... some people believe that military might [of the UDA] brought the IRA to the negotiating table for the first time ever to discuss peace.[34]

Respondent D, a UDA brigadier, provided his interpretation of the effects of political representation for the UDA:

> Well on reflection and when I look back at the people who have tried to represent the organisation over the years they never got a fair crack of the whip; the people on the paramilitary side shafted them to a certain extent. They tried to set out to do things and they were certainly politically capable of competing with other people like the DUP and other unionist parties, whatever, SF and the SDLP. But they didn't run on parallel lines like the IRA does with SF; the republicans would try to make sure that whatever they were doing politically would run in the same direction as what they were doing militarily and vice versa.

When pressed further on reasons behind the lack of cooperation with the political side of the organisation he replied:

Well violence seemed to be getting SF or the IRA where they wanted to go and they thought that was the best way. There was a time in the organisation when there was an inner council and an outer council. The outer council would have been the military people and the inner council would have been more – not politicians – but they realised the importance of politicians and the political way. The two things came together and as time elapsed and things moved on the inner council became the outer council and more military thinkers; the more assassinations that the IRA carried out the more the Loyalist paramilitaries thought there was a need to retaliate.

Sammy Duddy highlighted further insights into the effects of political representation for the UDA:

Well there have been so many splits within the organisation that political representation could only have worked in the early seventies. It couldn't possibly work now; it couldn't possibly work now because everyone seems to have their own agendas in loyalism.

It is evident that the Ulster Defence Association's attempts to create a political party that will *represent* their views have proved futile. The organisation has been unable to successfully convert the political thinking of key members within its ranks into policies that the organisation as a whole can support or believe in. This can be attributed to many factors: first, the fact that the organisation is so large and has virtually autonomous leaders, in the different brigade areas of the Inner Council, which coincides with the ambitions – personally and collectively – of the brigadiers. Second, and perhaps most importantly, there have been successive inabilities to convince the military-minded members of the organisation that a political route to achieving an exit from armed conflict was the preferred outcome. Effectively, the UDA politicos have been unsuccessful in creating 'audience signals'. As Morrow discusses, issues of commitment can arise if the signals and bargaining positions are not followed through.[35] In a similar vein to the UVF in its earlier days, the UDA has failed to convince its membership and local communities of the overriding cost-analysis benefits of politicising.

The UPRG has more recently stepped up to fill the void in the political analysis available to the UDA and sought to keep grassroots members informed. Surveys of the UDA membership have been conducted, with a number of workshops organised by the UPRG to establish how they wish to proceed on certain pressing issues concerning the strategic environment in Northern Ireland, such as decommissioning demands, and within the organisation itself, such as internecine feuding and criminality. A Conflict Transformation Initiative: Loyalism in Transition (CTI) has been produced with a stated remit that:

> Consensus feeling was that the organisation should play its part in transforming Loyalism and helping to create a more stable and peaceful society. The UDA leadership asked its political advisors, the Ulster Political Research Group (UPRG) to design a process which would facilitate such a development. From this the Conflict Transformation Initiative (CTI) emerged ...[36]

Interestingly, a member of the UPRG states that they want to play a role in achieving reconciliation but stated, '[w]e don't believe that Republicans really want reconciliation, so we intend to test them on it'.[37] During the discussions at various CTI workshops it became clear that the UDA, via the influence of political analysis provided by the UPRG, was concerned with how it signalled in the strategic environment to ensure that it manoeuvred itself into a position that could ensure maximum cost–benefit results in terms of upholding its belief systems. A UPRG member responded to a Palestinian delegate's question, 'what practical things do you want from Republicans to move towards peace?'

> We want Republicans to recognise our identity, which is reflected in the Loyal Order parades, the Union flag, the Ulster flag ... everything that gives expression to our identity as a people. The more they call for the removal of those things which signify my identity the more threatened I feel. And the more threatened I feel, the more I want to react to that threat by conflict.[38]

As demonstrated, the UDA has moved to consider conflict transformation or post-conflict exit strategies at a much later stage than the UVF.

CONCLUSION

The disillusionment of the Good Friday Agreement's implementation recorded in interviews obtained for this study, combined with the 'commitment' the IRA has demonstrated in remaining on ceasefire and decommissioning, have meant that loyalist paramilitaries have been able to concentrate on 'exit' strategies and sell these to their membership as viable options. So long as their 'loyalty' is being upheld to the 'brand' they espoused, it no longer obscures possible exit. The fact is that it has taken the UDA longer to accept the futility of electoral politics based solely on trying to represent the views of the whole organisation than consider political analysis and other avenues of exit.

NOTES

1. See Spencer, G., 'Constructing Loyalism: Politics, Communications and Peace in Northern Ireland', *Contemporary Politics*, 10, 1 (2004), pp. 37–55, for signalling using media. See Harris, L., 'Introducing the Strategic Approach: An Examination of Loyalist Paramilitaries in Northern Ireland', *British Journal of Politics and International Relations*, 8, 4 (2006), pp. 539–49, for further information on strategic theory.
2. Hirschman, A., *Exit, Voice and Loyalty: Responses to Decline in Firms, Organizations and States* (Cambridge, MA: Harvard University Press, 1970).
3. Ibid., pp. 21–9.
4. Ibid., p. 30.
5. Ibid., p. 37.
6. See Harris, L., 'Duck or Rabbit? The Value Systems of Loyalist Paramilitaries', in M. Busteed, F. Neal and J. Tonge (eds), *Irish Protestant Identities* (Manchester: Manchester University Press, 2008).
7. See, for example, Nelson, S., *Ulster's Uncertain Defenders: Loyalists and the Northern Ireland Conflict* (Belfast: Appletree Press, 1984) and Bruce, S., *The Red Hand: Protestant Paramilitaries in Northern Ireland* (Oxford: Oxford University Press, 1992). Empirical research was carried out for the author's doctoral thesis and included fifty interviews with ex-UVF and UDA members across Northern Ireland between January and September 2005.
8. Bruce, S., *The Edge of the Union: Ulster Loyalist Political Vision* (Oxford: Oxford University Press, 1994).
9. Morrow, J. 'The Strategic Setting of Choices: Signalling, Commitment and Negotiation in International Politics', in D. Lake and R. Powell (eds), *Strategic Choice and International Relations* (Princeton, NJ: Princeton University Press, 1999), pp. 77–114.
10. Ulster Political Research Group, *A New Reality? Loyalism in Transition 1* (Belfast: Regency Press, 2006); BBC News Online, 'Hain Backs Loyalist Project Grant' (http://news.bbc.co.uk/1/hi/northern_ireland/5357534.stm), 18 September 2006.
11. Gillespie, G., 'The Origins of the Ulster Workers Council Strike', *Etudes Irelandaise*, 29, 1 (2004), pp. 129–44 and Bruce, S., 'Terrorists and Politics: The Case of Northern Ireland's Loyalist Paramilitaries', *Terrorism and Political Violence*, 13, 2 (2001), pp. 27–48.
12. Ulster Volunteer Force, *Combat*, 1 (1974).
13. Bruce, 'Terrorists and Politics', pp. 29–30.
14. For more in-depth details of this period see Bruce, *The Red Hand*, pp. 117–36 and Garland, R., *Gusty Spence* (Belfast: Blackstaff, 2001).
15. Garland, *Gusty Spence*, pp. 194–216.
16. Ibid., pp. 178–9.
17. Ibid., p. 268.
18. Progressive Unionist Party, *Proposed Democratic Devolved Administration for Northern Ireland* (Belfast: PUP, 1979), p. 4.
19. Such as David Ervine, Billy Mitchell and Billy Hutchinson.
20. Bruce, 'Terrorists and Politics', p. 30.
21. *Irish News*, 27 June 1992.
22. Interview with Respondent A, County Down, 2005.
23. Ibid.
24. Interview with Respondent B, County Armagh, 2005.
25. Interview with Billy Mitchell, Belfast, 2005.
26. Interview with Respondent P, County Antrim, 2005.
27. Interview with Respondent M, County Down, 2005.
28. Prisoners' Aid and Post-Conflict Resettlement Group, *A Brief History of the UDA/UFF in Contemporary Conflict* (Belfast: Prisoners' Aid and Post-Conflict Resettlement Group, 1999).
29. Bruce, 'Terrorists and Politics', p. 31
30. Prisoners Aid, *A Brief History of the UDA/UFF* (1999), pp. 16–20.

31. Bruce, 'Terrorists and Politics', p. 32.
32. Ibid.
33. See Bruce, 'Terrorists and Politics', and McAuley, J. 'From Loyal Soldiers to Political Spokespersons: A Political History of a Loyalist Paramilitary Group in Northern Ireland', *Études Irlandaise*, 21, 1 (1996), pp. 165–79.
34. Interview with Respondent F, County Antrim, 2005.
35. Morrow, 'The Strategic Setting of Choices', pp. 77–114.
36. Hall, M., *Conflict Transformation Initiative: Loyalism in Transition 2: Learning from Others in Conflict: Report of an International Workshop* (Newtownabbey: Island Pamphlets, 2007), p. 3.
37. Ibid., p. 24.
38. Ibid., p. 11.

Chapter 6
Bridging the Militarist-Politico Divide: The Progressive Unionist Party and the Politics of Conflict Transformation

Stephen Bloomer

INTRODUCTION

This chapter begins with a critical overview of the internal and external pressures on the PUP from 1994, highlighting both opportunities and threats as the party navigated through the peace process balancing its role of maintaining the UVF/RHC ceasefire and at the same time vying for position within the peace process as a minor player within the unionist bloc. The chapter will argue that, from its zenith in 1994 when it was lauded for its role in facilitating the ceasefire, the party was intentionally sidelined, by both the British state and the unionist bloc, over the subsequent years as the peace process became ever more focused on facilitating the engagement between the mainstream unionist bloc with the SDLP, Sinn Féin and the Provisional IRA, down-grading the PUP's role to that of superintending the UVF and RHC.

By focusing on the 'big picture' the PUP was able to maximise its political impact for a number of years, although as a result the party failed to maximise its potential. In many ways its internal structures were insufficiently developed to build a modern political party. Consequently the party was dominated by a limited number of high-profile members involved in the 'high' politics of the peace process at the expense of developing the party at branch and association level. As a result the influx of new members after 1994 became a burden the party was unable to cope with, and membership haemorrhaged over the following decade.

Against this background a number of ideological currents within the party are examined, particularly the vexatious question of the party's relationship with the UVF/RHC, the development of a clear socialist position within the party and the related ideological debate within the party on electoral strategy and community politics, which in turn clarified its position in favour of an approach wedded to conflict transformation. To illustrate the development of conflict transformation a case study is provided on the East Antrim Conflict Transformation Forum which illustrates the benefits of real partnership between the political, military and community elements of the movement. This is followed by a discussion on the nature of the 'politico'/'militarist' debate within the wider movement.

The research for this chapter is somewhat unique in that it draws on both an ongoing research partnership with Aaron Edwards and also on the author's ethnographic insights into the PUP from within, in terms of my role as a party member who sits on the party's review team and its ruling Executive Committee (EC).

A CRITICAL OVERVIEW OF THE PROGRESSIVE UNIONIST PARTY FROM 1994

In the wake of the 1994 paramilitary ceasefires the PUP found itself centre stage. It had become more attractive to potential new members and consequently found itself under immense pressure to expand its organisational structure across Northern Ireland. The lead-up to the Belfast Agreement was a 'galvanising period' for the party, a period when many discussions took place between different hues of loyalism throughout the province and when the 'politicos' were dedicating their time to trying to sell a political deal to those with a more 'militarist' outlook. It produced a sense of political excitement, the allure of the 'end game', a time when a spirit of compromise between the communal blocs seemed possible. The period also demonstrated that internal and external pressures on the party were effectively retarding its progress. Developing the membership base of the PUP was by no means an uncomplicated task. PUP EC member Colin Robinson recalled how:

> The party at this time did have difficulty in coping with the influx of new members. Perhaps in the period after the ceasefires, we were all too enthusiastic, maybe we took on members who were not best suited to the party, but the momentum was genuine. The party was not equipped to deal with such quick expansion and the more mundane aspects of developing a party in terms of constitutions and structures were not in place.[1]

Similarly Dawn Purvis, who replaced the late David Ervine as party leader in January 2007 following his untimely death, recalled how '1995–1996 saw a rush of applications to the party for membership. It was clear at the time that the party was not ready for all the new members.'[2] Despite this influx the period up to 1998 was one in which 'the PUP rode the crest of a wave' according to Purvis. In hindsight, however, while policing a still fragile peace process it is clear that the PUP failed to address the more mundane issues of party structures and systems. Although an advanced blueprint had been drawn up in the 1990s to develop the PUP's branch structure, it never left the drawing board. In fact it was 2002 before a comprehensive reorganisation process was finally begun, which saw a new Executive and leadership structure installed. This rationalisation process led inexorably to a reduction in membership.

With the problems generated by a breakdown in the Provisional IRA ceasefire between February 1996 and July 1997, great strain was placed on both the party and the movement as a whole. The PUP can at least be credited for its work in maintaining the loyalist ceasefire. There can be little doubt that a reinstatement of the IRA ceasefire served to boost morale within progressive loyalist ranks. Colin Robinson summed up the buoyant mood prevalent in the run-up and immediate aftermath of the signing of the Belfast Agreement, which quickly began to dissipate:

> You could characterise the 1990s thus: after the 1994 ceasefires there was a feeling within militant loyalism that 'we had won'. In 1998 the spirit was more one of compromise; to give politics a chance; we had all to work together for a solution. The PUP worked very hard for the Agreement ... went head to head with the DUP on occasions which was difficult. Many people in the party suffered emotional strain.[3]

Another member of the PUP EC, Billy Hutchinson, is convinced that the period immediately prior to the Belfast Agreement provided ample evidence that not only was the PUP being sidelined but that the then much larger Ulster Unionist Party (UUP) and the British government were engaged in a campaign to destroy any influence that the party might accrue.

> I asked [Tony] Blair on a number of occasions how he was going to engage with loyalism. He had sent his aides to work with republicans. Where was the same process for loyalism? He never actually delivered on this; they did not send anyone to work with us. This begs the question ... and I warned him that just because the Provos do something loyalists will not necessarily do the same. We tried to tell him our difficulty is not with the weapons, it's with the mindsets.[4]

The PUP's standing among its support base was further undermined by the ineffectiveness of the UUP in delivering the peace dividends promised to the people of Northern Ireland, which led directly to considerable disillusionment within the wider UVF–RHC–PUP constituency. The PUP lost many members when it became apparent that the Agreement had failed to deliver what most people thought was owed to them: a stake in the political process. The two PUP MLAs between 1998 and 2003, David Ervine (party leader from 2002 until 2007) and Billy Hutchinson (MLA from 1998 until 2003), while they could exert some political influence, were already increasingly peripheral to the body politic.

This constituency-wide despondency – in both the political and military circles of progressive loyalism – has a long genesis. In fact it can be traced back to friction between loyalism and unionism in 1991 and the refusal by mainstream unionists to acknowledge the efforts undertaken by the Combined Loyalist Military Command (CLMC) to create space for political dialogue to emerge. William Smith, a senior PUP member in the 1990s, recalled that:

> A key problem during the ceasefire was that the move received no reciprocal gesture from mainstream unionism; neither the UUP nor DUP felt the need to engage with loyalism. That's when the CLMC decided that it would no longer have the mainstream unionist parties speaking on its behalf – we would have our own political representation.[5]

The brand of loyalism propagated by the PUP needed its own identity, not just as a junior partner within unionism but as a progressive working-class version of unionism. The waning of PUP influence continued over the next few years, an analysis recently accepted by the PUP leadership.[6] From the preliminary talks in Stormont, and the engagement with senior government officials, to the Forum elections and further negotiations, the PUP operated almost to its maximum potential, in the main due to the party's position in the balance of power between pro- and anti-Agreement unionists. The leverage afforded from this position explains to a great extent how the PUP manufactured the deal on the prisoner releases and the party victory in ensuring that six seats per each electoral area became institutionalised within the new electoral system.

Post-Agreement there was still a belief in the party that it was effective politically but was powerless to prevent pro-Agreement unionism from walking away from the Agreement. The PUP analysis of the immediate post-Agreement period is that the failure was one of implementation, rather than of fundamental problems in the Agreement. As the Agreement started to unravel, the smaller parties were increasingly sidelined in the run-up to the Weston Park talks in July 2001. A new *realpolitik* began to emerge wherein numerous developments and political deals were devised outside the confines of the Agreement. As Smith pointed out:

> At Weston Park they brought the UUP and SDLP over on the Monday for two days of serious talks and then brought the smaller parties over on the Wednesday for an hour. That's why we walked out of Weston Park, no point us being there. It was the same in Hillsborough [March 2003]; it was a smokescreen. In effect the SDLP, Sinn Féin and the UUP were making deals which were outside the Agreement.[7]

The dilemma remained for the PUP that even with the contribution to progress it had made in its important maintenance work it could not translate this into voter recognition. By 2004 the PUP had effectively been sidelined, in the main due to the failure of mainstream unionism to deliver on the Agreement, and in part because of two major shortcomings. The PUP had both failed to become an organised and effective political operator and to deliver the decommissioning of UVF weaponry. Inevitably two key issues dominated intra-party debates and discussions; the first concerned the future political and electoral direction of the party, and the second its relationship (or at least the nature of its relationship) with the UVF and the RHC.[8]

During 2004–05, as a result of formal and informal discussions within branches and at Executive level, the party was presented with an opportunity to clarify and accentuate its political direction. Alternatively there was support within the party to shy away from electoral politics in favour of an approach which was more issue-based, effectively winding down the PUP as a political party. In a series of interviews conducted by the author and Aaron Edwards a decade on from the paramilitary ceasefires,[9] a range of senior activists within the PUP discussed the future direction of the party. The overwhelming consensus arising from the interviews was the need for the party to (re)establish itself as avowedly socialist; the debate was on how to move to such a position.[10] The prevailing orthodoxy in the party was that the PUP should accentuate its contribution to community politics, where it could be seen to be making a difference. Dawn Purvis summarised this key new dimension for the PUP, which had been debated within its ranks for some time, particularly at branch level: 'The PUP needs to re-focus on community activism, for example the water charges offer a good opportunity to take the lead on the opposition campaign. The Party needs to overcome the notion within the Protestant working class that the working class are "no good" at politics.'[11] Billy Mitchell had been a key advocate for some time of a move away from 'high' politics towards community activism, arguing that the only way forward for the PUP was to refocus on class politics as the means to situate the party within a regionalised Britain. In terms of outlook the PUP had to undertake something of a paradigm shift away from issues it 'supported' to issues it was prepared to 'campaign' on:

> Would we be better as a working class socialist lobby group, rather than a party worrying about elections? This debate is necessary and needs to happen; is it a question of being afraid of alienating our support groups/potential voters? If they don't like us do we really need their votes; we could end up like the Workers Party.[12]

This was emphasised by Billy Hutchinson,[13] who was convinced that the PUP could be a socialist party but not until such time as the conflict was settled to the satisfaction of all parties, leading to realignment in terms of class rather than the nationalist/republican and unionist/loyalist groupings. David Ervine also reinforced the sceptical view that the politics of the PUP had been conservative in the extreme, too focused on the 'big picture', and had thus failed to attract electoral popularity. According to his analysis the PUP had not risked destabilising the UVF and the RHC by forcing a socialist ethos on an organisation with a conservative political outlook: 'Clearly there is a price to pay for the relationship with the UVF and Red Hand, unlike the nationalist community who seem to be more sophisticated in their electoral judgements. The PUP remains avowedly socialist; there are no other socialist parties in Northern Ireland.'[14] The social class dimension of 'new loyalism' has been explored in detail by James McAuley.[15] McAuley interprets the PUP's discourse as a 'coherent analysis of the class structure of traditional unionism' which challenges 'the old Stormont system of privilege and patronage' (see Chapter 1 of this volume). The PUP's democratic socialist credentials are enshrined in its Constitution (1996), which still retains Clause 4 of the old British Labour Party Constitution. The dual ideological preoccupation with the Union and socialism has been the historical burden of Protestant working-class politics since the rapid industrialisation of Belfast in the late nineteenth century. The PUP is the latest in a long line of working-class parties which have sought to transform the material fortunes of the Protestant working class.[16]

From February to June 2005 the party undertook an internal review of a number of key issues with all its branches and with external 'critical friends'. The review team was headed up by Dr John Kyle (who later assumed David Ervine's council seat in Belfast Pottinger after the latter's death) and focused on a range of issues central to the future direction of the PUP, including the nature of the party, its core political principles, the political message the party needed to convey, the challenges it faced, its links to the UVF/RHC and challenges to loyalism generally.[17]

The review team recognised that the party faced significant challenges and emphasised the need to reposition itself in the mainstream political process. In determining this view it effectively rejected the notion developed within some branches that the party should disavow electoral politics. However, in moving to this position the party adopted a new realism which dictated that electoral politics would be scaled down to ensure that it would field fewer candidates to guarantee that resources were more effectively employed. Hence the approach drew from both the main prevailing views at branch level: an emphasis on community politics and a more realistic approach to electoral politics. In reaffirming its core values the party reiterated that it was a socialist party, rooted in working-class communities, and committed to tackling poverty, social injustice and inequality of opportunity.

The report emphasised that the connection with the UVF and RHC was an electoral liability, catching the prevailing mood in the party that the time was ripe for a redefinition, precluding a more complete decoupling in the longer term. Accepting that loyalism had effectively been downgraded to a pejorative term, particularly within the wider unionist bloc, the report outlined potential areas of operation designed to ameliorate the perception of working-class unionism. In order to legitimise loyalism the party was called upon to instigate a number of practical measures including the promotion of restorative justice programmes, support for anti-drug and anti-racism programmes, promoting women office-bearers and increased engagement with Churches and community groups. Again the party direction was carefully crafted to balance community and electoral politics:

> The sub-group believes that we should focus more on local issues that affect the communities from which we come. A track record of effective involvement in the concerns of local residents will ultimately be our best strategy. This will be achieved by workers who are motivated by a social conscience rather than merely seeking an electoral endorsement ...[18]

The timing of the review was judicious, bearing in mind the PUP's dismal performance in the May 2005 local government elections. The PUP failed to put forward a single candidate for election in the Westminster contest, and at local government level over-extended itself by fielding thirteen candidates who returned only 4,591 votes.[19] Billy Hutchinson (Belfast Oldpark) and Tommy Sandford (Castlereagh Central) lost their seats in an election which saw the obliteration of pro-Agreement unionism in favour of 'the politics of fear and negativity'.[20] For many political commentators May 2005 was viewed as the unofficial date stamped on the PUP's electoral death certificate. To PUP insiders, however, it was regarded as a political interlude. Fortified by the review and its recommendations, and buoyed by the relative success of conflict transformation initiatives in areas such as Mount Vernon in North Belfast and East Antrim, the party confirmed that it was founded on the belief that the most effective way of dealing with a violent conflict is to transform it into a peaceful democratic one:

> We advocate the pursuit of conflict transformation. In Northern Ireland we accepted that it was not possible to resolve the conflict between those who believe in a United Ireland and their opponents who seek to maintain Northern Ireland's place within the UK. Thus we sought to transform the argument from an armed violent one to a peaceful democratic one. Though there is still some way to go, we believe that our ideas are now generally accepted by the mainstream.[21]

A key feature of the transformation approach was that it was an effective vehicle in which the PUP and the UVF, the politicos and the militarists, could move forward together with a view to redefining future relationships. As evidence of the type of transformation work discussed above I will now turn my attention to the case study of the East Antrim Conflict Transformation Forum (EACTF) in order to demonstrate the effective development of these new relationships within the ranks of progressive loyalism.

THE EAST ANTRIM CONFLICT TRANSFORMATION FORUM[22]

It is possible to trace the genesis of EACTF back to 2002, when the *Principles of Loyalism*[23] document was written by Billy Mitchell, a leading PUP member and former UVF prisoner, generally acknowledged as the PUP's senior strategist. The document attempted for the first time to set loyalism within a historical context, to distil its key principles and to address the current political landscape in which loyalism had become discredited. The *Principles* was then employed as the key discussion document during the UVF internal consultation phase as the context within which the organisation had to define its future. In parallel to this consultation exercise Mitchell was keenly aware that a theoretical discussion was too limited: a practical model had to be devised which could demonstrate the bona fides of the conflict transformation approach being commended to the progressive loyalist constituency.

Two key developments in 2004 helped create the conditions to embed a working model in East Antrim, an area where Mitchell remained a key player in the community development and political worlds. Following a long-term UVF internal investigation in East Antrim, a new UVF commander, fully supportive of conflict transformation, was installed, and the PUP in East Antrim reorganised at association level, creating a new dynamism in the party. EACTF aimed to tackle the conditions which gave rise to paramilitary activity, to challenge these and to provide young men, in particular, with an alternative route into more community-orientated enterprises. Crucially, the EACTF model was based upon a belief that the PUP should not break the link with the UVF until the conflict transformation process had been completed within loyalism.[24] The model seeks to bring politics, community and military together into a joint process; partners include the local leaderships of the Ulster Volunteer Force and Progressive Unionist Party in conjunction with various community-based groups. Additionally, a range of 'critical friends' from academia and the Church sector were invited to work with the EACTF Focus Group, a role envisaged as providing honest critical analysis as well as providing guidance and expertise. Critically, whilst the initiative is a partnership, overall leadership is provided in the main by the community representatives.

This approach is embedded within a critical framework and includes the task of encouraging the UVF to face up to the uglier aspects of its military actions. It does not seek to enrapture militarists with politics or to bolster local PUP support. In a post-conflict phase following a time when many communities were controlled by loyalist paramilitaries, the aim now is to enrich and enhance those areas and the lives of the people in them. The driving force behind EACTF is the Focus Group, which has four stated aims:

- to support the Conflict Transformation Programme;
- to liaise with government, public bodies and the business community;
- to lobby and engage with civic society to empower local people; and
- to engage with policy developers and funding agencies.[25]

The Focus Group is uniquely positioned in that it has the support of the various aspects of the movement it seeks to represent. It has the experience of key players to draw upon and provides the time and opportunity for serious consideration and debate on those issues which progressive loyalism must address. It also has the opportunity to broaden the horizons of the movement beyond the everyday management of local political issues to consider the bigger picture, to facilitate the movement from 'small p' to 'big P' politics in which the PUP's socialist credentials can be more fully developed and positioned within the broader unionist family. It is from this focal point that interaction can be promoted with aspects of civil society and the broader political community. The Focus Group has established a number of locally based transformation groups that have engaged both internally, with the several components of its own constituency, and externally with the wider community.

The outworking of the 'East Antrim Model' as the vanguard of progressive loyalism has been a test-bed for the wider movement across the province. Its success merits closer attention and replication because success has meant that, arguably, for the first time the PUP and its associated community representatives have been able to engage the UVF on equal terms. Success has been tangible: the model has centralised the work of various community groups which has facilitated more coordinated community development; funding has been made available which has enabled the project to employ a full-time coordinator; consultants have been engaged to draw up area plans and funding strategies; paramilitary activity has been reduced (this has been independently verified); a number of protocols are now in place, for example a flags protocol agreed with local PSNI which has dramatically reduced both the scale and timeframe of flag-flying in the summer months; and community representatives have reported that paramilitary 'control' in local areas is much reduced.

EACTF failures have not proved insurmountable to date, despite a number of setbacks including the loss in July 2006 of the project's architect, Billy Mitchell, whose role had been pivotal in liaising with the various partner groups. Failure could well give creative licence to an apolitical rump seeking only to line their own pockets and lower the expectations of a susceptible working class. At the time of writing (summer 2007) the EACTF has endured its most difficult period to date as a result of another change in the UVF leadership at a local level, an event played out over many months in the Sunday newspapers. The impact of this loss of key UVF personnel has yet to be fully analysed, but evidently any transformation initiative's greatest weakness lies in the lack of stability in one of the key partners. Loyalist paramilitarism has proved inherently unstable in the post-Agreement environment.

Yet, as Steve Bruce once noted: 'It is such a matter of routine for a para-military leader who falls from grace to be accused of having defrauded his organisation that it is difficult to have confidence in such claims.'[26]

In parallel with the development of the EACTF, the PUP in East Antrim has also been revived and re-energised. In late 2004 party activists re-formed their Constituency Association, heralding a change in the political character of the party and a more professional approach. Following preliminary discussions in the EACTF Focus Group, it was agreed that the party should instead operate mainly at constituency level, with close liaison with EACTF members. Key to the success to date of EACTF and the regeneration of the PUP in East Antrim have been the close ties developed between all the relevant constituencies which have provided the pool of resources necessary for any serious transformation initiative. The relative success of the EACTF is monitored very closely by the leaderships of both the PUP and the UVF, both of which encouraged the 'rolling out' of the model in other areas of Northern Ireland. To date the EACTF has facilitated the development of a number of similar conflict transformation initiatives in places as diverse as Belfast, Ballymena and North Down. The EACTF was additionally involved in the early months of 2007 when two of its members played an active role in the UVF's so-called internal consultation process, which led to its announcement to put its arms beyond reach from 3 May 2007:

> Following a direct engagement with all the units and departments of our organisation, the leadership of the Ulster Volunteer Force and Red Hand Commando today make public the outcome of our three year consultation process. Commensurate with these developments, as of 12 midnight, Thursday 3 May 2007, the Ulster Volunteer Force and Red Hand Commando will assume a non-military, civilianised, role. To consolidate this fundamental change in outlook we have addressed the methodology of transformation from military to civilian organisation by implementing the following measures in every operational and command area.[27]

Although the headline reactions to the UVF statement concentrated on the merit (or otherwise) of the UVF position on weapons, i.e. 'all ordinance has been put beyond reach and the IICD instructed accordingly', a potentially more interesting line of thought was generally ignored. Few commentators questioned the detail of what the organisation meant when it stated that it had 'addressed the methodology of transformation from military to civilian organisation', the only available information having been drip-fed to the public over the previous three years via the journalism of Brian Rowan. To many within the PUP, the EACTF and their communities of interest, who had been working on conflict transformation initiatives for some years, this was a missed opportunity to focus the *movement* as a whole, i.e. the political, community and military partners, on future reorganisation and development, rather than simply drawing a line under the military campaign which was supposed to have finished in 1994.[28]

Behind the headlines many activists within the PUP and the EACTF, and the cadre of community workers, were alarmed at the thought that from 4 May onwards they alone, i.e. in the absence of state support, were responsible for transforming the UVF into a new civilianised form, perhaps bearing in mind Steve Bruce's stark phrase: 'Terrorist organizations often do other things but their main point is to kill.'[29] To many activists it was clear that the EACTF, along with the range of transformation initiatives it had instigated, remained too weak and underdeveloped to take on the huge responsibility of civilianising the UVF. Whilst the statement rationale focused on the ending of the mainstream republican offensive, it seemed to downplay, indeed ignore, the fact that, certainly from 2000 onwards, there have been two key dynamics at play within loyalism: rivalry between loyalist paramilitary organisations, resulting in at least four rounds of feuding in, for example, the Shankill area in 2000 and in East Belfast and East Down in early 2004; and internal disputes within loyalist organisations.

The result of these dynamics is severely fractured working-class communities in which tensions between and within loyalist organisations, again evident in summer 2007, are replicated in community relations. Bruce noted that, while the Provisionals were transforming from violence to politics, Sinn Féin was able to offer former combatants a role in its political success or a role in the network of community organisations, the choice facing loyalist organisations attempting to transform in a peaceful society was severely limited. The PUP cannot offer the same opportunities as Sinn Féin and in loyalist and unionist communities the 'problem for a pro-state terrorist organization is that its intended supporting population feels less need to create a range of institutions outside or against those of the state'.[30]

Two main outcomes are notable from the legacy of ongoing UVF political violence. In the first instance, whilst the militarists have entered regularly into rounds of bloodletting, the pragmatic non-combatant style of politics advocated by 'politicos' and community representatives has been tarnished, perhaps irrevocably. The effects of the schism between militarist and politico attitudes concerning the superintendence of progressive loyalist strategy continue to undermine the development of loyalist politics and ideology. Second, and as importantly, the ramifications of ongoing violence and tensions continue to be the detrimental effect these actions have on attempts by politicos to transform loyalist communities.

The state continues to be steadfast in its refusal to give support (not just financial support) to any meaningful conflict transformation initiatives in the community sector, punishing working-class communities as a whole for the actions of a small minority; indeed, state funding of loyalist areas has been criticised by some commentators[31] as actively perpetuating the role and influence of paramilitarism, despite the rigorous checks and balances maintained by various funding bodies. The absence of genuine state engagement with the PUP and the UVF belies the need for inclusivity evidenced by a multiplicity of academic and practitioner experience from a range of peace processes in the late twentieth and early twenty-first centuries.

The nature of the relationships between 'politico' and 'militarist'[32] within the PUP–UVF axis remains in a constant state of flux and as a result the conflict transformation work undertaken by the 'politicos' remains tentative and weak due to the asymmetrical relationship between the armed and political wings of the movement.[33] While most political violence of a left-wing or even nationalist hue in Western Europe has been played out with politics to the forefront, if not exactly in the classic Marxist situation where politics is primary and political violence seen as a last resort, for the PUP its influence on the pro-state UVF is limited to an advisory capacity. Consequently the PUP has the responsibility of transforming the UVF without the benefit of being an equal partner in the venture. Since the PUP conference in 2005, when David Ervine announced that the PUP 'is committed to conflict transformation and the processes that empower and build a strong, confident and vibrant loyalist community',[34] the party, in effect, embarked upon squaring the circle of transforming, from the bottom up, an organisation which had, since its inception, adopted a strong centralist leadership style, i.e. 'top-down'.

The ambiguous relationship between 'militarists' and 'politicos' within the progressive loyalist movement continues to confuse those outside progressive loyalism; the financial sanctions imposed on the PUP as a consequence of International Monitoring Commission reporting on the UVF are evidence of this. The state has refused to appreciate fully the salient differences between the combined Sinn Féin–PIRA axis and the less formalistic UVF–RHC–PUP relationship. Simply put, the PUP is a separate organisation. Indeed there is plenty of evidence to show that many UVF volunteers don't vote for the PUP, so it would be inaccurate to say that the PUP is *the* political voice of the UVF.[35] The UVF regards itself as a military machine, prepared and ready to defend the constitution and more concerned with ensuring that the six points of the 1994 CLMC statement are adhered to.[36]

Case evidence from a range of peace processes across the world has demonstrated the need for a comprehensive and inclusive conflict transformation strategy to be implemented to ensure that the effects of political violence, or the threat of political violence, are minimised. John Darby, in analysing five areas of conflict (Northern Ireland, South Africa, Sri Lanka, the Basque Country[37] and Israel/Palestine), has outlined the dangers to peace processes of spoiler groups, defined by Stedman as 'leaders and factions who view a particular peace as opposed to their interests and who are willing to use violence to undermine it'.[38] It is suggested here not that UVF violence is designed to undermine the peace process but rather that the effects of its violence, and the potential to return to violence (its refusal to decommission weapons) have the same net effect. This is supported by a belief within the PUP that the government approach is to criminalise, rather than politicise, loyalism.

John Darby argues that violence will not disrupt peace processes if those willing to engage in it are supported and provided with the opportunities to become part of any peace initiatives. Groups within the process must be assisted in isolating zealots and those out for personal gain. Darby outlines five propositions for keeping peace processes on track in the face of violence:

1. Cease-fires are more durable if they can make it through the first few months.
2. Peace processes will only be sustainable if a sufficient number of those who have the capacity for violent obstruction are included.
3. The cooperation of former militants is necessary to neutralize the violent potential of zealots.
4. Leaders should be primarily concerned with bringing their own people to the table and only secondarily to assisting opponents.
5. Former fighters, both government and militants, must be integrated into normal society if peace is to last. As a corollary, the peace agreement needs to address victims' needs as well.[39]

Failure by the state to fully address propositions 2, 3 and 5, which if fully implemented would mean in effect that the PUP and the UVF were *central* to the peace process, has consequently resulted in a failure by the PUP and UVF to fully implement proposition 4. The state's asymmetrical attitude towards republicanism and loyalism has perpetuated a view within loyalism that while the state facilitates the politicisation of republicanism it is content to deal with loyalism through its security apparatus whilst conterminously turning a blind eye to positive developments within the community sector, e.g. the EACTF or the work undertaken by Billy Hutchinson in the Mount Vernon estate in North Belfast,[40] wherein progressive loyalist initiatives have met with some success. Indeed the state, via the regular reviews of the International Monitoring Commission, has managed to financially handicap the PUP in its work while at the same time encouraging the party to redouble its efforts to transform the UVF. Despite the growing evidence that transformation initiatives within loyalism have produced measurable benefits, this work continues to be undertaken by individuals within the UVF, the PUP and the community sector on a voluntary basis in the absence of adequate funding.

CONCLUSION

Currently the PUP, with its associated range of conflict transformation initiatives and community developers, is tasked with the near impossible. Political pressures, both internal and external, militate against significant progress in the near future. Loyalism continues to be undermined by the failure of the British state to support the Union and its unwillingness to address the phenomenon of pro-state terrorism. Whilst it can be argued that the Belfast Agreement represents a unionist victory, this message was never transmitted into unionist working-class areas. Furthermore, to many it is painfully obvious that political change is more advantageous for Irish nationalism and republicanism than for unionism.

The mainstream unionist bloc, to which many progressive loyalists continue to look for leadership, continues to shy away from any meaningful engagement with its working-class constituency, adopting a finger-wagging paternalism reminiscent of a bygone age. Only when it came to the possibility of contributing to UUP Assembly aspirations was the PUP courted, and David Ervine situated again, briefly, within mainstream unionism. That marriage was quickly annulled and forgotten by all; for the UUP it was of no more political benefit, for many PUP activists the convergence with the right-of-centre UUP had been unpalatable at a time when the PUP had made considerable progress in establishing its socialist credentials.

Internally it must be recognised that the PUP has significant shortcomings; it failed to harness the influx of new members after 1994, it remained structurally underdeveloped, ideologically immature and politically unfocused, caught between the 'big picture' politics of the peace process and superintending the UVF and the RHC. As the socialist tendency within the PUP becomes more pronounced under the aegis of Dawn

Purvis's leadership, so it becomes all the more difficult to 'sell' the party, with its socialist outlook, to the UVF and the RHC, neither of which share that outlook. Progress has been made in the community sector, where conflict transformation initiatives, based on an equal partnership, have enjoyed significant success, albeit gradually, and despite a lack of funding. It is clear that a reassertion of community-based leadership is what is needed to enable the UVF and RHC to transform into purely political organisations, if that is what they want. These new politico-driven groupings must employ the weaponry of dialogue and legitimate lobbying as a means of communicating and engaging with rivals and opponents. The positive undertakings of principled activists to develop collective responsibility in loyalist working-class areas – combined with an emphasis on social justice and human rights – must be supported by the state.

In Chapter 1 of this volume McAuley points out that, alongside reproducing sectarian ideology and action, loyalist paramilitary organisations have also provided an important channel for articulating social grievances and political ideologies. Yet despite these reinforcing tendencies there remains a lack of any genuine principled leadership at grassroots level, an issue which permits paramilitarism to degenerate into organised crime. In the absence of a desire for the vigilantism that paramilitarism once provided, working-class Protestants have become increasingly intolerant of paramilitarism, and associated criminality, repeatedly exposed by the local media, as well as the role played by the new breed of 'ceasefire soldier'. Within loyalist paramilitarism the lack of a clear political outlook and a positive role to play, allied to an innate resistance to change, remain major challenges to the PUP. These challenges are not insurmountable, as previously stated. The PUP has attracted many new members since Dawn Purvis succeeded David Ervine as party leader in January 2007. They have been welcomed into a party that now has a much more solid structural base and a clearer political direction. Given the right resources, further transformation is achievable.

NOTES

1. Interview with Colin Robinson, 20 August 2004.
2. Interview with Dawn Purvis, 23 August 2004.
3. Interview with Colin Robinson, 20 August 2004.
4. Interview with Billy Hutchinson, 20 September 2004.
5. Interview with William 'Plum' Smith, 25 August 2004.
6. PUP, Confidential Minutes of Executive Committee Meetings. In author's possession.
7. Interview with William 'Plum' Smith, 25 August 2004.
8. Edwards, A. and Bloomer, S., *Democratising the Peace in Northern Ireland: Progressive Loyalists and the Politics of Conflict Transformation*, Conflict Transformation Papers, Vol. 12 (Belfast: LINC Resource Centre, 2005).
9. Edwards, A. and Bloomer, S. *A Watching Brief? The Political Strategy of Progressive Loyalism Since 1994*, Conflict Transformation Papers, Vol. 8 (Belfast: LINC Resource Centre, 2004), available at http://cain.ulst.ac.uk/issues/politics/docs/edwardsbloomer04.pdf.
10. Ibid.

11. Interview with Dawn Purvis, 23 August 2004.
12. Interview with Billy Mitchell, 17 August 2004.
13. Interview with Billy Hutchinson, 20 September 2004.
14. Interview with David Ervine, 21 September 2004.
15. McAuley, J.W. and Hislop, S., '"Many Roads Forward": Politics and Ideology within the Progressive Unionist Party', *Etudes Irlandaises*, 25, 1 (2000), pp. 173–92; McAuley, J.W. 'The Emergence of New Loyalism', in J. Coakley (ed.), *Changing Shades of Orange and Green: Redefining the Union and Nation in Contemporary Ireland* (Dublin: UCD Press, 2002), pp. 106–22; McAuley, J.W., '"Just Fighting to Survive": Loyalist Paramilitary Politics and the Progressive Unionist Party', *Terrorism and Political Violence*, 16, 3 (2004), pp. 522–43; see also McGlynn, C., *How New is New Loyalism?* (unpublished PhD thesis: University of Salford, 2004) and Edwards, A., 'Democratic Socialism and Sectarianism: The Northern Ireland Labour Party and Progressive Unionist Party Compared', *Politics*, 27, 1 (February 2007), pp. 24–31.
16. Mitchell, B., *The Principles of Loyalism* (Belfast: Unknown Publisher, 2002). Archived at: http://www.pup-ni.org.uk/loyalism/principles.aspx. Accessed 1 June 2007; Edwards, 'Democratic Socialism and Sectarianism'.
17. Progressive Unionist Party, PUP Strategy Sub-Group Report, June 2005
18. Ibid.
19. For the full spread of election results see http://cain.ulst.ac.uk/issues/politics/election/rd 2005.htm.
20. Interview with Dawn Purvis, 4 August 2005.
21. http://www.pup-ni.org.uk/loyalism/conflicttransformation.aspx
22. For more detailed discussion of the EACTF model see Edwards and Bloomer, *Democratising the Peace in Northern Ireland*.
23. Mitchell, *The Principles of Loyalism*.
24. Edwards, A. and S. Bloomer, 'Loyalism at the Crossroads', *Fortnight*, No. 444 (May 2006), pp. 7–8.
25. EACTF, Confidential EACTF Document, 2005. In author's possession.
26. Bruce, S., 'Turf War and Peace: Loyalist Paramilitaries since 1994', *Terrorism and Political Violence*, 16, 3 (2004), p. 508.
27. Excerpts from UVF statement, 3 May 2007.
28. The UVF has been implicated in twenty deaths since 1996. See 'UVF Calls End to Terror Campaign'. Archived at: http://news.bbc.co.uk/1/hi/northern_ireland/6618371.stm. Accessed 4 May 2007.
29. Bruce, 'Turf War and Peace'.
30. Ibid.
31. See Mark Langhammer, 'Cutting with the Grain in the Protestant Community', *Fortnight*, No. 425 (May 2004), pp. 13–15.
32. For a full discussion on 'politicos' and 'militarists' see Irvin, C., *Militant Nationalism: Between Movement and Party in Northern Ireland and the Basque Country* (Duluth, MN: University of Minnesota Press, 1999).
33. For an interesting discussion on the two 'wings' of the movement, see 'The Ta Power Document: An Essay on the History of the Irish Republican Socialist Movement'. Archived at: http://irsm.org/history/tapowerdoc.html. Accessed 7 July 2007.
34. *Sunday Times*, 16 October 2005.
35. Bruce, S., 'Terrorists and Politics: The Case of Northern Ireland's Loyalist Paramilitaries', *Terrorism and Political Violence*, 13, 2 (2001), pp. 27–48.
36. Edwards, A., 'The UVF Abandons its Campaign of Terror', *Fortnight*, No. 452 (May 2007), pp. 12–13
37. Darby, J. *The Effects of Violence on Peace Processes* (Washington, DC: United States Institute of Peace, 2001).
38. Stedman, S.J., 'Peace Processes and the Challenge of Violence', in J. Darby and R. MacGinty (eds), *Contemporary Peacemaking: Conflict, Violence and Peace Processes* (Basingstoke: Palgrave, 2003), Chapter 9; see also Zahar, M.J., 'Reframing the Spoiler Debate in Peace Processes', in Darby and MacGinty, *Contemporary Peacemaking*, Chapter 10.
39. Darby, *The Effects of Violence on Peace Processes*, Chapter 5.
40. See *Observer*, 22 July 2007.

Chapter 7
Of Myths and Men:
Dissent within Republicanism and Loyalism

Anthony McIntyre

About three years ago the then Sinn Féin councillor Eoin Ó Broin made the point to me that it was a relatively cost-free exercise to dissent within the republican constituency. He held up the fact that I had been openly and vociferously critical of the Sinn Féin strategy for a decade or more yet was still alive and well, standing on the Falls Road alongside him, to tell the tale. While I was hardly enamoured of the supposed implicit generosity of the O'Broin perspective it nevertheless caused me to reflect. Arguably, had I lived in an area permeated by a strong loyalist paramilitary subculture, the freedom to express opinions contrary to the 'regime of truth' established by the dominant paramilitary power structure would have keen seriously circumscribed.

Later, the former republican prisoner Laurence McKeown pursued a similar theme when he openly lauded the tolerant nature of republican politics.[1] The fact that I was allowed to live in West Belfast despite having annoyed my neighbours with my thoughts on the Sinn Féin leadership was a courtesy that would not be extended to me in another community – by implication, the loyalist one. Seemingly I, a malcontent, as *An Phoblacht/Republican News* once put it,[2] should be grateful that I had not been murdered for pursuing the dark art of thought crime in West Belfast.

The sub-current in the discourse of both Sinn Féin members needs little in the way of decoding. The republican community is open and democratic and is tolerant of other views. This exists in sharp contrast to the loyalist world, where dissent can on occasion be literally suppressed with a hammer blow.

An accurate reflection of the state of play or yet another self-serving Sinn Féin myth? Certainly when I came to work with Billy Mitchell, a former UVF leader, on the editorial board of *The Other View* magazine, it struck me that Mitchell was acutely sensitive about criticisms in the magazine of the UVF or the PUP, whereas republicans on the editorial board were laid back about open discussion and free enquiry. But like was not being compared with like. Mitchell represented the view of the UVF/PUP leadership whereas the republicans had a long history of dissenting from the leadership line of the movement they once belonged to.

In some respects it is an easy matter to depict the loyalists as a brutish, thuggish lot equipped with Neanderthal minds and who are readily given to clubbing down the competition. The late Lenny Murphy would appear purpose built. With imagery going global that depicts grown men with well-endowed beer bellies screaming taunts such as 'Fenian bastards' into the faces of four-year-old schoolgirls, the world is disinclined to view the tattooed 'bellies' as urbane intellectuals who espouse the values of liberal tolerance.

The calibre of the 'bellies' confirms for many that loyalism suffers from a serious disadvantage the minute it sets foot in the recruiting pool. Those who join loyalist paramilitaries float to the top only once the British army, RUC, prison service and UDR have creamed off the military-oriented talent within the unionist community.[3] The lumpen gravitate towards the loyalist militias. Johnny Adair, later to become one of the most ruthless figures of the loyalist militia world – coupled with more than a passing interest in the drugs trade – admitted: 'I tried to join the UDR ... but because of a few minor criminal convictions they wouldn't let me in.'[4]

By contrast, republicans have managed to package themselves much more alluringly. With no competitors for the military services of the nationalist working class, the IRA had first pick of the militarily inclined within their own communities. Often their volunteers appear well read and cerebral, often given to a discourse of tolerance. The Queen's University academic Richard English, in his erudite survey of the H-Block library compiled by republican prisoners, commented on the lack of any equivalent on the wings of loyalist prisoners.[5]

That many of the books on the republican wings did little more than decorate the shelving they occupied seems to have escaped notice in the hype of intellectual excitement generated by the 'discovery' of an extensive library. And the pornography that was widely available, if not officially read, on republican wings (like the pot that was smoked) made it only to the alternative library. That repository of cruder literature was not the one that the republican jail leadership wanted put on public display.

In spite of the well-stocked shelves it is not difficult to see how shallow the absorption of republican history, Marxism or revolutionary socialism was on republican prison wings when all of it was expelled and expunged without as much as a collective sigh of protest as part of accommodation with the politics of the peace process. What socialist revolutionary would remain silent when their party leadership embraces that most quintessential capitalist concept of Private Finance Initiative (PFI)? What republican armed with a sense of their own history would stay stum while their leadership trades in all of republicanism's ideological tenets in exchange for inconsequential office in the Paisley government? None other than the H-Block revolutionaries! Curiously, the 'unsophisticated' and western-reading former loyalist prisoners of the PUP rejected PFI.

While loyalism has produced spokespeople much more articulate than the morons of Glenbryn, it has maintained an openly violent stance in relation to dissent. The public street confrontations at Garnerville and the Lower Shankill show the mobilisation of loyalist paramilitary organisations in general in a manner now almost unthinkable within the republican constituency.

In spite of this the central contention in this chapter is that dissent within both the loyalist and republican militia worlds and those of their satellite agencies such as the PUP, the UPRG and Sinn Féin is viewed as a boil that needs to be lanced. Republicans are not more tolerant of dissenting voices but rather have been forced to adopt more sophisticated methods of suppressing them. No longer is the IRA reported to be involved in murdering other republicans such as the Real IRA member Joseph O'Connor,[6] or kidnapping and maiming opponents such as Kevin Perry[7] and Brendan Shannon.[8]

DEFINING DISSENT

In the academic literature, while plenty has appeared about the loyalist and republican militias and the clandestine world they inhabit, little has emerged about the phenomenon of dissent.[9] For the most part it is mentioned in passing. Dissent is a vastly under-researched area, testimony perhaps to the extent to which its suppression has succeeded. Has academia facilitated the marginalisation of these strands of thought, even unwittingly?

Northern Ireland's armed militias have been engaged in such a wide form of factional rivalry and disciplinary procedures over the decades that to include internecine feuding or punishment attacks as examples of suppressing dissent would render the concept so seamless that its value would be negligible. For present purposes, where one established group enters into a feud with another like group, such as the Provisional IRA assault on the Official IRA in 1975 or the UVF strike against the UDA in the same year, this will not be regarded as a suppression of dissent. Quite often such feuds are personality-driven or about territorial control. There is often a longstanding ideological division between feuding groups but finer ideological points rarely cause feuds.

However, where one organisation moves against another when the latter is just in its formative or embryonic stages such as the UVF initiative to quell the LVF and the Provisional IRA effort to stymie the Real IRA, these will be regarded as acts of suppressing dissent. Likewise, where one established group moves to curb another in order to facilitate a political initiative of its own, that too falls under the rubric of suppressing dissent. Moreover, when individuals in a particular group come together for the express purpose of leaving the group they belong to, their reasons are usually in opposition to some political policy or strategic direction. Consequently the attempt by the 'mother' group to challenge them at that point is an act of suppression of a dissenting opinion or tendency.

Furthermore, there are those individuals who share the constituency of the militias although not associated with the militias and who are suppressed for their views; this too must be regarded as an act of dissent. People in the opposing community who have been murdered by a militia, such as Robert Bradford, killed by the Provisional IRA, or Sheena Campbell, killed by the UVF, are not regarded as victims of acts of repressing dissent, although friends of both may claim with justification that both individuals were killed for nothing other than expressing their views.

Dissent has taken different forms. On occasion it has been the emergence of individuals at the grassroots level of an organisation who were unhappy with elements of strategy or elements of leadership. On the other hand, dissenting voices may emerge from within a dominant bloc at the centre of a movement. Sometimes it can be violent but quite often amounts to nothing more than the expression of an opinion contrary to the dominant line.

For long enough the Provisional republican movement has been spoken of in terms of its ability to maintain unity and discipline; the odd voice that broke the silence was all too easily slotted into the crank category. Yet it is hardly true to say that republicans have produced fewer vocal dissenters than loyalism. The difference between John Kelly and Martin Cunningham on the republican side and Johnny Adair and Billy Wright on the loyalist side lies in the form that dissent took. For these loyalists it was violent, whereas the republicans mentioned pursued a non-violent strategy of dissent. But again there is no one size that fits all models. The writer David Adams hailed from a UDA-shaped culture but remains passionately committed to peaceful approaches, whereas Michael McKevitt in the republican camp has long been associated with military strategies.

There is such a rich history of dissent within the world of Northern Ireland's militias waiting to be written that one chapter addressed to both 'sides' is grossly insufficient to explain it. It is by necessity restricted to showing that dissenting thought has a history, to outlining some of its contours, and to giving names to voices. Perhaps most importantly, it will prompt others to explore the 'dark continent' of dissent and put an end to the taboos that often exist in relation to what 'mysteries' it holds.

REPUBLICANISM

The Provisional IRA is an organisation that the French writer Michel Foucault might have asked the following question of: 'How is it that at certain moments ... there are these sudden takeoffs, these hastenings of evolution, these transformations which fail to correspond to the calm, continuist image that is normally accredited?'[10] From its outset the Provisional IRA was not an organisation constrained within a strait-jacket of tradition. Its attitude to dissent has not been to democratical-ly embrace those who engage in it as colleagues but to smear and mar-ginalise them in a manner that resembles a totalitarian mindset. Imperatives of the power-pursuing present rather than an intellectual tolerance towards republicanism's own rich history of dissent have come to rule the roost within Provisionalism.

Traditionally within the republican community it was always much less tempting to express dissent during the war. A siege mentality con-jured up an imperative for self-censorship. While the republican organ-isations are top-down authoritarian bodies, the anonymous pressure of the group lessened the need for leadership to be more proactive in curbing dissent. With the enemy at the gates few wanted to be heard shouting that maybe those defending the citadel might be wrong in some aspects. Eddie Gallagher's courtroom outburst against certain republican leaders[11] and Maria McGuire's critical book on her year in the Provisional IRA[12] merely served to reinforce their isolation.

The formative years of the Provisional republican movement lent themselves to a structure that was not highly centralised. While the first chief of staff, Seán Mac Stíofáin, may have told the world he had devised a three-phased strategy[13] which was being implemented by his subordinates, the simple truth is that he followed the war on the ground: 'We were a pack of wild horses that nobody could hold back. GHQ didn't realise they were in a war. I felt they had an attitude of two years waiting, training, educating and then there would be a war.'[14] The commanders on the ground in the North both shaped and paced the war. In doing so they were not dissenting from the leadership. They were actively creating the line for the leadership, and the latter was prepared to tail the war on the ground. The real significance of empow-ered war regions and decentralisation would take a number of years before it made itself felt in serious strategic changes.

On occasion in the opening decade of the life of the Provisional IRA Derry republicanism could be found dissenting from the leadership strat-egy. Key IRA figures at national level felt that Derry was to the fore in pushing both the 1972 and 1975 IRA cessations. On the first of these events, 'Martin McGuinness himself made the suggestion that we should go for a week-long ceasefire.'[15] In relation to the prolonged 1975 truce:

The Army Council got a letter from the Derry Brigade saying they were going to have a ceasefire. Twomey snapped and went up and pulled Derry. Shane Doherty, I think, was behind it. There were more Derry internees getting released than from anywhere else, and I think some in Derry felt they could all be out if the war was to end.[16]

While there were clearly other factors influencing ceasefires the existence of dissent within republicanism cannot be dismissed. For the leadership, the concerns of certain republican power blocs had to be taken on board. This underscores the view that regional dissent, if located in the North where the war was fought, and if representative of sufficient military power, could impact on leadership direction. Nor could it be easily suppressed.

Nevertheless, in the opening years of the IRA campaign, vigorous dissent came in fact less from the war regions and more from within the leadership. Ruairi Ó Brádaigh and Daithi Ó Conaill were two senior IRA figures who were politically at odds with Mac Stiofáin. At the risk of gross oversimplification they believed that tailing the northern brigades was not quite the most strategically prudent way to advance.

Mac Stiofáin had built strong relationships with the Belfast IRA leadership under Seamus Twomey and had also included Martin McGuinness, the Derry IRA commander, in an all-IRA delegation to take part in talks with the British government in London in 1972. McGuinness claims not to have known why he was chosen, as he certainly did not regard himself as a member of the national IRA leadership.[17] Mac Stiofáin seems to have selected him for internal management reasons rather than for his ability to negotiate. It strengthened his hand against dissenting voices.

Ó Brádaigh and Ó Conaill would frequently speak to the press and encourage dialogue with other strands of political thought. In the case of Ó Conaill he was involved in talks with John Hume of the SDLP. Ultimately both were outmanoeuvred by Mac Stiofáin. His ability to do so rested on the relationships he had built with the people at the centre of the armed struggle, those in the North who wielded military power.

Although Ó Brádaigh was on the Army Council his ability to speak publicly on IRA matters was heavily circumscribed. Mac Stiofáin, eager to placate the Belfast leadership and marginalise the opposition to his position at leadership level, bluntly stated:

I warned him that if he ever did so again he would go off the Army Council. In any event he went off the Army Council when he came out of jail. I also suspended Ó Conaill for a month after the truce for a breach of discipline. With both he and Ó Brádaigh off the Army Council, I was able to tell Twomey and Adams that the leak on the Army Council had been plugged. Belfast was seriously concerned about this leak.[18]

The IRA was very much the dominant force. People with a Sinn Féin role, even if they served on the Army Council, were not viewed as having the same gravitas. Mac Stiofáin said of his Army Council colleague Ó Brádaigh: 'He was quite sincere and well-meaning but he really did not have the ability to operate at that level.'[19] According to Jimmy Drumm: 'The problem for Sinn Féin was that it was always getting directives to protest about this and protest about that. It had little time to become involved in the type of politics of later years.'[20] While the dissent on this occasion was dealt with *sans* recourse to violence, the fears of Ó Conaill were not allayed. At one point he expressed the view to Maria McGuire that 'I'll be shot', as a scapegoat if things go wrong.[21]

However, during the armed struggle dissent was more frequently to be found in prisons. Developments such as the League of Communist Republicans[22] emerged but were effectively policed or marginalised by a prison leadership which functioned as an extension of the leadership on the outside into the prison environment. On one occasion in the H-Blocks shortly after the emergence of the LCR, the IRA volunteer in charge of jail education, and very much viewing himself as the arm of the leadership rather than the representative of the prisoners, took it upon himself to veto any suggestions that might come from the general republican prisoner population destined for the leadership.[23] He would protect the leadership's ears from 'bad' ideas.

When Ivor Bell, as part of a wider dissenting tendency within the prison in the mid-1970s, challenged the then officer commanding of Long Kesh, Davy Morley, in an election he was defeated in a straight vote. Subsequently, the IRA leadership outside the prison abolished all future elections for jail leader (local cage/compound elections could still take place) and stated that from that point on all camp commanders would be appointed by the IRA leadership. This removed the decision-making process, in relation to who would lead prisoners, from the prisoners themselves and placed it solely with the IRA leadership, which would always ensure that jail leaderships invariably remained on message.

While in prison Bell and his fellow former Belfast IRA commander, Gerry Adams, were continuously at odds with the then IRA leadership both inside and outside the prison. In particular they were concerned about the ongoing ceasefire of 1975 and the sectarianism that the republican struggle had descended into.[24]

Because both men were imprisoned, much of their overt activity was conducted through the Adams-penned Brownie columns in *Republican News*. Adams wrote these columns from 1975 right up until he was released eighteen months later. Both dissenting voices were assisted by the fact that Adams had important allies in the IRA leadership, such as the chief of staff and the quartermaster general, both of whom served on the Belfast Brigade staff alongside Adams and Bell before the latter two found themselves in prison.

The Adams/Brownie columns were important because they helped irrigate the thought processes of the Provisional movement, mark Adams out as a left-wing radical and form an important intellectual bridge between imprisoned opinion-formers and the wider activist network. The leadership that was being dissented from made no attempt to suppress the Brownie columns.

On their release both men quickly moved to senior positions within the IRA. At different periods in time both served as the organisation's chief of staff.[25] This allowed their dissent to become more safely entrenched within leadership discourse. When Adams eventually completed his bloodless coup and seized control of both the IRA and Sinn Féin the exercise was a process rather than an event. The Adams faction had begun seizing commanding heights on the strategic terrain long before it became the undisputed hegemony.

A curious phenomenon of dissent is that it is not merely one side dissenting and the other being dissented against. In the battle by Adams to seize control of the Provisional movement there were to be found on the Ó Brádaigh side elements who adopted the traditional role of the dissenter *vis-à-vis* the Adams faction. As Adams grew stronger *vis-à-vis* Ó Brádaigh and was able to make important changes to the Ó Brádaigh direction, this placed him not yet in the hegemonic position but in a position where he was facing a form of rolling hegemony in which the roll was very much in his favour. Christin Ni Elias, who was in the Ó Brádaigh camp, was one of the more forceful critics of the Adams position. Her colleagues in the Ó Brádaigh camp described her as 'our Dreyfus'. Her dissent from the emerging Adams power bloc, in the view of some, almost cost Ni Elias her life. She fled the country.[26]

Once Adams had become the hegemonic force within Provisional republicanism his attitude towards dissent was shown to be self-serving and instrumentalist. When his erstwhile ally Ivor Bell, arguably the most important IRA chief of staff and a man of almost unrivalled intellect within the Provisional movement, began to question the strategic direction in which he felt Adams was taking republicanism he began to organise dissent. Although he had sought to remain above board and on the right side of IRA legality, Bell found himself outmanoeuvred by the Adams faction, who did not share Bell's adherence to legality. Bell was court-martialled and expelled from the republican movement. It was made clear to him that future acts of dissent would be viewed in a very dim light.[27]

Whatever concession may have been made to this type of behaviour it rapidly lost currency once the war ended. With no need to baton down the hatches, dissent may have been expected to flourish. This was not to be. Arguably the Provisional leadership had concluded a war in which its volunteers and supporters had suffered considerably, so far short of any of its stated republican goals that deceit became the new imperative towards censorship. The leadership needed to conceal from its own grassroots how closely it resembled all those it had previously labelled traitors. 'Traditionally, every previous generation of Irish revolutionaries has taken this road ...'[28] A culture of secrecy was maintained, and as the party became more dominant within the Provisional republican movement the ethos of the army continued to rule the party.

In the run-up to the Good Friday Agreement dissenting opinion manifested itself in the formation of the Real IRA and its political associate, the 32 County Sovereignty Movement (32CSM), while in the Provisional IRA the strategy of these people was to mobilise opinion against the Adams leadership mainly through stacking dissenting voices in the IRA Executive, a body tasked with appointing Army Council members. In large part the dissident group was responsible for forcing general army conventions of the IRA every matter of months. Given that only one such convention had been held between 1969 and 1986, the power of this dissident lobby should not be downplayed.

A sign of its ability to influence events, even in a manner not calculated, was when the Adams IRA leadership, left with no option for outmanoeuvring the dissidents, unanimously decided to break the 1994 ceasefire in February 1996 rather than face a new army convention at which a demand for the ceasefire to be broken would almost certainly win the day. The outcome would be a new IRA leadership.[29] Over the next eighteen months, because of its ostensible willingness to reengage in armed conflict, the Adams leadership won the trust of many doubters and was able to fortify its position and regain control. The dissident faction withdrew from the IRA to form the Real IRA. The Provisional IRA leadership, its flank freed from internal snapping, entered into a further ceasefire in the middle of 1997.

On its formation the Real IRA drew some quality people but, significantly, from no region in the North where the war had been fought. Initially the IRA response was to vilify its members by spreading rumour and innuendo. They were accused of being property owners and smugglers.[30] But once the Omagh bombing had been carried out by the Real IRA the Provisionals became more heavy-handed, visiting the homes of Real IRA and 32 CSM members and ordering them to desist from their activities: 'Some members and supporters were threatened with violence and in some cases the threats were read to their wives or children.'[31]

Eventually the attempt to suppress the Real IRA perspective resulted in the Provisional IRA murder of a Belfast Real IRA leader, Joseph

O'Connor, in October 2000. The killing took place not in the context of a feud between the two organisations. The Provisional IRA denied the killing and then ordered the homes of critics belonging to the Irish Republican Writer's Group, but not associated with the Real IRA, to be picketed by mobs on the pretext that those critics had falsely accused the Provisionals of having murdered O'Connor.

Throughout its ceasefire the IRA maintained its policy of kidnapping dissidents and intimidating its own membership. It conducted numerous acts of violence and intimidation against political opponents. This was almost exclusively concentrated on republican opponents rather than on the main nationalist rivals within the SDLP. Nevertheless, as the Provisionals have been drawn more and more into the service of the British administration in the North the need to deal with dissent has been no less paramount, although the methods are not as severe.

When the policing debates were taking place Sinn Féin, in an extraordinary volte-face, began to debate the matter with their critics in the concerned republican tradition in open public discussions in Toome, Derry and Belfast. At the same time the undermining of dissenting opinions was systematically conducted. Homes were visited, and critics were told not to deviate from the line.[32] Rumours were put around that one prominent critic, a former Sinn Féin director of election and one-time IRA prisoner, Tony Catney, was said to be forming a new army. Members of Sinn Féin and the IRA were briefed by a prominent Sinn Féin MLA that Catney posed a serious and ongoing threat to the Sinn Féin leadership. Catney rubbished the allegations and his accusers refused to debate the matter publicly with him.[33]

With less room for violence the Provisional leadership has opted for a more covert approach which is captured succinctly by Martin Cunningham, a former Sinn Féin councillor who left the party after repeated attempts to muzzle him: 'Dissident is like a disease. They definitely do not want you talking with people who are viewed as dissident republicans just in case you might catch the disease that the dissidents have. They are hated more than the RUC, the British Army or the SAS.'[34] Former founding member of the Provisional IRA John Kelly adds to this with his description of marginalisation and rumour spreading, whispering campaigns ensuring where possible that critics remain unemployable, ostracism, mobilisation of hate and the manufacture of bias ensuring that people are barred from pubs and clubs.[35]

LOYALISM

Two main paramilitary bodies, the UVF and the UDA, have for the most part represented loyalism. The origins of the UDA are pretty much undisputed. The organisation arose from a discourse in working-class unionist constituencies articulating the need for some sort of extra-parliamentary defence. There is no grand tradition that the organisation lays claim to in order to seek legitimacy.

Although the UVF claims to have a history and tradition, it effectively sprang into existence in the mid-1960s and, like the Provisional IRA, was almost exclusively working class in composition. A further characteristic it shares with the Provisionals is that it is better understood if analysed through the prism of discontinuity rather than continuity. Its conditions of existence are to be found in the conjunctural factors rather than traditional ones. In this sense there is no real history for any of the loyalist organisations to draw upon when it comes to the issue of handling dissent. Their respective approaches to the issue of dissent are revealing as they provide a window on the motives behind it.

THE UDA

The UDA throughout its history has had the appearance of being an organisation in which muscle rather than strategic acumen was the driving force. Although Michael Stone would later claim that he refused orders that 'could easily be deemed blatantly sectarian',[36] such disobedience would seem not to have been the norm. In its early years 'clever opportunists would rise to the top; hardened street fighters were clearly going to do well too'.[37] Sammy Smyth was said to be a rarity among the UDA leadership in that he had an interest in broader ideological issues.[38] Charles Harding Smith, the organisation's first leader, is reported to have said: 'I'm the boss, I take orders from no one.'[39] Jim Craig, a one-time military commander, 'was a brutal boss who imposed discipline through violence, sometimes with a lump hammer he kept for the purpose'.[40] John Gregg, the would-be assassin of Sinn Féin leader Gerry Adams, was ruthless with his local units and was renowned for 'kneecapping anyone who transgressed him'.[41] With this snapshot the UDA is hardly the type of organisation that would inspire dissent from its strictures.

Harding Smith, when replaced as leader, became one of the early UDA dissidents. The issue he chose to dissent on was his new leader's approval of links with the Gadafy regime in Libya.[42] The dissent almost cost him his life. After two assassination attempts, in which he was injured, he fled the country.

In the 1990s, prior to the ceasefires, there is evidence of dissent within the UDA. Some leading figures were opposed to attacks on the SDLP.[43] But even with the advent of the ceasefires, opposing the writ of the UDA was fraught with danger. Mark Langhammer, a left-wing councillor in Rathcoole, had a bomb placed beneath his car for calling for more efficient policing in the UDA-run estate. When the organisation's George Legge began to speak out about the lifestyle of some UDA leaders he was brutally murdered in a move which 'showed how desperate the East Belfast UDA was to stamp out internal criticism of their leaders'.[44] David Adams, despite having been a member of the UDP talks team in the lead-up to the Good Friday Agreement, found himself subject to a prolonged campaign of intimidation when his involvement in politics lessened and he became a public commentator and writer of some renown.[45]

When the 1994 Combined Loyalist Military Command(CLMC) ceasefire was first proposed a majority of UDA prisoners, led by Adie Bird, opposed it. Bird was replaced as the UDA's Maze commander by Johnny Adair on the orders of the leadership and he quickly won the prisoners over to the ceasefire proposal.[46]

Earlier, the major change in the UDA which allowed Adair and the Shankill element to come to power was the result not of dissent but of a vacuum largely created by the arrests made by the Stevens inquiry team. However, it propelled Adair to a position of such influence that in a bid to maintain it he ended up being one of the organisation's most prominent dissenting voices.

From hero to zero: the leadership of the UDA is trying to airbrush Adair out of its history,[47] having already dismissed him from the organisation in 2002 for 'treason'.[48] As someone who insisted on being obeyed, Adair came to fly the banner of dissent. He felt that the UDA leadership's pursuit of peace process politics was limiting his ambitions, which according to Michael Stone amounted to becoming supreme commander 'whatever it took'.[49] He began to explore possible alliances with a UVF breakaway group, the LVF. Bizarrely, at one point he approved talks between John White and the Sinn Féin Lord Mayor of Belfast, Alex Maskey.[50] He also tried to get the UDA to decommission while secretly arranging an arms deal for his own C Company. This would have strengthened his power over the rest of the organisation and placed him in a virtually unassailable position.[51]

In a bid to produce tension between the LVF and UDA, Adair tried to entice the LVF to kill fellow UDA 'brigadier' Jim Gray.[52] He also began expelling former loyal colleagues from the Shankill, such as Winky Dodds, as well as resorting to intimidation and threats of execution.[53] Eventually the faction that fell in behind him was responsible for the death of John Gregg.

The UDA leadership's strategy for quelling Adair's dissent was to split his forces in the wider Shankill area. Once this was achieved the leadership took openly to the streets and physically and violently expelled the opposition. Adair and his colleagues, now exiled in

Scotland, live under the threat of death. As a reminder to them of the sinister intent of the UDA leadership, it murdered Adair's colleague Alan 'Bucky' McCullough in May 2003.

Prior to Adair the peace process had thrown up another UDA dissident, the vociferous Alex Kerr. His position was that the UDP and the PUP had been used as dupes merely to give cover to a Sinn Féin entry into the talks process.[54] In a bid to undermine the UDA-sponsored UDP he began calling it the Ulster Drugs Party. As part of his aim to build a new loyalism he formed an alliance with Billy Wright out of which emerged the LVF.

The UDA sentenced Kerr to death for his dissent and proposed that the UVF do likewise with Billy Wright.[55] Prisoners supportive of Kerr on the UDA wings were expelled. The CLMC eventually ordered both men to leave Northern Ireland or face death.[56] Kerr was later labelled an informer by the organisation.[57]

UVF

When the UDA was finding its feet, whatever reservations the UVF had about it, it was a much too popular and unwieldy organisation for the UVF to do anything about. The longer-established loyalist militia had to share its space in the loyalist constituency with the newcomer. Sheer force of UDA numbers made any attempt to quell that body impractical. At one point a member of the UVF stated that in East Belfast there were thousands of UDA, whereas the UVF amounted to about eighty members.[58]

Prior to the UDA becoming its rival the UVF faced dissent from within its own ranks. The Tyrone UVF had been critical of the Belfast leadership's bombing campaign in the late 1960s.[59] In the 1970s Lenny Murphy often operated independently of the leadership.[60] Although the UVF engaged in moves that were highly radical for their time, such as the meeting with the Official IRA in July 1971,[61] it seems that these were leadership initiatives. Even when there was debate within the organisation it was invariably the 'brigade staff which decided policy'.[62]

In the early 1970s, when former UVF internee Ken Gibson headed up a new party to front for the UVF, there was suspicion. One senior UVF figure later claimed: 'There was a Pol Pot approach to politics. If you wore a beard and glasses and read books you were suspect among some members of the organization.'[63] Joe Bennett, who later became a UVF supergrass, was one of the Belfast UVF team labelling Gibson a communist.[64] In a move that was to foreshadow the Adams method of seizing control within the Provisionals, Gibson moved to a dissenting position and attempted to stack the UVF with his 'political' people, but after an election débâcle he was pulled back into line and 'the military people took over'.[65]

The UVF leadership appeared open to dissent if that dissent was likely to lead where the leadership desired to go, something which can be inferred from the views of Chris Hudson, who was instrumental in facilitating contact between the UVF and the Dublin government.[66] Although some in the organisation viewed Gusty Spence as a traitor for his views, the leadership listened to both him and David Ervine.[67] Spence appreciated the lack of freedom of debate within the UVF when he said that on his release:

> I didn't want any involvement in the UVF. I wanted to be in a position to criticise when criticism was required ... I remember one UVF man saying to a councillor 'you'll do what you're told'. That took away any freedom of movement. I wanted a free hand. But I did consult the UVF.[68]

The main dissident challenge to the UVF came from one of its most senior commanders, Billy Wright. Wright began to challenge the UVF leadership over its role in the peace process. Among other things he felt the process was ceding too much in terms of the role in Northern Irish affairs it permitted the Dublin government. He also believed the UVF in Belfast was too Marxist. Although supportive of the 1994 UVF ceasefire – he actually travelled to the home of David Ervine in September that year to demand that the UVF should call one[69] – Wright began to dissent when he read the Framework document of February 1995.[70] 'Loyalism had been shafted ... the game was up and that it was all about a united Ireland.'[71] He was particularly critical of the Belfast leadership's lack of support for the Drumcree march. Wright also opposed the idea that UVF men would have to vote for the PUP. He wanted it to be left to the individual conscience. And he disliked the notion that only Belfast could be represented on the brigade staff.[72] He eventually came to view the PUP leadership not as loyalists: '[t]hey may have emanated from within loyalism but they are no longer loyalists. They are in a prominent political position within the movement and are controlling it.'[73]

After the Portadown UVF murder of Catholic taxi-driver Michael McGoldrick the UVF stood down the unit responsible. As with the UDA handling of Adair, the UVF leadership moved to hive off support from the Wright faction and increase the isolation of Wright. He was ordered to leave the country inside seventy-two hours or face death.[74] Mid-Ulster UVF members appeared at rallies in Belfast expressing support for the UVF leadership. In order to maintain dissent Wright called a public rally which received substantial support. He played on the fact that the IRA had tried to kill him on a number of occasions. The UVF exploited his appearance with Willie McCrea of the DUP. The DUP had been lambasting loyalist groups and calling for the decommissioning of

UVF and UDA weapons. 'Here was Billy Wright aligning himself to the DUP who wanted the UVF to give up all their guns.'[75] Shankill graffiti accused Wright of being an MI5 agent. As one LVF member stated: 'It's always been the same of the UVF in Belfast. Once you stand up to them or question their authority they start using black propaganda. You are either a drug dealer, child molester or a tout. They try to discredit you within your local community and set you up for assassination. That's what they did with Billy Wright.'[76] As part of its attempt to maintain control the UVF leadership also killed the dissident Frankie Curry, in addition to attempting to assassinate other leading figures in the dissent world such as Jackie Mahood, Clifford Peoples and Kenny McClinton.

CONCLUSION

The militia-dominated groups, loyalist and republican, essentially operate in accordance with a totalitarian impulse. Rather than defend and empower the communities they originate from, their primary goal has been to empower themselves within those communities. The UVF, however, has remained anchored to the values of its formative years.

The Adams takeover, compared to the marginalisation of Billy Wright, suggests that dissent is more likely to succeed if those vocalising it are rooted in power centres, are at senior leadership level and have military prowess.

Loyalism is no more prone to curbing dissent than republicanism. It has certainly been more violent. While brute force seems to come instinctively to the UDA, the UVF is more calculating in its application of it as a means of suppressing dissent.

The Provisionals – shaped by the logic of the peace process and their feverish desire to be part of the establishment and in government – have placed limitations on dissidents in a way that loyalism has not yet faced. A parallel can be drawn with the issue of decommissioning of weaponry. The more the Provisionals were drawn into the peace process the less freedom they had, compared to the loyalists, to hold on to their weapons. Hence, apart from one act by the LVF there has been no loyalist decommissioning. It is likewise with the suppression of dissent. The Provisionals can no longer expect to be given a 'get out of jail free' card if they decide to murder a republican opponent. The loyalists who are generally not institutionally included within the power chambers of the peace process suffer from no such constraint. Where they are included, in the case of the PUP's one assembly seat, the imperative to hold on to that seat has opened up the UVF to certain pressures that the UDA remains largely impervious to. Hence the UVF has moved much further in its public statement of 2007 than has the UDA in any of its public pronouncements.[77]

Because the loyalist leaderships have deviated much less from the core constitutional issues that have featured at the centre of the conflict discourse than have the Provisionals, it is possible to suggest that, for the UVF at least, the perceived need to control dissent was linked to the securing of its constitutional objectives. In the case of the UDA and the IRA, both must answer the accusation that their primary interest in suppressing dissent may have been directly linked to the accruing of bureaucratic power.

NOTES

1. Laurence McKeown writing in *Daily Ireland*, 24 June 2006.
2. *An Phoblacht/Republican News*, 29 August 2002.
3. Former loyalist activist expressing opinion to author in the course of a conversation about such matters.
4. Johnny Adair, quoted in Lister, D. and Jordan, H., *Mad Dog: The Rise and Fall of Johnny Adair and 'C' Company* (Edinburgh: Mainstream, 2003), p. 39.
5. English, R., 'Revolutionary Writing', *Fortnight*, No. 404 (May 2002), pp. 22–5.
6. McIntyre, A. and Gorman, T., *Irish News*, 17 October 2000.
7. McIntyre, A., 'Hammering Dissent', *The Blanket*, 5 January 2003.
8. McIntyre, A., 'Living In Fear', *The Blanket*, 15 September 2003.
9. The present author wrote a chapter exclusively focusing on the suppression of dissent within republicanism. See 'Provisional Republicanism: Internal Politics, Inequities and Modes of Repression', in McGarry, F. (ed.), *Republicanism in Modern Ireland* (Dublin: UCD Press, 2003).
10. Foucault, M., 'Truth, Power and Sexuality', in V. Beechey and J. Donald (eds), *Subjectivity And Social Relations* (Milton Keynes: Open University Press, 1985), p. 89.
11. See McCann, E., 'Herrema's Kidnapper Explains Motive', *Sunday Tribune*, 23 October 2005.
12. McGuire, M., *To Take Arms: A Year in the Provisional IRA* (London: Macmillan, 1973).
13. Mac Stiofáin, S., *Memoirs of a Revolutionary* (Edinburgh: Gordon Cremonisi, 1975).
14. Martin Meehan, interview with the author, 1995.
15. Sean Mac Stiofain, interview with the author, 3 October 1995.
16. Former president of IRA Army Council, interview with the author, 1 July 1995.
17. Martin McGuinness, interview with the author, 26 June 1995.
18. Sean Mac Stiofáin, interview with the author, 3 October 1995.
19. Ibid.
20. Jimmy Drumm, interview with the author, 12 October 2005.
21. McGuire, *To Take Arms*, p. 127.
22. Ó Ruairc, L., *The League of Communist Republicans, 1986–1991* (2001). Available at: www.fourthwrite.ie/lcr.pdf.
23. The author was one of the people who opposed this move in 1987.
24. Brendan Hughes, interview with the author, July 2007.
25. Moloney, E., *A Secret History Of The IRA* (London: Penguin, 2002).
26. Ibid., p. 195.
27. Former IRA Volunteer, interview with the author, September 2006.
28. Holland, J., 'Savouring Romantic Ireland from the Shores of Donegal', *Irish Echo*, 5–11 February 2002.
29. Moloney, *A Secret History of the IRA*, p. 440.
30. The current adjutant-general of the Provisional IRA made this observation to the author at the end of a meeting staged by the 32 County Sovereignty Movement in west Belfast in 1998.
31. Bernadette Sands-McKevitt, quoted in Anthony McIntyre, 'The Struggle Goes On', *Parliamentary Brief* (November 1998).
32. Laurence O'Neill, interview with the author, March 2007.
33. Tony Catney, Interview with the Author, July 2007.
34. McIntyre, A., 'Sinn Féin and the Hate: Martin Cunningham Interviewed', *The Blanket*, 18 March 2004.

35. John Kelly, interview with the author, July 2007.
36. Michael Stone, quoted in Dillon, M., *Stone Cold* (London: Hutchinson, 1992), p. 68.
37. McDonald, H. and Cusack, J., *UDA: Inside the Heart of Loyalist Terror* (Dublin: Penguin, 2005), p. 23.
38. Ibid., p. 27.
39. Ibid., p. 34.
40. Ibid., p.110.
41. Ibid., p. 348.
42. Ibid., p. 85.
43. Ibid., p. 242.
44. Ibid., p. 368.
45. Reference from David Adams.
46. McDonald and Cusack, *UDA: Inside the Heart of Loyalist Terror*, p. 273.
47. Ibid., p. 211.
48. Lister and Jordan, *Mad Dog*, p. 249.
49. Stone, M., *None Shall Divide Us* (London: John Blake, 2004), p. 265.
50. Lister and Jordan, *Mad Dog*, p. 239.
51. Ibid., p. 222.
52. McDonald and Cusack, *UDA: Inside the Heart of Loyalist Terror*, p. 372.
53. Stone, *None Shall Divide Us*, p. 265.
54. Cusack, J. and McDonald, H., *UVF* (Dublin: Poolbeg, 2000), p. 343.
55. McDonald and Cusack, *UDA*, p. 282.
56. Ibid., p. 284.
57. Ibid., p. 286.
58. Ibid., p. 341.
59. Cusack and McDonald, *UVF*, p. 87.
60. Dillon, M., *The Shankill Butchers* (London: Arrow, 1990).
61. Boulton, D., *The UVF: An Anatomy of Loyalist Rebellion* (London: Torc, 1973), p. 139.
62. Sinnerton, H., *David Ervine: Uncharted Waters* (Dingle: Brandon, 2002), p. 37.
63. Quoted in Cusack and McDonald, *UVF*, p. 151.
64. Ibid., p. 349.
65. YCV leader, quoted in ibid., p. 153.
66. Sinnerton, *David Ervine*, p. 139.
67. Ibid., p.126.
68. Gusty Spence, quoted in R. Garland, *Gusty Spence* (Belfast: Blackstaff, 2001), p. 268.
69. Sinnerton, *David Ervine*, p. 165.
70. Anderson, C., *The Billy Boy: The Life and Death of LVF Leader Billy Wright* (Edinburgh: Mainstream, 2002), p. 47.
71. Billy Wright, quoted in Sinnerton, *David Ervine*, p.165.
72. Anderson, *The Billy Boy*, p. 65.
73. Billy Wright, quoted in Dillon, M., *God and the Gun* (London: Orion, 1997), p. 66.
74. Anderson, *The Billy Boy*, p. 47.
75. UVF commander, quoted in Cusack and McDonald, *UVF*, p. 350.
76. LVF member, quoted in Anderson, *The Billy Boy*, p. 51.
77. UVF statement, 3 May 2007.

PART III

NGOs, STATE STRATEGIES AND CONFLICT TRANSFORMATION

Chapter 8
Ordering Transition: The Role of Loyalists and Republicans in Community-based Policing Activity

Neil Jarman

The declaration of the paramilitary ceasefires in 1994 marked the beginning of a period of transition in Northern Ireland that has been marked by recurrent outbursts of public disorder and rioting. This violence has in particular been associated with protests against some loyal order parades, and inter-communal clashes at many of the interfaces that segregate working-class nationalist and unionist communities. Protests against the parades began in the spring of 1995, but erupted into serious violence the next summer following the police decision to restrict the Orange Order from marching down the Garvaghy Road as part of the Drumcree church parade.[1] The cyclical nature of the parades has served to stimulate the unresolved antipathy and political rivalry between the two main communities, and has ensured that tensions and hostilities resurface each summer. The rise in tensions in turn impacts on relations between the two communities and has frequently resulted in outbursts of violence at various interfaces. The marching season and social segregation thus exist in a symbiotic relationship of tension and distrust which is too often expressed through outbursts of inter-communal violence.

The cycle of tension and disorder has remained a feature of the Northern Irish summer for more than a decade. However, despite some similarities between the violence associated with the marching seasons of 1996 and 2005, there were in fact considerable differences in the reality on the ground. In 1996 when nationalists objected to the Tour of the North parade passing along Clifton Park Avenue in north Belfast, Sinn Féin's Gerry Kelly was at the heart of the protest. He was in the midst of the crowd that sat down to block the road and he was arrested by the police as they cleared the road to allow the parade through. In 2005 Kelly (now an MLA) was again on the streets as nationalists gathered to protest against a section of the Tour of the

North parade completing their route up the Crumlin Road to Ligoniel. But on this occasion Kelly was working to ensure that the protest passed off peacefully and he was one of many senior republicans trying (unsuccessfully) to prevent youths from the neighbouring Ardoyne from attacking the Orangemen, their supporters and the police. This chapter explores the changing and developing roles that members of the loyalist and republican communities have played in the crowd events and outbreaks of disorder on the streets through the period of political transition. It looks in particular at the increasing responsibility that has been taken in trying to control the potential for violence, and it discusses the impact that the practical work on the ground has had on building a foundation for more constructive relationships with the police. It does so within a framework structured by a critical perspective on current understanding of vigilantism and community-based policing activities.

TRANSITION AND ORDER

The transition from militarised violence to peace in Northern Ireland has been a problematic and difficult process. The armed conflict came to an end without a clear victor, with no sense of conciliation between the wider British unionist and Irish nationalist communities and without any general agreement over the next steps that were needed to consolidate the peace. One result of this was that the 'peace process' progressed along a number of interlinked but distinctive paths. One path involved the political elite in a drawn-out process of discussions and negotiations around the content and implementation of the peace agreement and the creation of the new institutions and structures of governance. Another involved the business and commercial community in attempting to build on the 'peace dividend' to regenerate and redevelop the economy and infrastructure. Yet another path involved a grassroots process, which was often played out on the streets and in the different communities and organisations of civil society, as communities sought to influence the direction and content of the new institutions and to maintain momentum in the process of peace-building. The various strands of the peace process were intimately linked, but they were rarely synchronised. Events on the ground have often had a negative impact on the attitudes and actions of political leaders, and on the potential for economic regeneration, while the words and actions of the political leadership have at times encouraged, but at other times restrained or deterred, the actions of local activists and community leaders.

The violence that dominated Northern Ireland for a generation left a legacy of suspicion, mistrust and antipathetic relationships between members of the nationalist and unionist communities. It generated strong feelings of mistrust and hostility towards the state and towards the security forces within both loyalist and republican constituencies. The early years of the transition witnessed not so much a 'peace process' as a continuance of the conflict, albeit by other means. Violent attacks were scaled down, but hostilities were sustained at a lower level. Protests against parades and disorder at the interfaces sustained tensions, while young people were often encouraged to participate in outbreaks of disorder. The period of transition also deepened the vacuum that existed in law and order, particularly in many working-class areas. Policing has long been a contentious issue for republicans, and over the course of the Troubles loyalists also became increasingly alienated from the RUC, as it became a more militarised and prominent arm of the security forces and sought to restrict their 'traditional' civil liberties and other activities. In the period immediately following the ceasefires the police did initiate some reforms and began to make attempts to build relations with the wider nationalist community, but the policing of the Drumcree protests in 1996 instantly undermined any progress that had been made. Thereafter public order policing, the most visible experience of policing for many people, became a major source of contention and the demand for policing reform became a key element of the political negotiations that were to lead to the signing of the Agreement in 1998. The political transition was thus a period of uncertainty, a time of optimism that was frequently tinged with trepidation. In many ways the peace had to be built from the bottom up as much as from the top down and this process involved diverse groups, organisations and activities, and included managing tensions and disorder on the ground and building relationships with erstwhile enemies and opponents.

PARAMILITARISM AND DIS/ORDER

The main paramilitary organisations have long taken a role in imposing forms of order and justice on 'their' communities.[2] During the Troubles paramilitary 'order' was largely delivered through the threat or practice of shooting, beating or exiling individuals who were accused of criminal or anti-social activities. Although this was sometimes done to enforce control and authority, it was also often carried out in response to demands from within the community in response to lack of legitimacy of the state or the criminal justice system. While such forms of order and 'justice' continued after the ceasefires, sections of the broad loyalist and republican communities also began to explore how they might move away from the reliance on the use, or threat, of force at a time when the police were still regarded by many as an unacceptable body. One outcome was the creation of community-based restorative justice projects in a number of areas, as a means of offering an alternative to punishment beatings but also to provide a more effective means of confronting criminal activity and antisocial behaviour through reintegration rather than further alienation of offenders.[3] At the same time there have been parallel developments involving members of loyalist and republican communities in developing practices and strategies to police crowd events and respond to inter-communal tensions and disorder.

Contentious parades often attracted members of various paramilitary groups, sometimes to defend the rights of the marchers, sometimes to confront them, sometimes to challenge the police. When the first protests over parades began in 1995 members of the Orange Order noted the prominent role of a number of republicans and ex-prisoners among the spokespeople for several of the residents' groups.[4] This was particularly significant in the three high-profile disputes in Belfast, Derry and Portadown, where the presence of republican ex-prisoners in the Lower Ormeau Concerned Community, and the Bogside and Garvaghy Road Residents' Groups, was used as an argument for avoiding face-to-face discussions and compromise. The prominence of republicans was cited as evidence that the protests were not only part of the ongoing Sinn Féin campaign against unionism, but also represented a shift to confronting Protestant popular culture. As a result unionists challenged the legitimacy of the residents' groups and their right to represent the views of the local communities. The unionist views of the protests and the protesters only hardened as they turned to more open confrontation and violence in a number of areas, and as the police began to restrict the parade routes in other locations. The visible presence of paramilitary actors on the ground further fuelled anger and suspicions.

From the opposite position, nationalists and republicans noted the presence of loyalist paramilitary symbols and regalia at many parades, with many of the bands, and even some Orange lodges and Apprentice Boys clubs, carrying flags and visual displays associated with the Ulster Volunteer Force (UVF), the Young Citizen Volunteers (YCVs), Red Hand Commando (RHC), the Ulster Defence Association (UDA) and Ulster Freedom Fighters (UFF). They also noted the presence of members of loyalist paramilitary groups on the ground in many locations, including the key contentious sites in Belfast, Derry and Portadown, supporting the rights of Orangemen to parade. The spring and summer of 1996 in particular was marked by escalating violence at a number of contentious parades, which snowballed to impact on many interface areas away from the parade routes and subsequently generated its own destructive momentum in urban and rural locations across the north. Neighbouring interface communities responded to violence with violence, which in turn generated further attacks. Disorder spread and continued through the summer and into the autumn months. Some members of the paramilitary organisations were undoubtedly involved in the violence and in provoking the disorder, but others were struggling to exert their authority and attempting to limit the conflict. This was most evident within loyalism, where contrasting positions were taken that reflected the divergence of views and attitudes amongst loyalist paramilitaries towards the direction of the peace process. Overall the UVF and the Progressive Unionist Party were more supportive of the process and tried to restrict random violence, particularly when it was likely to impact on loyalist areas, whereas the UDA and the Loyalist Volunteer Force were more unpredictable in their actions and responses. In general interface trouble in Belfast occurred more regularly in areas dominated by the UDA than in areas where the UVF was stronger, but even so at times the UDA sought to exert its influence and control the potential for violence when the political context demanded.

CREATING A COMMUNITY POLICE

There were two main forms of response to the threat and reality of outbreaks of public disorder by members of the republican and loyalist communities.[5] One involved organising people to act as marshals to try to control the more disorderly elements attracted to the contentious parades. The other involved mobilising local networks of activists to monitor the main interface areas and to intervene if trouble began to develop. In both situations a wide range of people were involved in the work. This included some individuals with a paramilitary background and others without; and in some cases such individuals were acting in a 'representative' capacity, while in others they were perceived as representatives of the wider community.

The attention that has been focused on the violence and disorder associated with the parade disputes, particularly following Drumcree in 1996, has largely obscured the work undertaken by people in both communities in Belfast to manage protests and prevent confrontation. In part this was because the 'marshals' were not always successful in stopping riots or attacks on the police, and in part it was because on occasions the paramilitaries had an interest in allowing or even encouraging violence. The tensions around the marching season fed into the wider political negotiations and rivalries both between and within the two communities. This meant that republicans might choose to mobilise marshals on some occasions but not others, or that the UVF attempted to limit the disorder in 'their' areas, while the UDA stood back or even encouraged people onto the streets in other parts of the city. However, when the main paramilitary groups all agreed that it was important to limit the violence and focus on peaceful demonstrations and protests they could be very effective. In June 1997, the Whiterock parade was confronted by protests from nationalists, and although the police agreed that it should proceed along the desired route, tensions were high in both communities. On the Shankill, the UDA and UVF worked together to limit disorder and as the parade passed along Workman Avenue the supporters, who were often responsible for initiating the disorder, were confronted by groups of men on either side of the road who simply blocked the pavements and refused to allow them to get near to the potential flashpoint. Similarly, republicans on the Springfield Road encouraged people to protest against the parade, but they also mobilised a line of 'marshals' to control the location and actions of the protesters. The practice of marshalling crowds at contentious parades became common in many areas and among both loyalist and republican communities after 1997. Within a few years it had become such a standard practice that the police and the Parades Commission increasingly took it to be the norm. In fact refusing, or threatening to refuse, to provide marshals to control the crowds became an evident indicator of community dissatisfaction and a warning of impending confrontation. But paradoxically the provision of marshals has also become widely acknowledged (and accepted) as a responsibility of the organisers of protests, and of those supporting the parades, which they have increasingly found difficult to abrogate.[6]

The relatively peaceful nature of contentious parades in Belfast between 2002 and 2005 was in large part due to the scale of the marshalling and management of crowds within both communities. But there were also ongoing discussions involving key actors, who recognised that any resolution to the disputes would require an agreement that was acceptable to the main communities of interest, and any outbreak of violence would only make it more difficult to reach such an agreement. Marshalling crowds was thus a means to an end, not an end in itself. The use of disorder, which in 1996 and the following years had been a means of mobilising support for a position and for pressurising decision-makers, was largely acknowledged as being no longer the most appropriate strategy and instead greater emphasis began to be placed on elaborating a discourse of human rights. Unfortunately, given the previously tolerated and even encouraged violence at protests, it has proved difficult to prevent some sections of the communities from continuing to advocate the use of force. For example, violent attacks were launched on Orange parades and the police on the Crumlin Road in the summer of 2005 despite the best intentions of the republican leadership, who mobilised senior figures, including Gerry Adams, in an unsuccessful attempt to ensure that the republican protests passed peacefully.

The violence and disorder of 1996 also stimulated community groups in north Belfast to consider how best to respond to the rising levels of tension at the area's many interfaces over the summer months. They noted the prominent role that rumour had played in creating fears and in mobilising people onto the streets, the impact that the presence of crowds of people on street corners or near interfaces had on people from the 'other' side, and the difficulty in maintaining communication between different areas and groups and the impact that this had on co-ordinating any effective response. As a result one local organisation, the Community Development Centre, decided to equip its existing network of community workers with mobile telephones. These enabled the activists to remain on the streets and monitor the situation at the various interfaces, but still stay in touch with members of their own community and with people on the other side of the interface. The phones enabled people to clarify and respond to rumours, helped them to calm fears and allowed individuals to synchronise their responses and co-ordinate initiatives to reduce tensions. The mobile phone network involved a diverse group of people, some, but not all, of whom had links with the republican and loyalist communities. They also linked with key people in statutory agencies such as the Housing Executive and in some areas provided a line of communication with the police.

The north Belfast network became a central element of community attempts to manage and control public disorder and reduce inter-communal tensions. In each of the main interface areas activists spent the summer nights on the streets until the early hours of the morning. In effect they were acting as a form of policing patrol, monitoring a small 'beat' and liaising with various people in an attempt to prevent trouble. When necessary they intervened to stop missiles being thrown or crowds gathering, and on occasion they liaised with the RUC over the strategy, tactics and timing of police interventions. The phone network was immediately acknowledged as a valuable addition to the conflict management repertoire in north Belfast, not only by the community sector but also by the key statutory agencies. As a result funding was made available to ensure that the network could continue, and the project expanded from twelve phones in 1997 to eighteen the following year. The model of a community-based mobile phone network rapidly became acknowledged as a fundamental element of local conflict management practice and, as mobile phones became more widely available, networks were established in most interface areas in Belfast and towns across the north. The north Belfast community network continued to form the basis of grassroots conflict management activities across the area, and it provided a foundation for a more extensive and formalised cross-community network, the North Belfast Conflict Transformation Forum, which was established in 2005 to develop more strategic approaches to dealing with interface issues.

The mobile phone networks were never explicitly linked with either republican or loyalist movements, although the various networks overlapped through individual co-membership. In north Belfast, for example, the initial mobile phone network was coordinated by a small team that included both a former republican prisoner and a former loyalist prisoner. The network was thus able to link unaffiliated community workers across the area with the more politicised groups, and this ensured that both unionist and nationalist groups had easy access to the local political leadership. As a result individuals such as Gerry Kelly of Sinn Féin and Billy Hutchinson of the PUP could be contacted and on the streets in a few minutes if a situation was becoming particularly problematic and required an input beyond the capabilities of the local groups. One of the factors that made the networks effective was that it crossed political and community boundaries, and could thus engage with and draw upon most if not all elements of the fragmented communities in north Belfast. The one limitation was with the somewhat tenuous involvement of the UDA, which as noted earlier, was often unpredictable in its response to tension and disorder. This matter came to a head in February 2005 when the UDA formally launched its own group, the Protestant Interface Network (PIN), which aspired to take a lead in dealing with interface issues across Belfast and elsewhere in Northern Ireland. Unlike the community networks, however, PIN announced that it would not engage with republicans, asserting that it would control interface tensions in loyalist areas and if republicans did likewise then the violence could be minimised. PIN never fulfilled its own aspirations, and although it provided additional resources in a number of areas it never flourished. PIN members eventually participated in the North Belfast Conflict Transformation Forum, thus implicitly acknowledging the importance of a broad cross-community strategy in managing interface tensions.

COMMUNITY POLICING AND VIGILANTISM

Research from several other locations has illustrated how communities often mobilise their members when there is a perceived or real threat to public order.[7] This is particularly common in situations where relationships with the police are poor: because the police are not considered to be a legitimate authority, or because they are perceived as hostile towards the community, or they are considered to commit insufficient resources to certain areas. However, while there might be a reasonable case to be made for community mobilisation and the creation of community-based policing, such initiatives are generally treated with suspicion by the state, and are considered as a form of vigilante activity and thus unacceptable. Popular understanding of vigilantism is largely based on models of the American west[8] or from popular culture, which has highlighted the figure of the urban loner seeking 'justice' or revenge, but academic studies have theorised vigilantism as a more complex range of activities.[9] Ray Abrahams has characterised vigilantism as activities that emerge at the physical, social or cultural boundaries of state authority, usually to impose a form of order that the state is incapable of providing. Les Johnston distinguishes between vigilantism and forms of 'responsible citizenship', which includes Neighbourhood Watch and similar crime prevention schemes. He argues that the distinctive elements of vigilante activity are that it is autonomous in form; maintains a distance from the state and state institutions; and most crucially it involves the use or the potential use of force. Vigilantism can thus be considered to fall within a 'grey area' of political activity,[10] in that it straddles the boundary between the legitimate and illegitimate, and the lawful and the unlawful, and in Abrahams's terms operates in 'the shadows rather than the bright lights of legitimacy and consensus'.[11]

The issue of the use of force is perhaps the element that for many people defines vigilantism and also categorises it as a problematic activity, since we have become used to accepting that the state and its agents have a monopoly on the lawful use of force. But Johnston's definition is problematic in so far as he requires only a potential for the use of force for independent activity to be categorised as vigilantism, not evidence of actual or even threatened use of force. In Northern Ireland paramilitary activities that have been undertaken in an attempt to impose order or control on their communities, such as the beating, shooting or exiling of people accused of criminal acts or anti-social behaviour, have been widely categorised as resorting to vigilantism and condemned as illegal and barbaric actions.[12] Hostility to paramilitary involvement in any forms of action, which might reasonably fall within the remit of the criminal justice system, continued even when such action aimed to challenge punishment violence; for example, the various community-based restorative justice schemes were at best regarded with suspicion, and at times with outright hostility, by the state and by some political parties. They were considered as attempts to by-pass state authority and retain or extend paramilitary control over working-class communities. They were too autonomous and too closely associated with paramilitary communities to be considered acceptable.

In contrast, few concerns have been raised about the role of people with connections to the paramilitary constituencies participating in community-based policing activity at parades and interfaces. Furthermore, there has not been any attempt to classify such actions as forms of vigilantism, even though the activities clearly fell within the boundaries of the definitions constructed by Abrahams and Johnston. This is surprising, not only because of the links with the broad paramilitary networks, but also because similar patrolling or community mobilisations in the UK, which have often been linked to issues such as prostitution or concerns about paedophiles, have been regarded with suspicion by the state and the media and classified as vigilantism.[13] There are two key aspects that need to be taken into consideration when analysing the sympathetic attitudes towards community-based policing in Northern Ireland: first, the diversity of participants in the community-based networks and, second, their relationships with the police. These factors in particular helped to create a blurring of the conceptual boundaries between vigilantism and responsible citizenship, and ensured a more positive response to policing community-based initiatives.

NETWORKS AND RELATIONSHIPS

One of the positive outcomes of the Troubles and the democratic deficit of rule from Westminster has been the prominence of the community and voluntary sector in Northern Ireland and the necessary recourse to self-reliance in diverse situations. People on the ground often did not rely on the state or its intermediaries to deal with their problems; rather forms of direct intervention, lobbying and service provision were developed in many areas. The broad community and voluntary sector includes networks that connect a wide range of geographical and interest communities, which integrated community development and community relations work and also connected local and horizontally based initiatives with vertically structured political and statutory networks. It was a key sector in the development of a solid basis of social capital that has been drawn upon to consolidate the peace and support a range of peace-building initiatives.[14] Thus the mobile phone networks were able to draw upon a diverse range of people from varied backgrounds and interests, and while some of them were working to a specific political agenda, others were primarily focused on protecting their communities from threat or violence. Members of the political/paramilitary movements were involved, but were not necessarily dominant or publicly prominent; rather they offered another dimension that helped to link individuals in different communities across north Belfast and helped to connect the community networks with the local political leadership. The ex-prisoners in north Belfast were part of a coordinating group that functioned as part of a fulcrum that mobilised social capital resources in response to the disorder. They were at the intersection of a range of single-identity, cross-community and statutory networks that were able to draw upon different elements of bonding, bridging and linking capital to reduce the scale and impact of the tension and disorder.

The marshalling work similarly drew upon a diverse range of people, and while members of the paramilitary groups were sometimes to the fore, other non-aligned activists were also involved. Furthermore, the loyal orders also developed and extended their own marshalling activities, such that exerting control over the management of events and activities on the streets came to be seen as an indicator of a growing and necessary social and civic responsibility.[15] As some communities and organisations sought to assert their freedom to assemble and the right to protest, other voices raised the desire for order and the need to continue to build the peace. Thus while the diverse forms of community mobilisation into grassroots policing activity remained autonomous from the state, both they and the police were largely working to a similar agenda, and this steadily developed into working to a common agenda. Furthermore, unlike the community-based restorative justice projects, the community-based policing work took place in the public eye; it did not seek to operate in the shadows, as Abrahams has suggested is indicative of vigilantism, but rather functioned in a way that was largely visible to the scrutiny of the police. There was thus a mutual transparency of approach, tactics and impact of both police and community workers, which helped lead to the development over time of some degree of trust and respect.

The police were initially only tenuously connected to these community networks because of the continued hostility towards the RUC and PSNI in many republican and loyalist communities. Nevertheless lines of communication were open from the outset. The diverse membership of the community networks included individuals who had established or developed working relationships with the police, often at senior levels, and it was generally known, if not publicly acknowledged, that a two-way chain of communication with the police was both available and being used. The availability of mobile phones enabled contacts between police and activists to be made even during outbreaks of rioting and disorder and the phones permitted an ease of communication, but with a degree of discretion, in order to hold conversations and exchange information in contexts and situations where this would previously have been impossible.

If the community activists were wary of engaging with the police, many police officers were also cautious about how far they could, or should, work with individuals and organisations that were connected to the political and paramilitary networks that contested their very existence. Initially work on the ground involved two parallel, but distinct and separate, networks of activity, with the police and community activists each aspiring to the same outcome, but at the same time treating each other with suspicion and mistrust. However, working relations soon began to be developed through practical work on the streets around contentious situations and events. The police recognised that the activists were genuinely attempting to reduce tensions and prevent disorder, while the activists also began to accept that the police were becoming more flexible in their tactics. Concerns about such matters as the timing of police intervention, the use of force, the location of vehicles, the scale of police presence and the recourse to riot gear were conveyed at various times and places by the community, and as the police began to respond positively some degree of trust began to develop. While the police were cautious about leaving themselves exposed to criticism for a failure to act or intervene quickly enough, over time they began to reduce their reliance on rapid and heavy deployment of officers and instead liaised with activists over the most appropriate form of intervention. Increasingly they gave space for the community monitors and marshals to try to calm situations down and held back from intervening until other options had been exhausted.

Working relationships between the police and community networks in the management of public order developed steadily over a decade, and although it is difficult to map out a clear path, it is possible to identify some key landmarks. One such landmark related to the use of force. Although no formal announcement was made by the police, an informal decision appears to have been taken in the late summer of 2002 to restrict the use of plastic baton rounds to extreme situations. In fact plastic bullets were not fired again until the summer of 2005, and then only in response to the use of blast bombs and live fire during extremely violent rioting in north and west Belfast. Instead the police used water cannon as their main crowd-control weapon, but also they appeared to accept the reality of officers getting injured in crowd situations and police injuries increased significantly for a couple of years.[16] A second landmark was that by the summer of 2003 working relationships had been increased to the extent that Gerry Kelly could publicly discuss the tactics of policing contentious parades with the local police commander on the street. And he could then report back directly to the crowd to explain the planned police approach and the republican response. A third landmark came in the summer of 2006, when the police were sufficiently confident of the capacity of the community networks that they agreed to reduce the visible police presence to minimal levels at the key parades. This was all the more significant as the previous summer republicans in Ardoyne and loyalists in west Belfast had launched furious attacks on the police at three contentious parades. However, it was clear from the approach taken in 2006 that the police were prepared to acknowledge the particular circumstances of 2005 and accepted that the community and political leaders had attempted to control the situation. This quiet and practical work, involving community-based networks and the PSNI working to a largely shared agenda in an attempt to maintain public order, was in turn one factor that helped prepare the ground for Sinn Féin's acceptance of the legitimacy of policing in early 2007.

CONCLUSIONS

The process of transition from conflict to a peaceful democracy involved not only reaching a political agreement and establishing new institutions but also addressing such matters as the continued presence of paramilitary organisations, inter-communal conflict, and the legitimacy of policing arrangements (among many others). In the early years after the ceasefires these factors all contributed to the extensive and repetitive outbreaks of public disorder and street violence, but over time the work of community-based networks (which included members of paramilitary groups) in challenging tensions and violence through taking greater responsibility for order management and policing has been a key factor in helping to embed the peace and pave the way for formal acceptance of the policing reforms.

The paramilitary involvement in community-based policing drew upon previous experience of attempting to 'police' their communities, which included the use of threat or force and also experiments in forms of restorative justice. Although sections of the broad loyalist and republican constituencies were undoubtedly involved in fomenting some of the street disorder in the late 1990s, the two constituencies were never homogeneous entities, and while some people were helping to sustain sectarian tensions, others were challenging them. This work initially focused on building links between loyalist and republican communities and networks and developing skills and capacities to intervene, but it was also evident that such work would require engagement with the police if it was to be more effective. Significantly some senior police officers also acknowledged the importance of building links with the community networks, and were willing to allow them space and time to work on the ground. Whilst it would have been relatively easy to demonise the community-based policing activity as vigilantism, the evident benefits of the work at community level, the largely transparent nature of the work on the ground, the common interests of community leaders and police in reducing violence and the developing range of contacts between activists and the police all helped to prevent this from happening. As a result community-based policing has been able to develop and has contributed to the relative reduction in public disorder associated with parades and interface areas.

The creation of community-based policing initiatives at times of crisis is not an unusual phenomenon, and has been experienced in a variety of countries and in response to a variety of contexts. But the experience of other countries also suggests that such initiatives are sustained for only a limited period of time, until the crisis has passed or the deficits in policing are addressed. In Northern Ireland community-based policing has been ongoing for more than a decade, and in some areas people have begun to shift their focus away from sectarian tensions and towards reducing expressions of anti-social behaviour within their own communities, while other forms of community-based policing work, such as marshalling at parades, have become an established part of the event-management process. It is unclear whether these activities will remain an accepted part of future policing and order management activities. However, there is extensive experience that community-based policing has been an important factor in embedding the peace in Northern Ireland and in facilitating the often difficult process of political transition.

NOTES

1.　See Bryan, D., *Orange Parades: The Politics of Ritual and Control* (London: Pluto, 2000).
2.　Bell, C., 'Alternative Justice in Ireland', in N. Dawson, D. Greer and P. Ingram (eds), *One Hundred and Fifty years of Law in Ireland* (Belfast: SLS Legal Publications, 1996), pp. 145–67; Knox, C. and Monaghan, R., *Informal Justice in Divided Societies: Northern Ireland and South Africa* (Basingstoke: Palgrave, 2002); Munck, R., 'The Lads and the Hoods: Alternative Justice in an Irish Context', in M. Tomlinson, T. Varley and C. McCullagh (eds), *Whose Law and Order? Aspects of Crime Control in Irish Society* (Belfast: Sociological Association of Ireland, 1988), pp. 41–53.
3.　See McEvoy, K., 'Human Rights, Humanitarian Interventions and Paramilitary Activities

in Northern Ireland', in C. Harvey (ed.), *Human Rights, Equality and Democratic Renewal in Northern Ireland* (Hart Publishing: Oxford and Portland, OR, 2001), pp. 215–48; McEvoy, K. and Mica, H., 'Restorative Justice and the Critique of Informalism in Northern Ireland', *British Journal of Criminology*, 42, 4 (2002), pp. 534–62; Jarman, N., 'Vigilantism, Policing and Transition: Informal Justice in Northern Ireland', in D. Pratten and A. Sen (eds), *Global Vigilantes: Anthropological Perspectives on Justice and Violence* (London: Hurst, 2007).

4. Jarman, N. and Bryan, D., *Parade and Protest: A Discussion of Parading Disputes in Northern Ireland* (Coleraine: Centre for the Study of Conflict, 1996).

5. Bryan, D. and Jarman, N., *Independent Intervention: Monitoring the Police, Parades and Public Order* (Belfast: Democratic Dialogue, 1999); Jarman, N., 'Managing Disorder: Responses to Interface Violence in North Belfast', in O. Hargie and D. Dickson (eds), *Researching the Troubles: Social Science Perspectives on the Northern Ireland Conflict* (Edinburgh: Mainstream, 2003), pp. 227–44.

6. See Bryan and Jarman, *Independent Intervention*. Also Bryan, D. 'The Anthropology of Ritual: Monitoring and Stewarding Demonstrations in Northern Ireland', *Anthropology in Action*, 13, 1–2 (2006), pp. 22–31; Jarman, N., 'Peacebuilding and Policing: The Role of Community based Initiatives', *Shared Space*, 3 (2006), pp. 31-44.

7. See Blagg, H. and Valuri, G., 'Aboriginal Community Patrols in Australia: Self Policing, Self-determination and Security', *Policing and Society*, 14, 4 (2004), pp. 313–28; Marx, G. and Archer, D., 'Community Police Patrols and Vigilantism', in H. Rosenbaum and P. Sederberg (eds), *Vigilante Politics* (Philadelphia: University of Pennsylvania Press, 1976), pp. 128–57; Sagar, T., 'Street Watch: Concept and Practice, Civilian Participation in Street Prostitution Control', *British Journal of Criminology*, 45, 1 (2005), pp. 98–112; Van der Spuy, E., 'The Emergence and Transformation of Civil Monitoring of Police Power: Some Trends from the Western Cape', in W. Scarf and D. Nina (eds), *The Other Law: Non-State Ordering in South Africa* (Lansdowne: Juta Law, 2001), pp. 169–87.

8. Brown, R.M., *Strain of Violence: Historical Studies of American Violence and Vigilantism* (Oxford: Oxford University Press, 1975); Rosenbaum, J. and Sederberg, P., (eds), *Vigilante Politics* (Philadelphia: University of Pennsylvania Press, 1976).

9. Abrahams, *Vigilant Citizens: Vigilantism and the State* (Cambridge: Polity Press, 1998); Johnston, L., 'What is Vigilantism?', *British Journal of Criminology*, 36, 2 (1996), pp. 220–36; Pratten, D. and Sen, A., (eds), *Global Vigilantes*.

10. Auyero, J., *Routine Politics and Violence in Argentina: The Gray Zone of State Power* (Cambridge: Cambridge University Press, 2007).

11. Abrahams, *Vigilant Citizens*, p. 7.

12. Kennedy, L., 'Nightmares within Nightmares: Paramilitary Repression in Working-Class Communities', in L. Kennedy (ed.), *Crime and Punishment in West Belfast* (Belfast: The Summer School, 1994), pp. 67–80; Silke, A. and Taylor, M., 'War without End: Comparing IRA and Loyalist Vigilantism in Northern Ireland', *The Howard Journal*, 39, 3 (2000), pp. 249–66.

13. Sagar, 'Street Watch'; Williams, A. and Thompson, B., 'Vigilance or Vigilantes: The Paulsgrove Riots and Policing Paedophiles in the Community', *Police Journal*, 77 (2004), pp. 99–119.

14. Varshney, A., *Ethnic Conflict and Civic Life: Hindus and Muslims in India* (New Haven, CT: Yale University Press, 2002).

15. Bryan, 'Anthropology of Ritual'; Jarman, 'Peacebuilding and Policing'.

16. Jarman, N., *Punishing Disorder: Sentencing of Public Order Offences in Northern Ireland* (Belfast: Institute for Conflict Research, 2006).

Chapter 9
For God and ... Conflict Transformation? The Churches' Dis/engagement with Contemporary Loyalism[1]

Claire Mitchell

The traditional view of loyalism is that it has both political and religious dimensions. There has been a long tradition of ideological overlap as well as some practical relationships between Protestant evangelicals and political loyalists. During the height of the conflict many loyalists cited Ian Paisley's sermons as firing up passions and stimulating their involvement in paramilitarism. But despite historical flirtations in times of conflict and crisis, in post-Agreement Northern Ireland many Protestant churches tend not to engage with loyalists. Ironically it is the conservative Protestant churches who are ideologically closest to traditional loyalism that now disassociate themselves the most from working-class loyalists on the ground, preferring to focus on more spiritual matters. In contrast it is left to liberal and left-leaning Protestants, who politically share the least with loyalism, to engage with the reality of socio-economic deprivation, paramilitarism and conflict transformation.

In a sense it may be unsurprising that most mainstream and conservative Protestant churches have disengaged from loyalism – because most contemporary loyalists have also disengaged from the churches. church attendance amongst Protestants in Northern Ireland is lowest amongst the working class,[2] and in the more deprived parts of Belfast that have come to be associated with loyalism it may be lower still.[3] Having said this, churches still occupy a central role in society, evidenced not least by the gospel halls and missions that punctuate the inner cities, housing estates and rural towns of Northern Ireland. And because of the strength of the historical relationship between traditional loyalism and Protestant evangelicalism, many loyalists continue to have a familiarity with, and in many cases a respect for, religion. However, as time passes and the churches have ever less to do with loyalists, their place in the loyalist imagination is becoming more ambiguous.

To point to the churches' disengagement from contemporary loyalism does not imply there is something unique about the religious sphere. It echoes the dissonance that has been developing for a long time between 'middle unionism' and loyalism. Loyalism is understood here to be a working-class, Ulster-oriented grouping, whilst 'middle unionism' is a term that is used to describe middle-class Protestant unionists in Northern Ireland. As social, economic and political changes have accelerated in Northern Ireland over the last twenty years, loyalists have increasingly felt removed from their middle class counterparts. In contrast to the early years of conflict, they have found that they are now no longer politically useful to unionists and have felt increasingly marginalised. They also inhabit very different social spaces. The legacy of conflict has left loyalist areas struggling with poverty, unemployment due to deindustrialisation, educational under-development, drugs, racketeering and paramilitary feuding. The middle classes, on the other hand, have enjoyed high standards of living and educational achievement, rising levels of equity in property and bountiful jobs in the pubic sphere.[4] Whilst middle unionists may not be entirely happy with the direction of political change, this is qual-itatively different from the sense of alienation and hopelessness expe-rienced by many working-class loyalists.

Another legacy of conflict has been prisoner release and the ongo-ing battle to transform loyalist paramilitarism. Pro-state paramilitaries usually have a more difficult relationship with their community of origin than do anti-state paramilitaries – the latter often being seen as freedom fighters whilst the former are often seen as 'thugs' in a context where the state has played a primary role representing a community's interests.[5] This is certainly the case in Northern Ireland, where former loyalist combatants have very little acceptance from their communities of origin.[6] Only 3 per cent of Protestants, for example, supported the prisoner release scheme in the 1998 Agreement (compared to 31 per cent of Catholics).[7] This has exacerbated the feeling amongst loyalists in general, including those actively seeking to transform paramilitarism, that they are seen as pariahs, outsiders in the new Northern Ireland.

These perceptions of hopelessness and outsiderness provide the context in which loyalist conflict transformation efforts take place in Northern Ireland. These efforts are the subject of much of this chapter, as they represent a crucial arena in which civil society and working-class loyalists now come into contact with one another. Although there is much to be said about how political unionism and statutory bodies engage with contemporary loyalism, this chapter focuses particularly on whether or not the churches have any significant relationship with loyalists and with conflict transformation at the coalface. Whilst it is accepted that different churches inevitably have different social priorities, this chapter explores how far they engage specifically with the gritty realities of socio-economic deprivation in loyalist areas and, particularly, issues around loyalist paramilitaries' transition out of recruitment and violence. The strong historical relationship between Protestantism and loyalism makes this line of enquiry pertinent, as does the continuing need for civil society to engage with conflict transformation in Northern Ireland.

The empirical parts of this chapter are based on my own experiences doing fieldwork with evangelicals and loyalists over the last eight years. The chapter draws on some interview material, but is primarily based on my observations of the relationship between the churches and loyalists. These observations are most heavily informed by a period of research with a network of loyalist conflict transformation groups in 2004–05[8] followed by observation and participation on a more informal basis that is still ongoing. It also utilises fieldnotes from earlier qualitative research projects about religion and politics, one with a cross-section of the population of Northern Ireland and another specifically with evangelicals.[9]

OLD-TIME RELIGION AND TRADITIONAL LOYALISM

Whether or not one believes that there is a connection between religion and loyalism in Northern Ireland rather depends on how one defines loyalism. The traditional way of defining loyalism has been to include a wide spectrum of Ulster-oriented 'ultra' Protestants, ranging from the Orange Order to the DUP to the old UVF.[10] This loyalism was based on a banding tradition, where groups of men would mobilise to protect their communities, and was also characterised by a contractual relationship with Britain. Loyalists would be ideologically faithful to the British monarchy, but their loyalty to the government of the day would be conditional on that government protecting Ulster loyalists' interests.[11] Defined in this way, traditional loyalism encompassed a broad sweep of Ulster Protestants, including different classes and denominations. A more recent approach, which probably reflects better the contemporary usage of the label, is to define loyalists as a working-class Protestant group, some but not all of whom have been or are associated with the paramilitaries.[12] This is sometimes referred to as 'new loyalism'.[13] In the former, more inclusive, definition a large number of connections between religion and loyalism have been identified – from preacher politicians to religious symbolism in Orange Order paraphernalia.[14] On the other hand, there is generally thought to be only a weak link between working-class loyalists in the latter sense and Protestant religion.

A number of commentators, however, have shown some degree of relationship in the contemporary period. Bruce, for example, argued in 1994 that there are two types of loyalist – evangelicals and gunmen.[15] For Bruce, the evangelicals provided the ideological backbone of loyalism, while paramilitaries were the footsoldiers. Bruce does not see loyalist paramilitaries as particularly religious, nor does he believe that there have been sustained practical relationships between loyalists and the churches, such as the Free Presbyterian church.[16] However, he has highlighted the symbolic role evangelical culture plays for Ulster Protestants, where religion defines group belonging, figures large in history, legitimises the group's advantages and radically distinguishes the group from its traditional enemy.[17] So for Bruce religion and loyalism often overlap at the level of ideas, in particular when justifying conflict and division.

Todd has also written about the religious dimension of loyalism in her seminal 'Two Traditions in Unionist Political Culture' article.[18] She uses the inclusive definition of 'Ulster loyalism' as a broad grouping of unionists who reach out to a local, Ulster sense of belonging, who have a traditional and conditional sense of Britishness and who are religiously motivated. This is in contrast to the 'Ulster British', who, she says, lean towards a broader UK imagined community and tend to be more middle class, sometimes liberal, and who are not primarily motivated by their Protestantism. The 'Ulster loyalists', in Todd's view, are often Calvinist, with a strong eschatology that focuses on sin and punishment and often interpret events in Northern Ireland from a biblical perspective. Todd follows this theme up in a later piece which puzzles over how far non-religious loyalists, including paramilitaries, might fall back on the certainties offered by a religious position in times of political insecurity.[19] Indeed, some of Mitchell's loyalist interviewees seem to describe such a process.[20]

This type of religiously informed loyalism has an even stronger, if marginal, variant in British Israelism. This is a belief that the people of Ulster are descended from the lost tribes of Israel, that they are a 'chosen people' and that Ulster is their 'promised land'.[21] It is essentially an ethno-racial mythology that is virulently anti-Catholic. British Israelism has influenced a range of Protestants from unionist politician Harold McCusker to an early loyalist paramilitary group, Tara. Tara, led by William McGrath, a Free Presbyterian, never had a wide membership and disintegrated in the mid-1970s, with members leaving for the UVF and the UDA. However, its ultra-Protestant interpretation of conflict and justification for violence have remained in small pockets of contemporary loyalism.

So there are clearly some ideological links between conservative Protestantism and loyalism in Northern Ireland, in both weaker and stronger forms. It is also clear that conservative Protestants have been ambiguous about loyalist paramilitarism at a practical political level. Paisley's associations with the Ulster Resistance militias in the 1970s and Willie McCrea's public appearance with the notorious loyalist paramilitary Billy Wright in the 1990s certainly indicate that this is the case. Ian Paisley is infamous for stirring up the passions of young loyalists, particularly in the 1970s as loyalist paramilitary organisations mobilised to defend their local communities as well as the union with Britain.[22] While Bruce[23] makes the case that Paisley and the DUP were never seriously involved in loyalist paramilitarism themselves, there was certainly strategic cooperation in times of crisis.

Ten years after the Agreement, however, the ideological and practical links that have been identified between religion and loyalism during the height of conflict appear to be much weaker. Many loyalist ex-paramilitaries can now be found expressing regret that they allowed themselves to be fired up by Paisley's apocalyptic sermons in the 1970s and now express a much more secular political vision.[24] The reduction in severe violent conflict means that loyalists may have less need for the explanatory power of religion. On a practical level, very few incidences of practical or personnel overlap between loyalist paramilitaries and conservative Protestant churches have come to light since the stabilisation of conflict in the 2000s. What therefore seems to be the case is that a strong relationship between Protestantism and loyalism in the early twentieth century was re-energised during violent conflict in the 1970s and 1980s, but may now be breaking down in the face of post-Agreement politics and rapid social change. The following sections explore this possible breakdown, asking how far any link between religion – particularly in its institutional form – and loyalism may now remain.

'RESPECTABLE' RELIGION IN CONTEMPORARY NORTHERN IRELAND

'Respectable', or mainstream, religion has always played a rather ambiguous role in conflict and post-conflict society in Northern Ireland. Throughout the years of violent conflict, clergy scarcely justified violence, in either Protestant or Catholic traditions. However, the churches have been accused of propping up conflict by their inaction.[25] By speaking exclusively on behalf of their own communities, sharing in their suffering and providing segregated spaces of sanctuary, churches inevitably became part of the pervasive social divide in Northern Ireland.[26] With a few notable exceptions,[27] churches rarely challenged their own flocks' sectarianism. Power's recent research shows how a variety of churches in Northern Ireland did focus on community relations by the 1990s, but argues that they were better at publishing reports on the subject than making radical inroads into dismantling the dominant social divide.[28] Moreover, churches that do have a streak of social radicalism sometimes choose to channel their energies in other directions and may often ignore the elephants in the corner of the · room – sectarianism and paramilitarism.

Given this reluctance to address the difficult issue of social division, it should not then be surprising that the dominant response of the mainstream Protestant churches has also been to give loyalism a wide berth. This is just as much the case in post-Agreement Northern Ireland, where loyalists, even those deeply involved in conflict transformation, are still seen as rather sinister. Clergy from mainstream Protestant denominations I have interviewed have expressed uncertainty about loyalist conflict transformation groups, speculating that they are just a front for paramilitarism. At one recent event showcasing local loyalist conflict transformation initiatives, over fifty local clergy were invited to see the work that was going on in their area; however, not one attended. Loyalists themselves feel acutely aware that they are seen as pariahs, and express frustration at the politicians and churches who were, in one former combatant's words, 'quite happy when I was dirtying my hands'.

Of course there are plenty of reasons why many 'respectable' Protestant churches would wish to disassociate themselves from loyalism – not least to avoid any implication in the actions of loyalist paramilitaries. It may also involve difficult and dangerous work that may not reap any immediate reward. But their estrangement also comes from the fact that many Protestant churchgoers are middle class and are unlikely to encounter the social, economic and cultural realities of loyalism in their own lives.[29] Some mainstream Protestant denominations, such as Presbyterian and Anglican, that are based in loyalist areas often have congregations composed of elderly locals, and rarely do they see local young people or loyalist paramilitaries coming for Sunday worship. However, loyalist areas have never been fertile ground for the mainstream churches. In contrast, it has been small gospel halls, independent evangelical churches, Pentecostalist and smaller conservative Protestant denominations that have thrived and built congregations amongst local working-class loyalist people. Many continue to be vibrant, and some have even been growing in the 2000s. The conservative Protestant Whitewell Metropolitan

Tabernacle on the Shore Road, for example, has around three thou-
sand members.[30]

In a sense, these conservative Protestant congregations have a much
better relationship with local loyalist communities than do mainstream
Protestant churches. They may provide important social services,
including organised activities for young people that provide an alternative to street culture. Some young people I have interviewed in inner-city
Belfast have attributed their religious conversions to these churches,
which resulted in them turning their backs on drug- taking and criminal activity. However, these churches' mode of engagement is often
primarily spiritual. Their *raison d'être* is to win religious conversions and,
whilst they may reach out to troubled young people, their goal may not
be to engage on a social level so much as to win their souls for Christ.
The Whitewell Metropolitan Tabernacle, for example, refers to its social
location only once on its website, and in revealing terms: 'The Tabernacle
is a truly exciting testimony of God's power at work regardless of the
history of violence, bloodshed, suffering and division here in Northern
Ireland [...] Some have called it, "A rescue shop within a yard of hell
and a hospital for sick souls".'[31] Whilst couched in strong terms, this is
typical of the way many churches see their mission – to tackle worldly sin
and save souls for God's kingdom, rather than simply to engage with the
murky socio-economic and political 'sickness' of this world. Of course the
line between social activism and proselytism is often blurred in practice,
but, for the conservative Protestant churches at least, no worldly concern
is as important as eternal salvation.

One of the only ways that mainstream and most conservative
Protestant churches may come into contact with loyalist paramilitarism
is through ex-UDA or ex-UVF figures who have turned their back on
their organisations and have become born-again. These ex-paramilitaries are often invited to church meetings to give their testimony,
which means to tell the story of their religious transformation. This
story usually follows a pattern of describing the old sinful ways, outlining the 'Damascus Road' moment of realisation, leading to religious
conversion via repentance and forgiveness.[32] This process tends to construct involvement in organised loyalism as 'sin', ignoring the social
and economic realities of the loyalist experience. It does not require the
congregation to engage outside of their comfort zones, and the 'happy
ending' of the testimony indicates that there is a spiritual solution to
loyalist violence (see for example Kenny McClinton's story of his transformation from a UFF leader and 'filthy, Hell-deserving sinner' to
born-again Christian).[33] Indeed it seems that churches that emphasise
the spiritual, rather than the social, dimension of their mission are the
least likely to engage with loyalists on their own terms.

This tendency to engage in the supernatural rather than the temporal realm is often accompanied by a pre-millennial eschatology in many conservative Protestant churches. Pre-millennialism predicts the imminent second coming of Christ, followed by the trials and tribulations of Armageddon, before God returns to establish his kingdom on earth. Conservative Protestants often describe their sense of loss after the Agreement, for example, as a 'sign of the end times'.[34] Each successive political loss or perceived moral unravelling has therefore been accepted as inevitable, even welcome, in the sense that they pre-empt the second coming of Christ. Thus many Protestants are inclined to sit back and give a biblical interpretation to their sense of political doom, rather than go out and engage with contemporary society. This helps explain how many conservative Protestants and their churches can share loyalists' sense of political loss, but yet are not inclined to do anything about it. Moreover, even if they were so inclined, working with loyalists towards the amelioration of paramilitarism and poverty may be seen as futile where such trials and tribulations have been divinely ordained.

However, as is argued above, the disconnection between churches and loyalists is not without its ambiguities. On a variety of occasions DUP personnel as well as other religious Protestants have, through sharing a platform, marching side by side or by a slip of the tongue, revealed connections with loyalists. An interview I conducted with a very religiously devout DUP politician ended with an encounter with a number of loyalists (of the born-again type mentioned above) where there was much mutual congratulation about the 'successful' picket at Harryville Catholic church.[35] Many former loyalist combatants who now run conflict transformation initiatives claim that the DUP often calls upon them to solve difficult situations in loyalist areas but refuses to publicly admit that such a relationship exists.[36] It is therefore important to note that when we talk of disengagement, this is not without grey areas where some contact with loyalists appears to be strategic and ongoing.

To summarise the argument being made: for a variety of reasons – spiritual, social, economic and related to differing experiences of conflict – most Protestant churches do not engage very much with contemporary loyalism. Whilst some churches and in particular small conservative Protestant denominations and gospel halls do attract working-class loyalist congregations, their primary goal is saving souls, and dealing with the gritty realities of paramilitarism, poverty and other social issues is usually not a priority. Loyalists themselves often highlight this lack of engagement and say that they feel abandoned by the churches both in practical terms and in the lack of political guidance in a divided society.[37] This is important because loyalists' perception of marginalisation plays an important, potentially destabilising, role in post-Agreement Northern Ireland. The churches in this sense are well placed to build bridges between loyalism and civil society, to help address issues around socio-economic deprivation, to help loyalists find a voice and place in contemporary Northern Ireland, and to help provide alternative analyses of the political situation.

CHURCHES AND LOYALISM AT THE COALFACE

Despite the widespread disengagement that has been identified, a small minority of Protestants work at the cutting edge of conflict transformation alongside loyalists in Northern Ireland. These include some specific congregations, some religious organisations and some committed Christian individuals who may come from larger, mainstream denominations or who may work independently. Some are themselves loyalists who come from the community they work within, some are former paramilitaries who have since become born-again Christians (sometimes having converted in prison), others may describe themselves as middle-class Protestants or as unionists. Some are modern-day Dissenters, part of the 2 per cent of Protestants in Northern Ireland who identify as Irish.[38] The level of relationship here is quite different from anything that has been described above. It largely centres around conflict transformation work, and deals with socio-economic realities as well as with the sensitive issues around paramilitarism.

In fact, a minority of church personnel have always played an important role in conflict transformation in Northern Ireland, and a handful of Catholic priests, Protestant ministers and other religious individuals were some of the early risk-takers in the peace process, realising that paramilitaries had to be involved at some level in the brokering of any lasting settlement. They met with both republican and loyalist paramilitaries behind the scenes long before local unionist and nationalist political parties had deemed this an acceptable approach to getting agreement.[39] From Father Alex Reid and Father Aiden Troy to the Reverend Ken Newell and the Reverend Sam Burch, there has always been a significant body of both Catholic and Protestant clerics who have been prepared to take risks for peace.[40]

Those religious individuals and institutions that do get involved with conflict transformation at the coalface often do so for reasons that are inherently religious. Christian socialism, for example, has been an influential tradition. This encompasses people who identify as Christians, who are also left-wing, and who see their religion and politics as informing each other. In this tradition the idea of the social gospel is central and Jesus is understood as a radical figure who was anti-authoritarian, who prioritised social justice and who had a special concern for society's 'outcasts'. It is closely informed by liberation theology. The late Billy Mitchell, for example, a former UVF prisoner and, until his untimely death in 2006, one of Northern Ireland's leading peace campaigners, saw himself as a Christian socialist. Writing in *The Other View* in 2000, he states, 'I see no contradiction in being a follower of Jesus Christ while, at the same time, seeking the social, political and economic emancipation of either the economic poor or the social outcasts. On the contrary, I believe [...] that that is exactly what Jesus Himself would seek to do.'[41] Billy Mitchell attended the church of the Nazarene, which is heavily involved in community work. Their flagship organisation, Local Initiative for Needy Communities (LINC), tries to encourage Christians in Northern Ireland to engage in social action at grassroots level.

A theology of peace and forgiveness is also important in informing some Protestants', as it is some Catholics', engagement with loyalism at the coalface. This entails a theological emphasis on reconciliation, grace and forgiveness that is very much at odds with some other Protestant churches' focus on sin and retribution. This is the primary focus of the Centre for Contemporary Christianity – formerly Evangelical Contribution on Northern Ireland – which since the early 1990s has provided an alternative theological analysis of the conflict in Northern Ireland that has presented a serious challenge to the lack of enthusiasm for conflict transformation amongst the mainstream churches.[42] Their summer schools, conferences, speakers and regular publication, *Lion and Lamb*, have provided important forums for debating issues of reconciliation in a divided society.

A theological rationale for reconciliation often leads to practical links between loyalists and religious individuals and churches of this persuasion. The Centre for Contemporary Christianity, for example, facilitates a 'Faith and Loyalism' group which brings together clergy and other Christians who work with loyalists in socio-economically deprived areas of Northern Ireland. This group is more radical than most in that many of its members accept the reality that conflict transformation requires a degree of engagement with paramilitaries and those young people caught up in their activities. Whilst these clergy and religious workers wholeheartedly oppose paramilitary organisations, their rationale is that ignoring the problem will not make it go away. Whilst not all of those associated with the 'Faith and Loyalism' group work at this level of conflict transformation, the fact that some are prepared to is significant.

There are many other practical connections between loyalists and specific churches. Northern Ireland Alternatives – a restorative justice organisation – enjoys good relationships with the churches in some areas and sometimes even gets referrals from them. In north Belfast, for example, Alternatives goes to the local Presbyterian church to do training for the local community around restorative justice, and the congregation meets one evening a month in the community centre. The LINK Family and Community Centre in Newtownards is a faith-based initiative that works closely with loyalists to help transform communities in their area. The Newtownards Community Forum meets in the local Presbyterian church on the Westwinds housing estate. The Methodist East Belfast Mission on the Lower Newtownards Road – now reformulated as the Skainos project – has had a long tradition of practical engagement with all shades of opinion in the local loyalist community. A senior Presbyterian clergyman heads up the Loyalist Commission – a forum for mediating relationships between paramilitaries and civil society in Northern Ireland. These are examples known to me, and doubtless there are plenty more. However, it must be underlined that this kind of activity exists in small pockets amongst handfuls of committed individuals, and certainly does not characterise the relationship between mainstream churches and loyalists in general.

The Progressive Unionist Party (PUP) also facilitates a relationship between loyalists and churches. Whilst the PUP is markedly secular in policy terms, amongst its rank-and-file are a significant number of born-again Christians who work in loyalist communities. Some of them have come from typically loyalist backgrounds, some are former loyalist paramilitaries, and others have joined the party from rather different backgrounds. For example, John Kyle, a PUP member on Belfast City Council, is a local GP who says his motivation 'springs from a strong Christian commitment and a desire to see communities damaged by conflict and deprivation transformed and renewed'.[43]

It would be inaccurate to classify all of the above organisations and individuals as 'liberal' Protestants. Many of them would reject this label and would place themselves squarely in the mainstream of Protestant evangelical culture. However, it is fair to say that scarcely any could be classified as conservative Protestants or come from the smaller conservative denominations. None, to my knowledge, is involved with the DUP or the Free Presbyterian church. They are often Presbyterians, Anglicans, Methodists, Nazarenes, charismatics and independent sorts of Christians. Whilst they may come from mainstream Protestant denominations, they are not typical of those denominations. Some may be involved with the PUP but most are politically uninvolved. It must also be underlined that the organisations and individuals working at the coalface are not simply nominal Protestants. Nearly all have an active, committed faith, and indeed it is this faith that they say compels them to engage with loyalists in these ways.

This engagement is important because churches have been able to provide an alternative analysis of the problem in Northern Ireland. Fearon,[44] for example, describes how in the early and worst years of conflict, a Belfast Methodist minister met with UVF members to offer an alternative way of thinking to that of violence. In a period of adjustment to a more politically stable society, as loyalist paramilitary groups grope around to find alternative ways of being and disbanding, this kind of contact and analysis continues to play an important role. churches cannot simply offer this analysis without also having a mutual relationship and open line of communication with loyalists. In a society where loyalists perceive themselves to be marginalised, this type of relationship with the churches also helps to build bridges with wider civil society. As class divisions continue to structure social relations, lifestyles and opportunities in Northern Ireland, contact between churches and loyalists may be important in crossing this other, equally pervasive, divide.

CONCLUSION

It is ironic that liberal Protestants in Northern Ireland are much more likely to engage with loyalism than their conservative Protestant counterparts with whom loyalists share such a long-standing heritage. To date, conservative Protestants have preferred to channel their political activism into voting for the DUP and their religious activism into saving souls. It is partially this focus on spiritual poverty rather than socio-economic deprivation that has led to most churches' disengagement from contemporary loyalism, and vice versa. Added to this is a class difference that is just as much of a chasm, with middle-class church attenders and clergy shying away from addressing socio-economic and political issues that do not really affect their own lives.

In this, the churches alone should not be held to account. Their disengagement is entirely representative of middle unionism, and of political unionism in general.[45] Nor should we expect all churches to begin to work with loyalists. Working for conflict transformation is often a frustrating and sometimes dangerous task that requires tireless persistence. It is often fraught with moral ambiguities, and engaging with the practical reality of loyalist paramilitarism may feel uncomfortably close to endorsing its existence. However, the wider question for churches must be whether this is a risk worth taking. Billy Mitchell saw it in these terms, arguing that 'in [his] own experience as a community activist [he had] come to realize that if the church gets involved in community development work it will require strong commitment and risky actions on the part of ordinary Christians [and] strong informed leadership on the part of the senior laity and clergy.' But as Mitchell saw it, 'risk-taking and informed leadership should be second nature to those who have answered the call to take up their cross and follow Christ.'[46]

Indeed, ultimately it seems that one's interpretation of 'God's work', as involving social justice or as something purely spiritual, underpins the churches' attitudes to contemporary loyalism. While some churches that focus only on the spiritual realm operate very successfully in loyalist areas, their reach and scope are essentially limited to those that they can convert to their religious position. While a handful of paramilitaries may come to turn their backs on their 'sins', this makes very little impact on the overall structures of social division, socio-economic deprivation or of paramilitarism in Northern Ireland. On the other hand, churches that concentrate less on souls and more on systemic divisions can probably expect only small rewards in terms of denominational growth, but will make a much bigger contribution to the overall project of conflict transformation in Northern Ireland.

NOTES

1. I would like to thank Philip Orr for his comments and suggestions on an earlier version of this chapter, in particular the theological aspects of conservative Protestantism.
2. In 2005, 42 per cent of professional and managerial Protestants said that they attended church, compared with 33 per cent of Protestants in unskilled manual jobs. Northern Ireland Life and Times Survey 2005; data archived at: http://www.ark.ac.uk/nilt/.
3. Morrow, D., Birrell, D., Greer, J., and O'Keeffe, T., *The Churches and Inter-Community Relationships* (Coleraine: University of Ulster, 1991).
4. See Coulter, C., *Northern Irish Society: An Introduction* (London: Pluto, 1999).
5. Rolston, B. 'Dealing with the Past: Pro-State Paramilitaries, Truth and Transition in Northern Ireland', *Human Rights Quarterly*, 28, 3 (2006), pp. 652–75.
6. Shirlow, P., Graham, B., McEvoy, K., Ó hAdhmaill, F. and Purvis, D., *Politically Motivated Former Prisoner Groups: Community Activism and Conflict Transformation* (Belfast: Northern Ireland Community Relations Council, 2005).
7. Northern Ireland Life and Times Survey 2000. data archived at: http://www.ark.ac.uk/nilt/.
8. Mitchell, C., 'The Limits of Legitimacy: Former Loyalist Combatants and Peace-Building in Northern Ireland', *Irish Political Studies*, 23, 1 (forthcoming 2008); Gribben, V., Kelly, R. and Mitchell, C., *Loyalist Conflict Transformation Initiatives*, Report for OFFDFM (2005). Available at http://www.ofmdfmni.gov.uk/conflict.pdf.
9. For more details of these projects see Mitchell, C., *Religion, Identity and Politics in Northern Ireland: Boundaries of Belonging and Belief* (Aldershot: Ashgate, 2005); Mitchell, C. and Todd, J., 'Between the Devil and the Deep Blue Sea: Nationality, Power and Symbolic Trade-offs among Evangelical Protestants in Contemporary Northern Ireland', *Nations and Nationalism* 13, 4 (forthcoming, 2008).

10. Miller, D., *Queen's Rebels: Ulster Loyalism in Historical Perspective* (Dublin: Gill and Macmillan, 1978); Stewart, A.T.Q., *The Narrow Ground: Aspects of Ulster, 1609–1969* (London: Faber and Faber, 1986 [1977]).
11. Miller, *Queen's Rebels*.
12. McAuley, J., 'Whither New Loyalism? Changing Loyalist Politics after the Belfast Agreement', *Irish Political Studies*, 20, 3 (2005), pp. 323–40; Howe, S., 'Mad Dogs and Ulstermen: The Crisis of Loyalism: Part One', *Open Democracy*, 28 September 2005. Archived at: http://www.opendemocracy.net/globalization-protest/loyalism_2876.jsp. Accessed 15 October 2005.
13. McAuley, 'Whither New Loyalism'; Ervine, D., 'Redefining Loyalism', in J. Coakley (ed.), *Changing Shades of Orange and Green: Redefining the Union and Nation in Contemporary Ireland* (Dublin: UCD Press, 2002), pp. 57–63.
14. Brewer, J. with G. Higgins, *Anti-Catholicism in Northern Ireland, 1600–1998* (London: Macmillan, 1998); Jarman, N., *Material Conflicts: Parades and Visual Displays in Northern Ireland* (Oxford: Berg, 1997).
15. Bruce, S., *The Edge of the Union: The Ulster Loyalist Political Vision* (Oxford: Oxford University Press, 1994).
16. Bruce, S., 'Fundamentalism and Political Violence: The Case of Paisley and Ulster Evangelicals', *Religion*, 31, 4 (2001), pp. 387–405.
17. Bruce, *The Edge of the Union*, p. 25; see also Bruce, S., *God Save Ulster: The Religion and Politics of Paisleyism* (Oxford: Clarendon Press, 1986).
18. Todd, J., 'Two Traditions in Unionist Political Culture', *Irish Political Studies*, 2 (1987), pp. 1–26.
19. Todd, J. 'Loyalism and Secularisation', in P. Brennan (ed.), *La secularisation en Irlande* (Caen: Presses Universitaires de Caen, 1998), pp. 195-206.
20. Mitchell, *Religion, Identity and Politics in Northern Ireland*.
21. Akenson, D.H., *God's Peoples: Covenant and Land in South Africa, Israel and Ulster* (Ithaca, NY: Cornell University Press, 1992).
22. Taylor, P., *Loyalists* (London: Bloomsbury, 2000); Fearon, K., *The Conflict's Fifth Business: A Brief Biography of Billy Mitchell*, Conflict Transformation Papers (Belfast: LINC Resource Centre, 2002). Archived at: http://www.linc-ncm.org/No.2.PDF. Accessed 25 June 2007.
23. Bruce, 'Fundamentalism and Political Violence'.
24. Taylor, *Loyalists*; Fearon, *The Conflict's Fifth Business*; personal interviews with author.
25. Morrow, D., 'Church and Religion in the Ulster Crisis', in S. Dunne (ed.), *Facets of the conflict in Northern Ireland* (Basingstoke: Macmillan, 1995), pp. 151–67.
26. Mitchell, *Religion, Identity and Politics in Northern Ireland*.
27. Power, M., *From Ecumenism to Community Relations: Inter-Church Relationships in Northern Ireland, 1980–1999* (Dublin: Irish Academic Press, 2005); Ganiel, G. and Dixon, P., 'Religion in Northern Ireland: Rethinking Fundamentalism and the Possibilities for Conflict Transformation', *Journal of Peace Research* (forthcoming, 2008).
28. Power, *From Ecumenism to Community Relations*.
29. Evans, G. and Duffy, M., 'Beyond the Sectarian Divide: The Social Bases and Political Consequences of Nationalist and Unionist Party Competition in Northern Ireland', *British Journal of Political Science*, 27, 1 (1997), pp. 47–81; Mitchell, C. and Tilley, J., 'The Moral Minority: Evangelical Protestants in Northern Ireland and their Political Behaviour', *Political Studies*, 52, 4 (2004), pp. 585–602.
30. Whitewell Metropolitan Tabernacle, http://www.whitewell.com/. Accessed 11 June 2007.
31. http://www.whitewell.com/about/. Accessed 11 June 2007.
32. Buckley, A. and Kenny, C., *Negotiating Identity: Rhetoric, Metaphor and Social Drama in Northern Ireland* (Washington, D.C: Smithsonian Institution Press, 1995).
33. Ulster American Christian Fellowship, http://www.ulsterchristians.org/kenny.asp. Accessed 7 June 2007.
34. Mitchell and Todd, 'Between the Devil and the Deep Blue Sea'; Mitchell, C., 'Protestant Identification and Political Change in Northern Ireland', *Ethnic and Racial Studies*, 26, 4 (2003), pp. 612–31.
35. Worshippers at the Catholic chapel in Harryville were picketed by an assortment of loyalists, and the chapel was sporadically attacked, from 1996 to 1998.
36. Gribben, Kelly and Mitchell, *Loyalist Conflict Transformation Initiatives*.
37. See, for example, Rankin, P., 'Loyalism and Me', *Lion and Lamb*, 33 (2002). Archived at: http://www.econi.org/LionLamb/033/loyalismandme.html. Accessed 13 June 2007.

38. Northern Ireland Life and Times Survey 2003. Data available at http://www.ark.ac.uk/nilt/.
39. Mitchell, *Religion, Identity and Politics in Northern Ireland*.
40. McCartney, C., 'The Role of Civil Society', in C. McCartney (ed.), *Striking a Balance: The Northern Ireland Peace Process*. Accord: an international review of peace initiatives, No. 8 (London: Conciliation Resources, 1999).
41. Mitchell, B., 'Christian Socialism', *The Other View*, 3 (winter 2000).
42. ECONI, *A Future with Hope: Biblical Frameworks for Peace and Reconciliation in Northern Ireland* (Belfast: ECONI, 1995).
43. The Progressive Unionist Party, www.pup-ni.org.uk. Accessed 13 June 2007).
44. Fearon, 'The Conflict's Fifth Business', p. 23.
45. A notable exception is when Reg Empey asked the late David Ervine, PUP, to sit with the UUP Assembly group in 2006.
46. Mitchell, B., 'Community Development and the Churches', Conflict Transformation Papers (Belfast: LINC Resource Centre, July 2004).

Chapter 10
'The Economic and Social War Against Violence':[1] British Social and Economic Strategy and the Evolution of Provisionalism

Kevin Bean

Trying to understand the ideological and organisational trajectory of the Provisional movement has been a central issue in Northern Irish politics since the 1970s. The formation of the Sinn Féin/DUP executive in May 2007 appeared to settle finally the question and marked the end of the Provisionals' remarkable transformation from armed insurgents into a party of government. As one DUP MP put it, Sinn Féin was now 'facing the unpalatable situation of being part of the British establishment' for the foreseeable future.[2] Although Provisional leaders continued to describe these developments as 'a new phase of our struggle', it was clear by this point that they had, in practice, 'embraced Northern Ireland' and were now settling down to make the new dispensation work.[3]

These events brought a final closure to the Provisional campaign to overthrow the Northern Irish state and, in doing so, produced a widespread feeling that a distinct historical period had come to an end. It also afforded political actors with an opportunity to draw up balance sheets and to assess how and why the Provisionals had so decisively abandoned the long-established goals of the republican project during the peace process. Although a wide range of explanations were advanced to explain this political transformation, one common theme that emerged from the otherwise opposed analyses was the significance of the relationship between the Provisional movement and the British state. Republican critics of the peace process, for example, saw the movement's transformation as a long-drawn-out process of surrender and political accommodation with British imperialism, secretly initiated by the Provisional leadership and developed through prolonged secret contacts with the state since the 1981 hunger strike.[4] Thus, some argued that 'at a time when the national struggle was at the height of its power Adams and McGuinness were plotting behind the scenes ... What foolish notions took possession of them? Was it because they were never republicans in the first place?'[5] This focus on the contacts between the Provisional leadership and the British state also accorded with other established journalistic narratives that similarly described the peace process and the political trajectory of the Provisionals largely in terms of the secret diplomatic history of Gerry Adams.[6]

These long-term perspectives also reflected the dominant British narrative of the Provisionals' history in the 1980s and 1990s: Britain's successful military and political containment of the republican challenge induced war-weariness and encouraged a new mood of political realism amongst the movement's leadership. For example, a review of British army operations in Northern Ireland since 1969 undertaken by senior officers reportedly argued that the 'military structures which "eventually defeated PIRA" were in place by 1980, although it took another 25 years for its armed campaign to be ended'.[7] Thus, whilst the exact sequence of events and the fine details of the new dispensation were not decided until the Good Friday Agreement in 1998, the Major and Blair governments had long been aware from the early 1990s that the Provisionals were prepared to accept a settlement that fell far short of their stated aims.[8] Given the long-term security service penetration of the Provisional movement at all levels, British ministers were probably in a better position to know the real intentions of both its military and political leadership during the peace process than were ordinary Sinn Féin activists and IRA volunteers.[9]

These explanations proffered by traditional republicans and British security strategists are useful descriptions of Provisionalism's incorporation into Northern Ireland's new political dispensation. However, as analyses they are limited by their failure to situate the Provisional movement in a broader political and social context. Thus, the traditional republican emphasis on the individual failings of the Provisional leadership reduces a complex series of political and social interactions to a simplified form of morality tale. Likewise, the British analysis understates the challenge that the Provisionals posed to the state and implies that British success was almost inevitable. As a result, these different narratives of betrayal and containment leave many unanswered questions about the nature of contemporary Provisionalism, both as an ideological form and as a social movement.

One way of answering these questions is to consider the Provisionals as a social movement organisation that has developed into a structure of power within nationalist civil society through a process of institutionalisation.[10] The processes by which formerly radical movements are absorbed by the status quo have long been debated. An extensive literature, both academic and activist, has developed over the last hundred years to explain how such parties have been transformed from revolutionary instruments to participants in establishment politics.[11]

Republican attempts to examine their own movement have been limited because they have largely understood the institutionalisation process as a product of conflicting conservative and radicalising impulses within the movement's own organisational culture.[12] However, in common with other social movement organisations and political parties, the Provisionals' evolution has been 'shaped more by interactions with other actors than by processes internal to a movement'.[13]

Whilst the British state is the single most important political actor in Northern Ireland, it is not the sole determining agency in the institutionalisation of the Provisionals. The political conflict between the state and Provisional republicanism over the last forty years has been mediated by and through a wide range of other factors such as Northern Ireland's distinctive forms of political economy and the rapidly changing structures of civil society. By considering how the British state interacts with these factors to define the political and social environment within which Provisionalism operates, it is possible to understand how this process of institutionalisation occurred and what its implications are for the future trajectory of the Provisional movement.

Much analytical attention has been devoted to the impact of British military and political strategy on the Provisional movement.[14] From the beginning of their campaign, Provisional leaders had recognised the British state's ability to define the military and political context and thus directly shape republican strategy.[15] Indeed, the movement's strategy, whether in its 'Long War' or 'Peace Process' mode, flowed from just such a recognition of this power as it attempted to overcome the imbalance between the Provisionals and the state.[16] Republicans also recognised that British counterinsurgency had a social and economic dimension targeted at the hearts and minds of the nationalist population.[17]

In this way, civil society became a battleground between the British state and the Provisionals. As a 'realm of social interaction, autonomous from both economy and state, that stands between the private sphere and the state' civil society provided the 'terrain where social movements organize and mobilise ... [and] diffuse their values and world views ... [forming] an intermediary sphere between social movements and political power, a sphere that does not so much lie outside political power bur rather penetrates it deeply'.[18] This process of penetration largely occurred through the 'soft' structures of state power which exerted a wide ideological and cultural influence over these 'autonomous' forms of civil society. Given the social and economic weight of the state in Northern Ireland, this meant that even the oppositional forms of republican politics were ultimately determined by the state in its various forms. In the mid-1980s, public expenditure accounted for 70 per cent of Northern Ireland's GDP, and some 45 per cent of the workforce was employed by the public sector.[19] Even after the Good Friday Agreement and the development of the private sector as part of the 'peace dividend' in the 1990s, some 40 per cent of employment in Northern Ireland is still provided by the British state.[20]

These figures reveal one aspect of contemporary state power. However, the definition could also be broadened to include the outer layers of para-state structures that surround the core state and are drawn into its orbit as it attempts to influence civil society. These ill-defined frontiers between the state and civil society were where the battle for hegemony between the British and the Provisionals was at its sharpest. It was here that the British state was to prove most influential in shaping the ideological framework of the Provisional movement. Such a definition of state power more accurately reflects the changing complexities of the relationship between the British state, the economy and civil society in Northern Ireland than does a simple focus on coercion and social control.

The importance of social and economic policy as a political instrument had been recognised by the British state since the beginning of the troubles. Successive governments had made a direct connection between social and economic deprivation and political conflict.[21] However, it was not until the 1980s that a range of policy initiatives were brought together to form 'the third arm of the British government's strategy ... the ... economic and social war against violence'.[22] In particular, during this period a discourse of normalisation and modernisation was conjoined with explicitly political arguments that were designed to weaken support for the Provisionals. As one long-serving British minister explained it, the rationale for this strategy was relatively simple:

> Arguments about a failed state could only be answered if you could see that the state was starting to succeed in terms of social and economic progress. Of course, [Gerry] Adams ... didn't want that because ... the more economic success began to show through, he would lose control of his own community because they were not reliant on him and his advice centres ... if people had jobs they would start to become independent.[23]

In this way counterinsurgency joined with conventional urban, social and economic policy concerns to form an *ad hoc* strategy closely reflecting policy models for dealing with social disorder and social exclusion already operating in post-industrial cities in Britain and the United States.[24] These 'shared visioning' models of urban planning were based on ideas of community development and economic regeneration as motivators for social cohesion and progress.[25] Urban policies of this type were to be later influential in laying the foundations of the post-1998 'reinvention of urban Ulster as normal, placeless and able to hold its own in a competitive global economy'.[26]

Initially British attempts to influence nationalist civil society were designed to marginalise the Provisionals rather than draw them into partnership with the state. In west Belfast in the late 1980s, for example, the aim was to create 'mini-areas of authority and administration' that used resource allocation to demonstrate British commitment to the nationalist population and act as an alternative pole of attraction and centre of power to that of the Provisionals.[27] Some ministers also later believed that this process could be the basis for wider political engagement, moving from a policy of conflict management and 'keeping the lid on the cauldron' to a political process that mobilised nationalist civil society to 'give back power to local authorities and local communities'.[28] The success of these policies in west Belfast encouraged these politicians to believe in the possibility of 'drawing them [the republican movement] into the net' and making Sinn Féin a 'part of that very different part-public, part-private partnership which was the essence of our long-term solution'.[29] This strategy presupposed that the republican leadership could be easily netted by the lure of funding and employment for west Belfast.[30] A more realistic assessment, perhaps, is to assume that both parties were aware of the others' motives and that in the case of the republicans any hooks that were being taken had been swallowed long before 1990.[31]

If the Provisionals were drawn into the net it was not quite in the way that Sir Richard Needham had expected. Their public response to this 'normalisation agenda' was to argue that it was a 'blatant attempt by the British government to control, through blackmail, community groups and self help schemes in the city [Derry]' as part of a conscious British strategy of controlling potential community resistance:

> Britain, having recognised the extent of the dependency it created, is now attempting to impose political and social control through the manipulation of these schemes. Britain has always feared the development of a community dynamic, believing it to be inherently subversive to establishment interests in the six counties.[32]

However, behind this confident opposition the Provisionals were well aware by the early 1990s that British strategy was successfully undermining republican influence in the nationalist community. As one republican community activist recalled:

> In the late 1980s some republicans argued that getting directly involved with community groups was one way of circumventing censorship and *going directly to the people in the local areas* ... Also that was the only way that we are going to have *some sort of contact with state agencies*: they won't talk to us directly, but would indirectly through community groups. Sinn Féin activity was also limited in that the state was refusing to have any contact with republicans, but *legitimate authority* such as councillors could be in contact with the state [my emphasis].[33]

Republicans had failed to establish a wider hegemony beyond their base areas and even there they were under threat. An internal conference of activists was told in 1991 that the state had penetrated local communities which had resulted in 'self-censorship' and the marginalisation of Sinn Féin because the 'British government are portraying themselves in a positive light'.[34] During internal discussions republicans argued that these British successes were the result of political and organisational weaknesses combined with a failure to develop 'empowering partnerships' with community activists.[35] One participant questioned whether the British strategy could be resisted:

> How many people outside our own base recognize the same things? And within our base, is recognizing the same as being able to resist? ... We have allowed the Brits to plant the doubt that we may be more of a liability than anything in all but restricted 'policing' roles within our areas ... We have left our people isolated and in fear of being associated with us or supported by us.[36]

The outcome was that republicans reorganised and reoriented their community activism in an attempt to broaden their base in the 1990s. Although it appeared to be successful in terms of building electoral support, this came at a price. Electoral and community politics drew the Provisionals and the wider nationalist community into even deeper contact with the state and further facilitated the Provisionals' institutionalisation.

The question posed to activists in 1991 – 'can our communities and our movement withstand another five years [of British strategy]' – was to be answered in the negative by the practice of republican community politics throughout the 1990s.[37] This was because the British state was not only capable of limiting the military and political options available to the Provisionals, but also had the power to define the ideological framework and thus effectively shape the political responses of other actors in Northern Ireland.

This was illustrated by the impact of the Fair Employment Act 1989 and the Northern Ireland Act 1998 on the emerging Provisional politics of equality. Republicans and other community activists were increasingly operating in an environment closely shaped by this legislation and the wider British policy agenda that created it. The Fair Employment legislation drew together a number of threads from the British social policy agenda that had emerged during the 1980s, as well as reflecting some of the initiatives resulting from the Anglo-Irish Agreement after 1985.

Perhaps the most significant feature of the Fair Employment Act was its explicit enshrining of the discourse of communal conflict into legislative form. This was in marked contrast to previous policy frameworks that had emphasised that discrimination was an individual issue rather than a structural product of collective discrimination. This analysis of inequality enshrined in the Act was congenial to the nationalist community not only because it corresponded to their own sense of legitimacy, but also because it saw political advance and the possible redress of nationalist grievances in communal rather than individual terms.[38] In this sense the underlying premises of the Act could be satisfactorily interpreted both through pre-existing frames of nationalist political culture and through the emerging themes of identity politics, which drew on structural and contextual explanations of identity.

This type of thinking was given added weight by the Good Friday Agreement and the resulting Northern Ireland Act (1998). Section 75 in particular required public authorities to actively promote equality of opportunity between and within categories of community defined by, amongst other things, religious belief, political opinion, race, gender and sexual orientation. Public bodies responsible for allocating resources had to work within this framework and ensured that, through their policies and 'equality impact assessments', there was equitable distribution and compliance with these aims. In establishing patterns of resource allocation and bureaucratic regulation this legislation increasingly defined the discursive framework and ideological context for nationalist community projects in the 1990s. This impact on Provisional politics can be seen in what was to become known in the 1990s as 'the equality agenda', which focused on gaining equality and parity of esteem for the nationalist population *within* Northern Ireland. This emphasis on immediate practical and achievable policy aims meant that inevitably the long-term project of reunification receded increasingly into the distance.

Although the Fair Employment Act was initially given no credibility by republicans, 'it later became some kind of marker beyond just winning individual cases because the act of revealing discrimination might create some imperceptible change. It was about doing some immediate good and revealing power structures. It was thought that the process of revealing resulted in politicization and activism.'[39] The Northern Ireland Act had a similar impact on the underlying discursive framework of republican politics: arguments that the 'equality agenda' was not being adhered to during the allocation of resources became commonplace in the everyday exchanges of politics in the 2000s. For example, Sinn Féin MLA Fra McCann argued that, by exempting many high-level decisions from 'screening' under Section 75 ' civil servants ... frustrate change in the North and implement policies which fundamentally undermine the chances of attaining a level social and economic playing field.'[40] Most significantly, a leading Provisional strategist believed that the 'human rights agenda' encapsulated within this legislative framework could be utilised as a significant constitutional and political dynamic to facilitate reunification. For the Provisional leadership the institutions and policy frameworks of the Good Friday Agreement had become yet another site of struggle for the 'equality agenda'.[41] These and other examples showed that what had previously been dismissed by the Provisionals as, at best, marginal and at worst reformist had, by the 2000s, moved centre stage in their politics.

The election of the Blair government in 1997 gave added impetus to British strategy by adding a communitarian gloss to social and economic policy. This reflected the government's domestic agenda of social inclusion and the rebuilding of the social capital of communities through a combination of partnership, empowerment and direct state intervention. Furthermore, these policies had the ambitious aim of transforming the region's economy *and* thus its social structure as the starting point for the creation of a new political dispensation.[42] The underlying assumptions of the Good Friday Agreement in particular strongly reflected this discourse.[43]

Another new strand in this policy drew on the international experiences of peace processes and defined civil society not as a site of contestation, but rather saw it as a conduit for transformation through the promotion of community cohesion and cross-community reconciliation.[44] These aims were also supported by a range of European Union and International Fund for Ireland programmes which were introduced after the Good Friday Agreement. The development of the International Fund for Ireland from 1985 reflected a dominant view in the United States that economic and social development was an essential underpinning to conflict resolution in Northern Ireland.[45] This economic intervention was supplemented by American political and cultural influence. Together they reinforced the idea that new forms of community could transform the conflict in Northern Ireland.

Likewise at both a discursive and material level the impact of the European Union was considerable. By drawing on a long-established culture of 'civil and social dialogue' involving NGOs and social partners, the European language of civil society and subsidiary was to enter the common currency of Northern Irish politics through funding regimes for the community and voluntary sector.[46] This increased engagement with the socially excluded and marginalised and mirrored the new forms of political engagement between the British state and the Provisionals in the late 1990s. These policies were a local example of a wider international pattern in which states increasingly engaged with anti-state insurgencies through social and economic mechanisms with the aim of creating 'a nationalism of responsible and recognized business management promoted by the construction of the European Union, which offers appropriate institutional tools [to take] the place of a nationalism of protest'.[47] The political impact of such interventions has been significant beyond the level of resources expended. These initiatives have brought insurgent forces into the mainstream of the European Union and helped to transform their politics from protest to participation and lobbying.[48]

By the late 1990s a combination of British government policies, European Union programmes, wider social and economic change and the concomitant strengthening of these community organisations had created a unique form of civil society in Northern Ireland. This was reflected in the development of what has been defined as 'the peace industry', a term that is said to conjure up images of 'hatchet-faced paramilitaries appropriating for their own dark purposes peace funds designed to promote healing and reconciliation'.[49] Given that it has been claimed that this sector is the region's largest employer, 'with 30,000 workers being paid by 4,500 community organisations which have benefited from £1 billion in handouts from the European Commission and the British and Irish governments' since 1994, it seems possible to quantify the social and economic power that this sector represents.[50]

This range of activities and employment gives the sector its significance as a network of social power and influence in the nationalist community and thus provides a framework for the institutionalisation of the Provisional movement. These structures draw both the nationalist community and Provisionalism closer to the state through a subtle process of active engagement/dialogue between partners within the many spaces where the state and sections of civil society meet and fuse. In a pattern that became familiar in Northern Ireland from the 1980s the community sector functions as a conduit for social resources as well as mediating between the state and the community. Given the political support and the social power that the Provisionals can exert within this sector, this process of mediation and resource allocation also acts to strengthen the Provisional movement through its deep roots and wide support base within particular nationalist communities.

Characteristically this scaffolding around the core structures of the state is not only drawn from the structures of the clearly defined quangocracy itself, but increasingly involves nominally independent non-governmental organisations as well as elements of the community and voluntary sector. In this way these organisations become increasingly independent of the communities that created them. This remoteness and lack of real accountability helps to further blur the distinction between state and civil society. Some republican activists see these developments as the continuation of a British counterinsurgency strategy by other means, albeit one that now *incorporates* republicans rather than *excluding* them on the margins. The typical forms of politics for these third-sector groups become those of the pressure group, petitioning for reform and the redress of grievances rather than organising movements for transformation and mobilising challenges to the state.

These structural factors, mediated through the British state, have shaped the political context for the development of Provisionalism since the 1980s. However, the relationship between social and economic forms and political ideology is not a simple one in which the societal base closely determines the political superstructure. Likewise the dialectic between the British state, nationalist civil society and the Provisionals has not resulted in a simple command relationship of subject/object. All interact with and shape each other, although the flows of power and influence are by no means equal. The nature of nationalist civil society is itself a significant determining factor on the future trajectory of Provisionalism. The state had a disproportionate importance in the nationalist community generally and amongst the most deprived groups in particular given the continuing high levels of unemployment, state-sponsored employment and social deprivation. Given this relationship and the complex structures of power that have emerged in Northern Ireland, civil society will continue to exhibit a contradictory character.

The social networks, which had initially provided the supporting frameworks of the Provisional revolutionary project in the 1970s and 1980s, have now become forces for stabilisation and channels for normalisation and integration. The formalisation of these networks into community organisations mirrors a process of institutionalisation and political adaptation by the Provisionals themselves. What has emerged in many of the base areas of Provisional republicanism is a structure of power that mirrors many of the characteristics of the formal state with which it is in partnership. Given the nexus of power and influence that has been created and the historical experience of other institutionalised movements, it is unlikely that such a significant structure will quickly disappear or be fully absorbed by the conventional state forms. Given the tendencies towards the further growth of the 'soft' power of the state and the increasing significance of the para-state penumbra in Western societies, the new political dispensation and the structures of its civil society will continue to exhibit these contradictory and yet essentially stabilising features for the foreseeable future. The importance of these structures to their political support and social power will ensure that this is one feature of the Provisional movement that will not be going away.

NOTES

1. Needham, R., *Battling For Peace* (Belfast: Blackstaff, 1998), p. 1.
2. DUP MP William McCrea quoted in 'SF is "part of the establishment"', *News Letter*, 30 May 2007.
3. 'We have Entered a New Phase of our Struggle – Adams', *An Phoblacht*, 28 June 2007; McDonald, H., 'Today the Provisionals Embrace "Northern Ireland"', *Observer*, 28 January 2007; for an account of the constructive attitude shown by Sinn Féin and the positive atmosphere within the executive and assembly, see McGinn, D., '"Chuckle Brothers" Enjoy First 100 Days', *News Letter*, 16 August 2007.
4. Ruddy, G., '1967–2007 Ireland: An Overview', *The Plough* (e-mail newsletter of the Irish Republican Socialist Party), 5 August 2007. Archived at: http://www.theplough. netfirms. com.
5. Knowles McGuirk, C., 'Republicans Here for the Long Haul', *Saoirse* (August 2007).
6. A central theme in Moloney, E., *A Secret History of the IRA*, second edition (London: Penguin, 2007).
7. McKinney, S., 'Structures that "Defeated" IRA were in Place by 1980', *Irish News*, 7 July 2007.
8. See, for example, John Major's reaction to the attack on Downing Street in February 1991 and his interpretation of the Provisionals' English bombing campaign as a means to increase political leverage. Major, J., *John Major: The Autobiography* (London: Harper Collins, 1998), p. 433. In a similar vein, Alastair Campbell's assessment of the Provisionals' position in 1997 was that 'Adams was OK [with a settlement that did not lead to a united Ireland], McGuinness was not'. See 'A Classic Moment in Downing Street', *Guardian*, 9 July 2007.
9. See, for example, '"A Man with Whom we can do Business": An Analysis of the Denis Donaldson Affair', *The Sovereign Nation* (February–March 2006).
10. Institutionalisation is a process where social movement organisations 'become players in the conventional political process, thereby losing their initial character as challengers to the status quo and the forces in power'. Amongst the classic characteristics of such parties are their bureaucratic structure and integration into the state. See Rucht, D., 'Linking Organization and Mobilization: Michel's Iron Law of Oligarchy Reconsidered', *Mobilization: An International Journal*, 4, 2 (1999), p. 155.
11. For some useful surveys of the literature, see Barker, C., 'Robert Michels and "the Cruel Game"', in C. Barker et al. (eds), *Leadership and Social Movements* (Manchester: Manchester University Press, 2001), Della Porta, D. and Diani, M., *Social Movements: An Introduction* (Oxford: Oxford University Press, 1999); Kriesi, H. and Rucht, D., *Social Movements in a Globalising World* (Basingstoke: Palgrave, 1999).
12. O'Hearn, D., 'A Radical Political Force for Ireland', *Left Republican Review*, 5 (May 2005).
13. Oliver, P.E. and Myers, D.J. 'The Co-evolution of Social Movements', *Mobilization: An International Journal*, 8, 1 (2003), p. 19.
14. See, for example, McIntyre, A., 'Modern Irish Republicanism: The Product of British State Strategies', *Irish Political Studies*, 10 (1995), pp. 97–121; Neumann, P., *Britain's Long War: British Strategy in the Northern Ireland Conflict, 1969–98* (Basingstoke: Palgrave Macmillan, 2003) and Smith, M.L.R., *Fighting for Ireland? The Military Strategy of the Irish Republican Movement* (London: Routledge, 1995).

15. Interview with Tom Hartley, former Sinn Féin general secretary, 10 August 2005.
16. Interview with Danny Morrison, former editor of *An Phoblacht/Republican News*, 5 January 2004.
17. Wilson, D. and Kearney, O., *West Belfast: The Way Forward?* (Belfast: Concerned Community Groups, 1988).
18. Casquette, J., 'The Sociopolitical Context of Mobilization: The Case of the Anti-military Movement in the Basque Country', *Mobilization: An International Journal*, 1, 2 (1996), pp. 211–12.
19. Coulter, C., *Contemporary Northern Irish Society* (London: Pluto, 1999), p. 65.
20. Ruddock, A., 'Northern Ireland: Where is the Bright New Future?', *Management Today*, 23 March 2006.
21. Neumann, *Britain's Long War*, pp. 179–88.
22. Needham, *Battling for Peace*, p. 1.
23. Interview with Sir Richard Needham, former parliamentary under secretary of state (Northern Ireland Office), 1985–92, 25 July 2005.
24. Interview with Sir Gerard Loughran, former permanent secretary in the Department for Economic Development (Northern Ireland), 1991–2000, 16 August 2005.
25. Hadaway, P., 'Cohesion in Contested Spaces', *Architects Journal* (November 2001).
26. Murtagh, B., 'The URBAN Community Initiative in Northern Ireland', *Policy and Politics*, 29, 4 (2004), p. 432.
27. Interview with Sir Richard Needham, 25 July 2005.
28. Ibid.
29. Needham, *Battling for Peace*, pp. 207–8.
30. However, Needham himself appears to contradict that impression by his references to republican scepticism about British motives. See *Battling for Peace*, pp. 207–8.
31. See, for example, a discussion paper prepared for a Sinn Féin internal conference on community politics entitled *Altering the Sea We Swim In: British Government Attempts to Change and Control the Community* (Belfast: undated – June 1991?), which indicates Provisional awareness of the aims of British strategy. Copy in author's possession.
32. Mitchel McLaughlin quoted in Plunkett, J., 'Community Groups Hit Back', *An Phoblacht/Republican News*, 13 February 1986.
33. Interview with F. Ó hAdhmaill, former republican prisoner and community activist, 31 August 2005.
34. *Altering the Sea We Swim In*.
35. Ibid.
36. Ibid.
37. Ibid.
38. Ruane, J. and Todd, J., *The Dynamics of Conflict in Northern Ireland: Power, Conflict and Emancipation* (Cambridge: Cambridge University Press, 1996), Chapter 6.
39. Interview with Claire Hackett, former monitoring and evaluations officer, USDT and local history project worker, Falls Community Council, 18 July 2006.
40. Hall, M. 'Equality Undermined', *Irish Democrat* (June–July 2006).
41. Anderson, M., 'The Great Experiment', *An Phoblacht/Republican News*, 16 October 2003.
42. Murtagh, 'The URBAN Community Initiative in Northern Ireland', p. 443.
43. 'The Good Friday (Belfast) Agreement: Rights, Safeguards and Equality of Opportunity: Economic, Social and Cultural Issues', in M. Elliott (ed.), *The Long Road to Peace in Northern Ireland* (Liverpool: Liverpool University Press, 2002), Appendix 6, pp. 227–30.
44. Guelke, A. 'Civil Society and the Northern Irish Peace Process', *Voluntas: International Journal of Voluntary and Non-Profit Organizations*, 14, 1 (March 2003), pp. 61–78.
45. Byrne, S. and Irvin, C., 'Economic Aid and Policy Making: Building the Peace Dividend in Northern Ireland', *Policy and Politics*, 29, 4 (2006), p. 416.
46. Wilson, R., *Continentally Challenged* (Belfast: Democratic Dialogue, 1997); and Murtagh, 'The URBAN Community Initiative in Northern Ireland'.
47. Crettiez, X., 'IRA, ETA, FLNC: l'agonie des illusions militaristes', *Le Monde*, 23 August 2005. I wish to thank Dr I. McKeane for the translation.
48. See, for example, 'MEP's Diary … Bairbre de Brún', *An Phoblacht*, 29 June 2006.
49. Meredith, F., 'Putting a Price on Peace?', *Irish Times*, 10 January 2006.
50. 'INCORE and Cresco Trust Report', quoted in Meredith, 'Putting a Price on Peace?'

Chapter 11
'A Tragedy Beyond Words':
Interpretations of British Government Policy and the Northern Ireland Peace Process

Paul Dixon

'In the second half of the 20th century no matter what has been the position in the past the British government has no political, military, strategic, or economic interest in staying in Ireland or in the exercise of authority in Northern Ireland. ...

We hope that this statement will clarify our present policies in Northern Ireland. We also hope that it will prompt the Provisional IRA to review their present policies and to see that the use of violent tactics against 'colonial interests' which in fact do not exist is a mistake and a tragedy beyond words not only for the people of Ireland generally but also for themselves. (Secret British Message to Gerry Adams, c.1986–88, quoted in Ed Moloney, *A Secret History of the IRA* (London: Allen Lane, 2002), pp.251–52)

INTRODUCTION

The misperception by republicans and loyalists of 'British'[1] policy is one of the most profound tragedies of the recent conflict in Northern Ireland. These misperceptions led both to reject a power-sharing settlement in 1974, which was similar to the Good Friday Agreement that republicans signed up to in 1998 and most loyalists had endorsed by 2007. In the intervening period republicans and loyalists carried out violent campaigns, republicans in the belief that this would remove the British presence and loyalists because they believed the British government was selling them out. By contrast this chapter argues, using a theatrical metaphor,[2] that British policy towards Northern Ireland since 1972 was characterised by continuity and tactical adjustments[3] in pursuit of a compromise settlement of power-sharing with some kind of Irish dimension. This settlement was pursued – and the options of Irish unity or integration into the UK rejected – because it was thought most likely to result in a *stable* Northern Ireland. For republicans and loyalists the Good Friday Agreement 1998 was, as Seamus Mallon aptly put it, 'Sunningdale for slow learners'.

During the recent peace process three interpretations of British policy – republican, loyalist and nationalist consociationalist – have been deployed in the propaganda war. These claim that there have been dramatic shifts in British policy. For nationalist consociationalists this occurred in 1975, for republicans in the late 1980s and for loyalists in the early 1990s.

The Sinn Féin/IRA, or republican, version of the 'pan-nationalist' script of the peace process is shared by much of the academic literature. This suggests that in the late 1980s the British government declared its *neutrality* for the first time, decided to *include* republican and loyalist paramilitaries in a peace process and did this reluctantly under 'pan-nationalist', including US, pressure. The developing *Irish* peace process was driving changes in British policy that would result in Irish unity. The Sinn Féin leadership was using this interpretation or script to persuade a key hard-line, IRA audience to abandon violence for a non-violent road to Irish unity.

Paradoxically, this republican script reinforced a key loyalist, anti-peace process script which also saw Irish unity as the end result of the 'peace process'. The Democratic Unionist Party and United Kingdom Unionists argued that the 'peace process' was driven by the IRA's bombings of the City of London in 1992, 1993 and 1996. These bombings damaged the British economy and broke the will of the British to remain in Ulster. The result was a 'surrender process', rather than a peace process, which appeased republicans and gradually delivered Ulster into a united Ireland by stealth. Anti-peace process loyalists were trying to win over the majority of the unionist audience to oppose those in the Ulster Unionist Party who were more accommodating towards the peace process and took a less negative view of British policy.

The republican and loyalist scripts had powerful political advocates and were deployed in the propaganda war to win over and mobilise key audiences – using violence if necessary – and gain political advantage over opponents. Their emphasis on *recent*, radical shifts in British policy was used to dramatise the conflict, raising hopes or heightening fears, in order to mobilise key audiences against their opponents. Dramatisation is also achieved through the demonisation of opponents by using crude and hostile stereotypes which emphasise the power and malignancy of British political actors. Propagandistic portrayals of British government policy and 'tactical adjustments' in that policy have served to obscure the constraints operating on British governments and the underlying, strategic continuity of a bipartisan approach.

The third interpretation comes from pro-nationalist, consociational[4] academics John McGarry and Brendan O'Leary[5], who have also argued against continuity in British policy. They suggest that with the appointment of Margaret Thatcher as Conservative leader in 1975 the Conservatives broke bipartisanship, adopted an integrationist stance and lost the sophistication of the pro-power-sharing approach of Ted Heath in 1974. The stupidity and 'contradictions and inconsistencies' of Conservative policy during the period 1975–97 were ironed out only by a process of 'painfully slow ethno-national policy learning'.[6]

In contrast to these three interpretations, it is argued in this chapter that the strategy of successive British governments during the recent conflict was to achieve a stable settlement to the conflict and contain its impact, whether this was within the Union or in a United Ireland or some compromise between the two. There were a range of options before successive British governments but only power-sharing, with some kind of Irish dimension, was perceived as likely to win widespread nationalist and unionist support and therefore provide stability. This bipartisan approach was attempted and failed during the first peace process (1972–74) and, with greater success, during the second peace process (1994—2007).

BRITISH POLICY AND THE UNION[7]

Since partition there has been an influential strand of loyalism which sees 'the British', or perhaps more accurately the 'English', in Great Britain as untrustworthy guarantors of the Union and has been highly suspicious of 'British' interventions in Northern Ireland. Loyalists were particularly sceptical of the Liberal and Labour Parties, which had traditional sympathies for Irish nationalism. The Stormont parliament was imposed on unionists to remove the 'Irish Question' from British politics. The unionists soon came to realise the advantage of having their own government and parliament as a means of safeguarding their interests from both nationalists and the perfidious British government. Successive British governments were unwilling to involve themselves in the politics of Northern Ireland even though there was discrimination by the unionist political establishment against Catholics. Some British politicians reassured themselves that some combination of history, geography, economics, European integration and modernisation would lead inevitably to the reunification of Ireland, it was hoped, within the British Commonwealth. During the Second World War both

Neville Chamberlain and Winston Churchill made, albeit ambiguous, offers of Irish unity to the government of the Irish Free State. The post-war Labour government, however, ignored nationalist sympathisers within its own party and gave Northern Ireland a guarantee that it would remain within the UK so long as its parliament consented.

The prospect of the return of a Labour government sympathetic to the demands of the emerging civil rights movement alarmed loyalists. There is some evidence that Harold Wilson, the British Prime Minister 1964–70, 1974–76, favoured Irish unity. The sympathy of the Labour Party for Irish unity was expressed publicly by leading members of the party as well as by party activists. In November 1971 Harold Wilson came out in favour of Irish unity and in March 1972 he met the IRA. In the early to mid-1970s the Labour leadership, in opposition and then in government, considered the option of British withdrawal from Northern Ireland. Such discussions took place 'behind the scenes' because the political elite feared that front-stage discussion of this option would further destabilise unionism and lead to an upsurge of support for loyalist violence as a way of either preventing Northern Ireland being coerced into a united Ireland or preparing for independence.

The Conservative Party had close links with the Ulster Unionist Party and traditional sympathies for the Union between Great Britain and Northern Ireland. Although the election of a Conservative government in 1970 may have reassured unionists, this was tempered by the Conservative Party's determination to pursue a bipartisan approach. There was also contemporary evidence – now supported by the release of government documents – that the Conservative Party's support for the Union was not solid. In his Guildhall speech in November 1971 Conservative Prime Minister Ted Heath declared that the nationalists' aspiration for Irish unity by democratic and constitutional means was legitimate and that if a majority in Northern Ireland wanted Irish unity, 'I do not believe any British Government would stand in the way.' There were also contemporary media reports of an emerging bipartisan consensus in favour of Irish unity. Cabinet minutes have since revealed that the Conservative cabinet was flexible about the North's position within the Union. In 1972 a Green Paper, *The Future of Northern Ireland,* asserted Britain's neutrality and willingness to accept the unity of Ireland by consent. British priorities were, first, peace and stability; second, prosperity; and, third, that the region should not offer a base for any external threat to the UK.[8] British policy attempted both to reassure unionists of their place within the Union while coercing them towards power-sharing by veiled threats to their constitutional position. In late 1971 the SDLP was arguing that the obstacle to Irish unity was not British imperialism but the fears of unionists.

The willingness of British governments and parties to contemplate Irish unity suggested that there was no *overriding* political, strategic or economic interest in Northern Ireland. Front stage, at any rate, the bipartisan approach of the British parties was based on the consent of the people of Northern Ireland even if behind the scenes the British political elite considered Irish unity. This was because, while the British had undoubted interests in Northern Ireland – in particular the stability of the island of Ireland – these might be met even if that region left the Union. Northern Ireland had become a 'drain' on the economy and the most deprived region of the UK. The consistent support of a majority of the British public for withdrawal suggested that the North was not an essential component of the British 'nation'.[9]

The ambiguities of Conservative government policy, and the pronationalist posture of the Labour Party, the alternative party of government, exacerbated the unease of loyalists, who feared that 'British' interference was undermining the Union. The loyalist backlash of 1971–73 saw the establishment of the loyalist paramilitary Ulster Defence Association (UDA) which, along with the Ulster Volunteer Force (UVF), carried out a vicious campaign of sectarian murder against Catholics. Ian Paisley's hard-line DUP was established in September 1971 and the Vanguard Unionist Progressive Party (VUPP), a pressure group principally within the UUP, was founded and these two parties occupied the grey area in loyalist politics between constitutionalism and paramilitarism. The British army came into conflict with the loyalist paramilitaries and, at one point in 1972, the UDA briefly declared war on the British government. The first peace process and the construction of a power-sharing settlement, with its Council of Ireland, was seen by its loyalist opponents as a device to, in the words of one nationalist, 'trundle Unionists into a united Ireland'.

Loyalist fears of British betrayal and withdrawal were strong until the mid-1970s. They were encouraged by the threats and declared exasperation of leading figures in the British political elite. This found its most notorious manifestation in Wilson's 'spongers speech', which precipitated the collapse of the Ulster Workers' Council strike in May 1974. Wilson drew a line between 'us', the British people, and 'them', the people of Northern Ireland. The 'British' had paid for Northern Ireland with the lives of their soldiers and in treasure but had been viciously defied 'by people who spend their lives sponging on Westminster and British democracy and then systematically assaulting democratic methods. Who do these people think they are?' The IRA ceasefire of 1975–76 further raised fears that the Labour government was planning to withdraw. After the ceasefire broke down and constitutional initiatives came to nothing, loyalist fears of a British withdrawal subsided.

Speculation about a withdrawal reached such a height that the Irish government raised its concerns with the British and US governments. The Labour government rejected the withdrawal option because it was thought likely to destabilise Britain and Ireland, leading to all-out civil war and repartition. The Conservative party also examined all the options – including a federal Ireland – and came to a similar conclusion. The parameters of British policy were being tested. The British could have withdrawn during this period but they were not willing to pay what they perceived to be the costs of that policy: further destabilisation and violence in Britain and Ireland. The unionist policy of integration was also tested during this period (see below) and also perceived as not likely to achieve the stabilisation of Northern Ireland. So in spite of the preferences of powerful actors within the Labour Party for Irish unity this policy was not pursued in government and, indeed, the 1974–79 period was seen by unionists as the most favourable to it since direct rule. The Anglo-Irish Agreement was signed in 1985 by the 'English unionist' Margaret Thatcher. Although she probably intended the Agreement to bring security benefits, others in her government believed it was a step towards a historic settlement along the lines of the first peace process. Unionists tended to interpret the deal as a further step towards a united Ireland, bringing Northern Ireland to the edge of the Union, and they mobilised to prevent any further movement in that direction.

LOYALISTS: A BRITISH SURRENDER PROCESS

Bob McCartney, leader of the UK Unionist Party, has been the most articulate exponent of the view – shared by the DUP until recently – that the 'peace process' is in fact a surrender process of appeasing the IRA and, through the Good Friday Agreement, delivering Northern Ireland into a united Ireland. His core claim is that British disengagement is 'fundamental Labour Party policy' but 'was also thought necessary, in pragmatic terms, by the Conservatives in order to resolve the conflict with Sinn Féin and safeguard the City of London'.[10] The British, he argues, have been trying to disengage from Northern Ireland since 1921 and the 'peace process' is just the latest attempt. Churchill's offer to de Valera of a united Ireland in 1940 is cited in support of McCartney's contention. The end of the Cold War in 1989 removed Britain's strategic interest in Northern Ireland. The bombing of the Baltic Exchange in 1992 created an economic interest in withdrawal. The 'surrender process' is one in which the bipartisan approach of British governments is capitulating to the IRA/SF and pushing Northern Ireland into a united Ireland.

The key problem with this account of British policy is that it fails to explain Britain's failure to withdraw. If the British have been trying to disengage from Northern Ireland since 1921 then why have they failed to pull out of Northern Ireland, when Britain has succeeded in withdrawing from the biggest empire the world has ever known? If Britain has been trying to disengage since 1921 then this would suggest that Britain has had no overriding selfish strategic or economic interest in Northern Ireland since then – long before even the start of the Cold War. If this is the case then the British had better opportunities to quietly slip Northern Ireland out of the Union during the past seventy-five years than through the current, high-profile, peace process. The most obvious opportunity for the British to withdraw from Northern Ireland was 1974–76, and the reasons they did not do so reflect what they have perceived are the 'hard realities' of the situation:

1. There is no purely military solution, something acknowledged since at least 1971.
2. The British cannot coerce one million unionists into a united Ireland and any attempt to do so was likely to increase violence and instability.
3. A stable Northern Ireland cannot be created without accommodating the legitimate demands of nationalists through power-sharing and an Irish dimension.

Another key problem for McCartney's account is that British overtures to Sinn Féin and the revitalisation of the British–Sinn Féin back channel contacts date back to 1989/90, well *before* the City of London bombings in 1992, 1993 and 1996. The lack of sympathy, or even empathy, for unionism of successive British governments is evident in their record on Northern Ireland. The result is that unionists have had to repeatedly demonstrate the strength of their beliefs and their determination to resist being manipulated out of the Union.[11]

REPUBLICANS: SELFISH, STRATEGIC AND ECONOMIC INTERESTS

Republicans have traditionally emphasised British imperialism's 'selfish, strategic and economic interests' in hanging on to its first and last colony. But if the above account of British policy is largely accurate, then loyalists have had greater reason to fear British withdrawal than the republicans have from British attachment to the Union with Northern Ireland. The difficulty for Sinn Féin/IRA in entering a peace process was how to justify such a major shift in republican ideology. Their script suggested that an *Irish* peace process had created such pressure on the British government that it had 'blinked first' in the stand-off with republicans, and that in response to the British government's declaration of neutrality republicans could revise and moderate their position.

The republican version of the 'pan-nationalist' account of the peace process is echoed in much of the academic literature, suggesting that there were three major developments in British policy towards Northern Ireland that account for the peace process.

1. In the late 1980s the British government dramatically shifted its policy by declaring its *neutrality* and claiming that it had 'no selfish strategic or economic interest' in Northern Ireland.
2. The British government shifted from excluding republican and loyalist paramilitaries to *including* them in a peace process.
3. These *reluctant* changes in British policy were partly brought about by EU integration, the end of the Cold War and pressure from a pan-nationalist front consisting of constitutional nationalists in the north and south of Ireland as well as US President Bill Clinton.

There are flaws in all three of these arguments:

1. As we have seen, in the early 1970s the British government declared its neutrality on Northern Ireland and its willingness to bring about a united Ireland if that was by consent. The consent principle underpinned the bipartisan approach of the British political parties (see below on bipartisanship).
2. On the issue of inclusion the question of whether the British government pursued an 'inclusive' or 'exclusive' approach to peace-making in Northern Ireland is too crude. The question is *under what circumstances* was the British government prepared to bring paramilitaries into a political process (and the British had considerable experience of talking to 'terrorists' in the retreat from empire)? To bring paramilitaries into a political process prematurely could undermine democracy and encourage violence by giving legitimacy to those with guns rather than those with votes. More pragmatically, bringing paramilitaries in ran the risk of alienating moderate unionist *and nationalist* opinion and driving it away from negotiation and the possibility of a power-sharing settlement built on the centre ground. During the recent peace process, it was not a question of *either* exclusive all-party talks *or* a process that included paramilitaries. The all-party talks acted as an incentive to get republicans involved in the peace process. The paramilitaries could be brought into negotiations, but this ran the risk of driving out unionists and even moderate nationalists if it was

not carried out in the 'right circumstances'. British overtures to republicans during 1989–93 probably exacerbated unionist insecurities and increased loyalist violence.[12]

Contrary to stereotype, British governments have regularly engaged with republicans during the recent conflict and have often been more 'inclusive' than some Irish nationalists. Leading nationalists, such as SDLP leader John Hume and Taoiseach Garret Fitzgerald, have in the past attacked British governments for engaging in talks with the IRA because this risked legitimising them and undermining the position of constitutional nationalists north and south. From early on in the conflict the British realised that there was no 'purely military solution' and that if paramilitaries could be brought into the democratic process they might be weaned off violence. Reducing violence might also allow some kind of power-sharing accommodation a greater chance of success. Lines of communication were kept open to the republican movement in order to investigate any significant developments in IRA ideology and the possibility of a negotiated end to the conflict. There were several periods of contact: in July 1972 there was a secret meeting between representatives of the British government and the IRA; during the IRA ceasefires of 1975–76; negotiations to end the hunger strikes in 1980–81; contacts in the mid-1980s between Sinn Féin and Secretary of State for Northern Ireland Tom King; and the renewal of 'back-channel' contacts in 1990–93. In 1972 the IRA – influenced by an anti-imperialist perspective on the conflict – may well have believed that they were on the verge of victory over the British and, therefore, had no need to involve themselves in negotiations which would not result in Irish unity. Given the ambiguities of British policy this perception wasn't entirely without substance.

The British government attempted to bring loyalists *and republicans* into the political process. The ban on the loyalist Ulster Volunteer Force was removed in April 1974 to encourage it to engage in electoral politics. In October 1975, following UVF involvement in violence which claimed the lives of twelve people, the UVF was once again declared illegal.

3. Pan-nationalism has exaggerated the role of the external dimension in order to claim that they have driven an Irish peace process. This conveniently ignores the efforts of the British Conservative government and Irish republicans to develop a peace process before the involvement of President Bill Clinton and the end of the Cold War.[13]

To what extent the republican leadership has, since the 1970s, believed its own propaganda about the British state is worth considering. The propaganda position is partly designed to mobilise support and encourage people to fight, kill and possibly die to drive the British out of Ireland. Complete victory and vindication are promised to fortify the movement and undermine the will of the enemy to resist. A 'dramatic', stereotypical, 'black and white' story about the British is, arguably, a more effective tool for fighting such a 'war' than a more nuanced and accurate portrayal of British policy. As Danny Morrison, former Sinn Féin director of publicity, later said, 'You have to fight a war from a fundamentalist position but you cannot fight a peace process from that position.' For example, front stage Sinn Féin opposed the Anglo-Irish Agreement but behind the scenes they were more welcoming of the deal, which could also be used to persuade hardliners in the IRA that British policy had shifted.[14] The repressive nature of British security policy, particularly during the early 1970s, may well have influenced republican perceptions of British policy.

In the mid-1970s the British government deliberately fooled the IRA into believing that it was about to withdraw. This suggests that the IRA leadership must have believed that Britain's interest in the Union was not so strong. The IRA leadership also appears to have believed that British withdrawal could result in a bloody civil war between unionists and nationalists, whereas in their propaganda they denied the 'bloodbath scenario'. Ruairí Ó Brádaigh, the president of Sinn Féin, warned Britain not to withdraw and leave behind a 'Congo situation'. In the 1980s the IRA demanded that the British army disarm the RUC and UDR before withdrawing. In *Towards a Lasting Peace in Ireland* (1992) Sinn Féin recognised both Northern Ireland's economic dependence on Britain and the possibility of a Protestant backlash following British withdrawal. Sinn Féin had developed a more sophisticated, less fundamentalist, analysis of the British state and acknowledged the possibility of divisions between British government actors by implication more supportive of the peace process than the 'securocrats' who were attempting to undermine it. Even republican dissidents who want to continue the 'armed struggle' have suggested that the British have no great interest in Ireland but that 'the Dublin government is scared of taking it [Northern Ireland] under its wing'.[15]

NATIONALIST CONSOCIATIONALISM: DISCONTINUITY AND PAINFULLY SLOW ETHNO-NATIONAL POLICY LEARNING

Nationalist consociationalist academics John McGarry and Brendan O'Leary argue that British policy towards Northern Ireland reached a peak in 1974 with power-sharing and the culmination of the first peace process. The election of Margaret Thatcher as leader of the Conservative Party in 1975 resulted in the abandonment of Heath's wise approach, a break in bipartisanship and a shift towards a more hard-line, integrationist unionist stance. After 1979, however, the 'inconsistencies and contradictions' of Conservative policy towards Northern Ireland gave way to a 'painfully slow learning process' of 'ethno-national policy learning which led to 'a more consistent and sensitive approach to the management of Northern Ireland'. They argue that the understanding of the conflict by British policy-makers was 'transformed' during the period 1979–97, with the result that by the end of that period the Conservative government had learnt 'what Edward Heath mostly understood in 1973'. By implication, the Conservatives had wasted, therefore, eighteen if not twenty-two years.[16]

Their interpretation of the 1975–97 period underestimates the degree of continuity in British government policy and is unconvincing on at least the following four counts.[17]

1. *Confusion on British Policy*
In McGarry and O'Leary's writings between 1995 and 1998 they provide inconsistent and confused accounts of British policy:

a. In 1997, O'Leary argues that in British policy there is a *dramatic break* between Conservative policy in 1974 and 1979 and that this was in a painfully slow way 'transformed' between 1979 and 1997.[18]

b. In 1995, McGarry and O'Leary suggest, British policy had more *continuity* and that the British had been trying to develop a power-sharing settlement since 1972.[19] In 1996 they were arguing slightly differently, that 'British policy-making between 1972 and 1975–76, and after 1982, was in favour of voluntary power-sharing ... and willing to consider an Irish dimension.'[20] They also acknowledged that the Anglo-Irish framework established in 1980 initiated 'the interactions between officials which would end in the Anglo-Irish Agreement'.[21]

c. Neither of these two accounts, a) or b), is compatible with the view, in 1997, that the Anglo-Irish Agreement 1985 represents a *'volte-face'*, an about face or policy reversal, in British policy.[22]

d. In 1998, O'Leary argues, it was the *influence of Margaret Thatcher* that constrained Conservative policy as opposed to his, altogether different, argument in 1997 that it was all about painfully 'slow policy learning'.[23]

e. McGarry and O'Leary do not define bipartisanship but in 1997 they claimed that *bipartisanship ended* in 1975, in 1989 that it ended in 1979, and in 1996 that it ended in 1981. But in no one place do they claim that it ended at all these different times.[24]

2. *Bipartisanship Not Broken, 1975–79*

Bipartisanship, although difficult to define, has remained intact throughout the recent conflict. It can be defined as a general agreement between the two main British political parties that if there is to be change in the constitutional position that should take place with the consent of the people of Northern Ireland. Bipartisanship limits party competition on Northern Ireland and contains the impact of the conflict on domestic politics and the threat of a populist movement for withdrawal.[25]

During the 1975–79 period the Conservative opposition did not break bipartisanship over Northern Ireland. Both the Labour government and the Conservative opposition moved their policy towards a more unionist stance in order to win the support of the Ulster Unionist MPs at Westminster, at a time when the House of Commons was finely balanced. In addition, the success of the Ulster Workers' Council strike in 1974 shifted the likely ground on which an accommodation could be achieved towards unionism and away from an Irish dimension. The Conservative opposition tried to strike a harder bargain with Labour for the continuation of bipartisanship, but the relationship survived and this was acknowledged by spokespersons for the Conservative opposition and the Labour government. The Conservative Party took an integrationist stance in its 1979 election manifesto, but was already moving away from this position before the election. This might suggest that, while an integrationist posture in opposition was acceptable, the responsibilities and constraints of government meant that it was unlikely to be implemented.

3. *Devolution Talks and the Anglo-Irish Process*

The integrationism of the Conservative Party's 1979 election manifesto was never implemented: within a year of being elected the Atkins initiative was launched to promote devolution and in May 1980 the British Prime Minister and the Irish Taoiseach met to develop a British–Irish dimension which developed into the Anglo-Irish Agreement of 1985. Although Margaret Thatcher was probably an instinctive English unionist/nationalist and later regretted signing the Anglo-Irish Agreement, her governments were constrained to reject integration by strong incentives to pursue a policy on Northern Ireland which was broadly in line with that of previous Conservative and Labour governments. Margaret Thatcher explains in *The Downing Street Years* that, after 1979, she realised that to defeat terrorism she had to undermine support for republicanism. This would not be achieved by introducing integration which would alienate nationalists in the North, the government of the Republic of Ireland (who Thatcher hoped would cooperate in fighting the IRA and pacifying the region) and international opinion.[26] On the other hand, Thatcher also needed to avoid alienating the unionists as the polarisation of unionist and nationalist opinion during the hunger strikes in 1981 again threatened to plunge the region into civil war. Mrs Thatcher's ignorance of Northern Ireland affairs may suggest a heightened vulnerability to the influence of the cabinet and the Civil Service. Leading political and bureaucratic actors in the British state saw the Anglo-Irish Agreement as part of a process that could be traced back to Sunningdale. The newly elected Conservative government did not need to embark on a 'painfully slow process' of 'ethno-national policy learning' because it contained leading politicians and civil servants from the Heath era – Willie Whitelaw, Douglas Hurd, Francis Pym, Quintin Hogg (Lord Hailsham) and Lord Carrington – who already had knowledge and experience of Northern Ireland and the Sunningdale policy. They were able to bring this experience to the Thatcher cabinet.[27]

4. Consistent 'Inconsistencies and Contradictions'

McGarry and O'Leary argue that during the 1979–97 period there were five 'inconsistencies or contradictions' in Conservative policy which had been ironed out through 'painfully slow' 'ethno-national policy learning'. Below, these 'inconsistencies and contradictions' are listed and explained in a more convincing manner:

a. *The contradiction of Conservative support for the Union with Scotland and Wales and a willingness to end it with Northern Ireland* – this arises out of the government's dual role to strike a 'balance' between the claims of both nationalist and unionist audiences. The British government has to play its role as *Champion of the Union* to reassure unionists of their place within the Union while insisting that they should reach an accommodation with nationalists. Simultaneously, the British government needs to encourage nationalists and republicans into negotiations by reassuring them that the British are playing a *neutral* role and that they will be fairly dealt with in any 'peace process'. This need to balance nationalist and unionist claims has been apparent since the late 1960s, when James Callaghan, then Home Secretary, attempted to 'calm the fears of the Catholic community without awakening those of Protestants'.[28] The emphasis of the British government on its role as neutral arbiter or champion of the Union changes with the political environment as one or other community is seen to be in more need of reassurance. In 1998 Secretary of State for Northern Ireland Mo Mowlam attempted to reconcile the dual roles of neutrality and champion of unionism: 'I value the Union. I have throughout my time in this job tried to facilitate an accommodation, and I have said at times therefore I am impartial. I value the Union but I am not taking one side or the other, because we need in this process to pull together.'[29]

b. *The contradiction between Conservative opposition to devolution for Britain but support for it in Northern Ireland* – the Stormont Parliament was imposed on Northern Ireland by Britain in 1920 and this marked out the region as an exception within the UK. Devolution was supported for Northern Ireland partly as a way of insulating it from British politics but then also since the start of 'the Troubles' as probably the most realistic compromise between unionists and nationalists. Northern Ireland is different from the rest of the UK because it has a significant minority that prefers to be part of another state.

c. *The Conservative government's opposition to the erosion of UK sovereignty by the European Union but support for an enhanced role for the Republic in Northern Ireland* – support for an Irish role in Northern Ireland dates from about 1971/72 and arises out of what British politicians perceive to be the most pragmatic and effective way of resolving the conflict.

d. *The Conservative government's public opposition to talking with terrorists contrasted with its private 'contacts' with terrorists* – as we have seen above, the British government has generally taken a relatively inclusive approach to dealing with terrorists. This contradiction arises out of the need to maintain the pressure on the republican movement in the 'propaganda war', by demonising its activists on stage as criminals and terrorists, and refusing to lend them legitimacy by negotiating with them. At the same time, British policy-makers realise that ending the violence is an important component in reaching a stable settlement to the conflict and that 'contacts' may be required 'behind the scenes' to assess the possibilities of finding a basis on which the violence can be stopped. Negotiations between the British and the IRA can also increase unionist suspicions that they are being 'sold out' and can provoke a violent loyalist response. This 'contradiction' has been apparent since at least June 1972 up until 1997.[30]

e. *The Conservative government's pursuit of free market policies in Britain whilst maintaining a strong interventionist role and high public expenditure in Northern Ireland* – this contradiction arises because since 1970 even Conservative governments have perceived that the extension of the free market would create further economic deprivation and that this would exacerbate paramilitary violence.[31]

This nationalist consociationalist interpretation of British policy is a caricature of British Conservative political actors which draws on a stereotypical and propagandistic understanding of Conservative attitudes and is belied by the practice and pragmatism of Conservative governments. The focus on stereotypes blinds the observer to the constraints that operate on British governments of all parties, and these have underpinned the bipartisan approach of the two major parties towards Northern Ireland.

CONCLUSION

The three interpretations of British policy presented here are crude portrayals of a much more complex reality. All three accounts have tended to see the British government as a single actor reflecting the intentions of that actor rather than a more complex process that is the result of various constraints and opportunities and affected by contingencies. The loyalist, anti-peace process account of British policy which suggests that Britain is an unreliable defender of the Union is more convincing than the republican view that the British are determined to hold on to Northern Ireland. The loyalist account, however, can't convincingly explain why the Union persists, particularly after the SF–DUP deal in 2007 to restore devolution. The nationalist consociationalist account is stereotypical in its account of Conservative policy, focuses too much on the claimed intentions and personalities of actors and fails to deal with the constraints and underlying continuities of British government policy. This propagandist, actor-oriented approach cannot explain why the pro-nationalist Wilson does not implement a more nationalist policy in government or why a unionist like Thatcher abandons integration, signs the Anglo-Irish Agreement and explores the back channel with the IRA. John Major and Patrick Mayhew, in spite of the traditional unionism of the Conservative Party, took considerable risks to push the peace process forward: talking to terrorists and trying to facilitate an IRA ceasefire.[32]

What is striking about British policy towards Northern Ireland throughout 'the troubles' is its *relative* continuity since at least 1972 in pursuing both power-sharing devolution and an Irish dimension. A focus on the 'tactical adjustments' can blind the observer to the strategic continuities.[33] The period 1974–79 stands out as an apparent anomaly, with both the Labour government and the Conservative opposition adopting a more unionist stance. But this was a 'tactical adjustment' in recognition of a more finely balanced House of Commons and to appease unionist power. The Good Friday Agreement is 'Sunningdale for slow learners', although the second peace process produced a more sophisticated document than the first and is the product of a very different context. Bipartisanship and the continuity of British government policy towards Northern Ireland is explained by the extent to which those governments are constrained. These constraints do not determine outcomes but provide strong incentives for successive Labour and Conservative governments to pursue a broadly similar approach to the resolution of the conflict, whether or not this is the personal preference of leading actors. Unlike the three, actor-oriented loyalist, republican and nationalist consociationalist accounts presented here, this approach sees actors as neither completely autonomous nor completely constrained. They have room to manoeuvre and the capacity to improve their scope for action, but there are nevertheless structural constraints which limit the power of agents. British government policy needs to be set in the wider social, economic and political environment.[34]

The theatrical metaphor has been deployed to explain the complexity of British policy and the way policy-makers have tried to manage various audiences. This helps to explain some of the ambiguities and apparent 'contradictions and inconsistencies' in British policy. These ambiguities give some substance to both republican and loyalist misperceptions of British policy, although the loyalist stereotype of British policy is closer to the mark, particularly during the 1969–76 period. The impact of the repressive nature of British security policy on nationalists in particular may have distorted the republican analysis of British policy.

Republican and loyalist misperceptions of British policy have probably fuelled the recent conflict in Northern Ireland. If this is the case, could the British government have been more successful in managing the conflict if it had been clearer and less ambiguous about its interests and intentions? In 1983 Padraig O'Malley argued that the lack of a long-term strategy for Northern Ireland and the ambiguity and inconsistency of British policy created constitutional uncertainty and an incentive for loyalists and republicans to use violence to shift policy in their direction. While he understands that these inconsistencies are partly due to the divergent claims of both nationalists and unionists, he argues that consistency and certainty could reduce constitutional insecurity and, therefore, the incentives for violence.[35] Alternatively, it could be argued that such consistency and certainty could have alienated either or both unionist and nationalist audiences. Only through *some degree* of 'creative ambiguity' and 'political skills' could the British – along with other partners – hope to bring widely diverging constituencies to an accommodation. Even during the recent peace process the British government has had an interest in not challenging too strongly the republican interpretation of British policy because it realised that this was an important script for the Sinn Féin/IRA leadership to win over their key activist audience to an unarmed struggle.[36]

The republican and loyalist 'misperceptions' of British policy presented here were not inevitable, and other nationalists and unionists had more accurate understandings of British policy. These misperceptions probably in part motivated the violence of loyalist and republican paramilitaries. That the IRA fought so long and claimed so many lives to drive the British state out of Northern Ireland when it had no selfish strategic or economic interest for being there is 'a tragedy beyond words'.

NOTES

1. The term 'British' in this article is used to describe the policy of the Westminster government and the people residing in Great Britain. This is not to deny that there are British people living in Northern Ireland.
2. For an introduction to the theatrical metaphor see Rigney, D., *The Metaphorical Society* (Oxford: Rowman and Littlefield, 2001).
3. Cunningham, M., *British Government Policy in Northern Ireland, 1969–89: Its Nature and Execution* (Manchester: Manchester University Press, 1991), p. 243.
4. Consociationalism is a top-down, elitist and segregation-oriented approach to conflict management. See Dixon, P., 'Paths to Peace in Northern Ireland (1): Civil Society and Consociational Approaches', *Democratization*, 4, 2 (1997), pp. 1–27.
5. McGarry and O'Leary prefer to be jointly responsible for their work.
6. O'Leary, B., 'The Conservative Stewardship of Northern Ireland, 1979–97: Sound-Bottomed Contradictions or Slow Learning', *Political Studies*, 45 (1997), pp. 663–76.
7. This section draws on Dixon, P., *Northern Ireland: The Politics of War and Peace* (Basingstoke: Palgrave, 2nd edition 2008).
8. Northern Ireland Office, *The Future of Northern Ireland: A Paper for Discussion* (Belfast: HMSO, 1972).
9. See Dixon, *Northern Ireland: The Politics of War and Peace*.
10. McCartney, R., *Reflections on Liberty, Democracy and the Union* (Dublin: Maunsel and Company, 2001).
11. Dixon, P., 'Contemporary Unionism and the Tactics of Resistance', in J. Coakley and M. Bric (eds), *From Political Violence to Negotiated Settlement: The Winding Path to Peace in Twentieth Century Ireland* (Dublin: UCD Press, 2004).
12. Dixon, *Northern Ireland: The Politics of War and Peace*, pp. 227–32.
13. Dixon, P., 'Performing the Northern Ireland Peace Process on the World Stage', *Political Science Quarterly*, 121, 1 (2006).
14. Mallie, E. and McKittrick, D., *The Fight for Peace* (London: Mandarin, 1997), pp. 35–6.
15. 'An address to the People of Ireland', February 2003, p. 2, www.rsf.ie.
16. O'Leary, 'The Conservative Stewardship of Northern Ireland, 1979–97', pp. 663, 664, 675, 676.
17. For more detail on this argument see Dixon, P., 'British Policy Towards Northern Ireland 1969–2000: Continuity, Tactical Adjustment and Consistent "Inconsistencies"', *British Journal of Politics and International Relations*, 3, 3 (2001), pp. 340–68.
18. O'Leary, 'The Conservative Stewardship of Northern Ireland, 1979–97'.
19. McGarry, J. and O'Leary, B., *Explaining Northern Ireland* (Oxford: Blackwell, 1995), p. 321.
20. O'Leary, B. and McGarry, J., *The Politics of Antagonism* (London: Athlone, 1996), p. 234.
21. Ibid., p. 216.
22. O'Leary, 'The Conservative Stewardship of Northern Ireland, 1979–97', p. 667; and O'Leary, B., 'Communications', *Political Studies*, 46 (1998), pp. 796–8.
23. O'Leary, 'Communications', p. 797.

24. O'Leary, 'The Conservative Stewardship of Northern Ireland, 1979–97'; O'Leary, B. ,'The Limits to Coercive Consociationalism in Northern Ireland', *Political Studies*, 37 (1989), pp. 571–2; O'Leary and McGarry, *The Politics of Antagonism*, pp. 184, 215.
25. For more detail see Dixon, P., '"A House Divided Cannot Stand": Britain, Bipartisanship and Northern Ireland', *Contemporary Record*, 9, 1 (1995), pp. 147–87.
26. Thatcher, M., *The Downing Street Years* (London: HarperCollins, 1991), pp. 384–7; see also Prior, J., *A Balance of Power* (London: Hamish Hamilton, 1986).
27. For details of this see Dixon, 'British Policy towards Northern Ireland 1969–2000', p. 353.
28. Callaghan, J., *A House Divided* (London: Collins, 1973) p. 70; see also pp. 78–9.
29. *Irish Times*, 28 February 1998.
30. Dixon, 'British Policy Towards Northern Ireland 1969–2000', pp. 360–1.
31. Cunningham, *British Government Policy in Northern Ireland, 1969–89*, pp. 249–52.
32. Dixon, *Northern Ireland*, Chapters 9 and 10.
33. Cunningham, *British Government Policy in Northern Ireland, 1969–89*, p. 243.
34. Marsh, D. et al., *Post-war British Politics in Perspective* (Oxford: Polity, 1999).
35. O'Malley, P., *The Uncivil Wars* (Belfast: Blackstaff, 1983), pp. 254–5.
36. Dixon, P. 'Political Skills or Lying and Manipulation: The Choreography of the Northern Ireland Peace Process', *Political Studies*, 50, 3 (2000), pp. 340–68. O'Malley, in a typically nuanced way, does recognise these difficulties.

PART IV

POST-CONFLICT NORTHERN IRELAND AND
THE INTERNATIONAL DIMENSION

Chapter 12
Talking to Terrorists: Political Violence and Peace Processes in the Contemporary World[1]

Aaron Edwards

I totally condemn the IRA terrorism that there has been over the past decades, but I don't think you can compare the political demands of Republicanism with the political demands of this terrorist ideology we are facing now. The political demands of Republicanism are demands that would be shared by many perfectly law abiding people who are Nationalists in the north, or citizens of the south in Ireland. These demands of this [Islamist] terrorist ideology are demands, it is not that they don't have demands, they are just none that any serious person could ever negotiate on, and that is just an end to it.[2]

We are not dealing with Sinn Féin and the IRA; what we have in Iraq is all IRA.[3]

INTRODUCTION

It could be argued that some of the world's most protracted intra-state conflicts[4] have been successfully settled by opposing groups entering into a process of political dialogue with one another. Yet the actual methodology by which such conflicts are resolved is often under-explored, especially when the main threat to stability within a state emanates from non-state military actors employing the method of terrorism to extract political concessions from democratic governments. Indeed, it has been a source of contention in the realist literature on international relations just how far states ought to venture in order to secure peace within their own borders.[5] Paul Wilkinson, in his book, *Terrorism versus Democracy: The Liberal State Response*, claims that there 'are very few clear-cut cases where conflict resolution has been used as a means of ending violence by factions using terrorism as their primary weapon'.[6] Instead of bringing these non-state military actors into the political process, Wilkinson recommends that states should utilise both the judicial and the extra-parliamentary resources at their disposal to suppress terrorist groups. Conversely, in a lively conceptualisation of this ongoing debate, Peter Neumann reminds us that, in practice, democratic governments *have* sometimes negotiated with terrorists. He maintains that exploring such options can often offset threats to internal security, while minimising the risk of setting dangerous precedents and destabilising a state's political system.[7] In a further contribution to the debate Martha Crenshaw notes that, even if 'the likelihood of negotiated settlement appears to be decreasing, it is critical to examine peaceful pathways out of terrorism, because political solutions do exist'.[8]

The aim of this chapter is to unpack these academic arguments and to ask at what juncture – if any – it is appropriate for states to enter into dialogue with non-state military actors such as terrorist groups. Therefore, the specific research question I wish to interrogate can be posed in two parts. First, if we accept Max Weber's sociological definition of a state as 'a human community that (successfully) claims the *monopoly of the legitimate use of physical force* within a given territory [original emphasis]'[9] – then what happens if, and when, a state loses that monopoly over physical force when challenged by a non-state military actor in the form of a terrorist group? Second, at what juncture should a state intervene to reclaim its monopoly? I propose to answer this question by drawing several lessons from the Northern Ireland peace process, a case-study which provides us with clear empirical evidence of a liberal democratic state (Britain) entering into peace negotiations with a terrorist group (the Provisional IRA) as a means of neutralising the latter's so-called 'armed struggle'.[10]

CONCEPTUALISING TERRORISM AND POLITICAL VIOLENCE: PROBLEMS OF DEFINITION

Before embarking on a detailed critique of the dynamics underpinning the seemingly asymmetrical relationship between state actors and terrorist groups, it is worthwhile conceptualising what I mean by 'terrorist group'. For decades leading experts in the field of terrorism studies have 'generally agreed that terrorism lacks an agreed conceptual framework'[11] from which to formulate an overarching generic definition of the phenomenon. Yet, as Walter Laqueur has pointed out, this 'is not surprising because there is no universally accepted definition as to what fascism and communism is or democracy and nationalism or virtually any other political phenomenon'.[12] Despite the lack of consensus about what actually constitutes terrorism, there have been many concerted attempts by scholars to explain the phenomenon. Mary Kaldor sees terrorism as 'a technique increasingly used by extreme religious and/or nationalist political movements as part of an array of forms of violence mainly directed against civilians'.[13] Meanwhile John Horgan employs a rather more nuanced definition, viewing terrorism as 'a conscious, deliberate strategic use of violence against a specific type of target to affect the political climate'. He prefers to see terrorism more as 'a weapon, capable of adoption by a very wide array of both non-state *and* state actors' [original emphasis].[14] Most academic and official state definitions focus on the targets and victims of terrorism, with the latter group comprising mainly unarmed civilians. By concentrating on victims, however, some analysts risk avoiding what Noam Chomsky terms the 'moral truisms'[15] arising from state responses to armed challenges to its authority. In other words states prefer to avoid confronting the reality of their role in the cycle of violence. Similarly, terrorist targets tell us little about the actual political or strategic goals of terrorist groups, and even less about how these groups might be dissuaded from their armed campaigns.

Chomsky's kaleidoscopic approach is somewhat at odds with the work of counter-terrorism experts, such as Wilkinson, who tend to view the threat in telescopic terms, with any adverse criticism of state terror being restricted to autocratic regimes, exemplified by Nazism or Stalinism.[16] Few would question the right of liberal democratic states to pursue the option of retaliation against non-state military actors (especially when its non-combatant citizens are targeted unashamedly); however, even to arch-liberals such as Michael Walzer, such actions can be 'legitimate responses to terrorism only when they are constrained by the same moral principles that rule out terrorism itself'.[17] Moving to a situation where non-autocratic states acknowledge their role in the cycle giving rise to terrorism may be impossible;[18] as Charles Townshend rightly notes, all 'attempts to go beyond the fundamental concept of murder are political, and few states will forgo their prerogative of interpreting such concepts'.[19] The problem, Townshend maintains, is that terrorism is 'not a war of evil against good, not a fantastic hydra-headed monster, nor a disease, but a real political strategy adopted in myriad circumstances with myriad intentions'.[20]

While one could argue that most state-sponsored research into terrorism fails to provide comprehensive situational awareness of the specific contexts which give rise to terrorism,[21] there has been a reciprocal, reactive tendency amongst the left to frame discussion of the state's role in equally absolutist terms. They suggest that any response to the threat of terrorism by states is bound to limit the individual freedoms of their citizens. Adrian Guelke occupies this sceptical position, suggesting that governments – when responding to the threat – 'will continue to manipulate the public's fear of terrorism to advance authoritarian agendas at home and aggressive policies abroad. This is why it is so important that the problem of terrorism is viewed objectively and in its proper proportion.'[22] It is a source of controversy just how far civil liberties have been diluted in Western liberal democracies, although what continues to differentiate them from authoritarian regimes such as Pakistan, Algeria, the Philippines and Uzbekistan is that the latter have attributed 'long-running local insurgencies to al-Qaeda, the newly discovered international bogeymen'.[23] In the West there has been a much more concerted effort to defeat terrorism 'at the levels of values as much as that of force'[24] although few concrete attempts to redress the grievances underpinning the propensity of groups engaging in such violence. However, the nascent 'global values' paradigm must be seen in light of flagrant human rights violations in places such as Guantanamo Bay and Abu Ghraib *vis-à-vis* calls by some British government ministers to replace the Geneva Convention.[25]

This chapter highlights one particular methodology by which state actors have tackled a particular variant of terrorism. In doing so it draws a conceptual distinction between those conflicts linked to ethno-national disputes (and which may have territorially separatist goals) and those broader conflicts that have emerged from the embers of the attacks on the Twin Towers on 11 September 2001. Too often terrorism – as a complex social and political phenomenon – has been reduced to mere caricature. Consequently, it is depicted as irrational; something perpetrated by sociopaths (or 'crazies') and delinquents with sexual inadequacies.[26] This is a simplistic misunderstanding of a serious threat. It leads political elites and counter-terrorist experts to under-appreciate the complexities of the phenomenon and make knee-jerk reactions in response. As the Northern Ireland case demonstrates, non-state military actors are complex and multi-layered organisations, with the ability to evolve, adapt and oscillate between progression and reaction. It also illustrates how some groups are motivated by a deep commitment to fighting for a political cause and how this can be accommodated by an emerging peace process.[27]

THE NORTHERN IRELAND CONFLICT IN COMPARATIVE PERSPECTIVE

On 8 May 2007, following forty years of sectarian violence and a decade of political turbulence, Northern Ireland's two largest parties – the Democratic Unionist Party and Sinn Féin – entered into a devolved power-sharing government, which saw the latter willingly pledge to support policing and the administration of British rule in Ireland and the former agree to sharing power with republicans subject to delivery on policing. This was a monumental decision because it showed how far these ethno-political forces – antipathetical to one another on ideological and individual levels – had moved towards each other during a protracted conflict when their public rhetoric would have suggested otherwise. Although various ingredients went into the mix that eventually produced a return to devolution – not least the signing of the Good Friday Agreement in 1998 – it was the British government's willingness to include the republican movement in the 'peace process' which informs the following analysis.

Roger MacGinty has argued that 'for much of the troubles, republicans had regarded the British Government as the most significant "political other" in Northern Ireland, with unionists as secondary actors'.[28] Similarly, Neumann considers the rapprochement between the British government and the Provisional IRA as an unsurprising dynamic in the latent stages of the conflict, with the former observing something of an 'open door' policy *vis-à-vis* republicans: 'At times, London has even engaged in a strategy of pro-active "politicization", aimed at encouraging a transformation from violence to constitutional politics.'[29] The extent to which the Provisional IRA was coerced into the 'peace process', or that it was eventually outmanoeuvred by the British, is a matter of controversy, with some critics, such as the former IRA volunteer Anthony McIntyre, forcefully arguing that:

> The political objective of the Provisional IRA was to secure a British declaration of intent to withdraw. It failed. The objective of the British state was to force the Provisional IRA to accept – and subsequently respond with a new strategic logic – that it would not leave Ireland until a majority in the North consented to such a move. It succeeded.[30]

Notwithstanding the Provisional IRA's own rationale for calling its original ceasefire in 1994, there were several other multi-causal reasons influencing its decision. These included: the shifts in the strategic environment after the end of the Cold War, demographic change in favour of the Catholic community, the successful targeting and assassination of republican activists by loyalist paramilitaries and, perhaps, more importantly, the military stalemate which ensued between the British army and the IRA.[31] It soon became obvious that the main parties in the conflict were conducive to pursuing the option of an appropriate exit strategy.

According to the internationally renowned expert on conflict resolution, I. William Zartman, one of the crucial factors for parties wishing to move away from protracted internal conflict is the 'timing' by which a transformation in the conflict takes place. Yet parties can move into a new, more peaceful, phase only once the situation is 'ripe'. Thus,

> the notion that when the parties find themselves locked in a conflict from which they cannot escalate to victory and the deadlock is painful for both of them (although not necessarily in equal degree or for the same reasons), they seek an alternative policy or way out.[32]

What precipitates this decision to enter into a negotiation process, according to Zartman, is the occurrence of a 'mutually hurting stalemate' (MHS). Applying this analytical framework to Northern Ireland one might suggest that such an MHS existed in the early 1990s. Yet it could be argued that Zartman overstates the predicative utility of his theory and somewhat underplays the value in the dialogue taking place during what Adrian Guelke has called, the 'pre-talks phase'.[33] In Northern Ireland, this dialogue had been ongoing – albeit away from public view – between representatives of the British government and the republican movement from the mid-1980s.[34] Leaving aside the debate over the predictive capabilities of Zartman's theory of ripeness,[35] it can be difficult for competing groups to move beyond their entrenched positions without some sort of endogenous transformation being matched by an exogenous reconfiguration of the state system within which they operate.

Apart from the invaluable investigative journalism of Ed Maloney, most empirically based explanations of the IRA's abandonment of the tactic of 'armed struggle' have tended to focus on either the internal or external dynamics underpinning the republican movement's 'peace strategy'. Few have considered the dialogue between the British state and the Provisional IRA. There are notable exceptions, including the academic work of Henry Patterson, Anthony McIntyre and Kevin Bean, who concentrate their gaze on the structural dynamics underpinning the IRA and its symbiotic relationship to the British state.[36] These authors (see Chapters 7 and 10 of this volume) emphasise how the current leadership of the republican movement subsumed the cutting edge of the IRA's 'armed struggle' in favour of a more explicit political direction.[37] The talks held between Harold Wilson and IRA leaders in London and Dublin in the early 1970s[38] – and the continuation of behind-the-scenes exploratory dialogue between the British state and the IRA during the 1980s and 1990s – certainly supports this view. Indeed, when juxtaposed alongside repeated efforts by the British (and later Irish governments) to marginalise Provisional republicanism by arriving at the Sunningdale Agreement of 1973 and the Anglo-Irish Agreement of 1985, one can see how the initial priority was to bolster constitutional nationalists in the SDLP. That this process failed in the aftermath of the Belfast Agreement necessitated a more direct engagement between the British government and the Adams leadership. However, following the breakdown in the IRA ceasefire in 1996–97, New Labour under Tony Blair sought to bring Sinn Féin in from the cold, judging inclusive talks as an important step towards securing lasting peace. Blair is often lauded for his risk-taking in talking to Sinn Féin, but it must be recognised that both Margaret Thatcher and John Major both held open secret channels with the party.[39] Despite Thatcher's rhetoric that 'I will have nothing to do with any organisation that practises violence. I have never seen anyone from ANC or the PLO or the IRA and would not do so',[40] communication between her successive Secretaries of State, Tom King and Peter Brooke, did take place.[41] It is simply disingenuous to prop up the mythology that Conservative governments refrained from negotiating with terrorists.

However, by themselves, dialogue and negotiations rarely bring an end to violence. The ending of violent conflict can also be precipitated as much by the long shadow cast by rejectionist groups or leaders opposed to a compromise deal between sworn enemies as by impending catastrophe caused by escalation. The case of the Real IRA (a Provisional IRA splinter group) – which carried out the 1998 Omagh bomb that murdered twenty-nine people a few months after the signing of the Belfast Agreement – is perhaps the most striking instance of what Stephen Stedman calls 'spoilers', that is to say, the presence of leaders or groups who oppose peace negotiations and who often employ violence to derail peace initiatives. According to Stedman, 'peace creates spoilers because it is rare for all leaders and factions to see peace as beneficial'.[42] In this respect, 'peace is most vulnerable in the short term'[43] and it is the challenges of making peace stick early on in an embryonic process which demands most scholarly attention. Stedman argues that 'the presence of spoilers, spoils and hostile neighbours pose the gravest threats to fledgling peace processes' and that we must take a more holistic approach to peace-making beyond the official start date of negotiations if we are to meet the challenge they pose.[44]

When placed in the context of the comparative ethnic conflict literature Northern Ireland is far from unique in its possession of these key
variables of peace-making. Conflicts in Israel-Palestine, Angola, Uganda,
Mozambique, Rwanda, Kashmir, Corsica and the Basque country – to
name but a few – have all exhibited similar trends, wherein two or more
groups have resorted to violence, followed by political dialogue, to settle
ethno-national differences. Reaching political accommodation in peace
settlements inevitably means developing institutional arrangements
acceptable to the parties in conflict. These have ranged from the partition
'solution' in Israel-Palestine, to power-sharing between unionists and
nationalists in Northern Ireland, to autonomy in Sri Lanka and
the Basque country. Much of the more rigorous comparative political
science work can illuminate our understanding of how and why ethno-
national conflicts occur at a sub-state level. One of the early pioneers of
'linkage theory', Frank Wright, stressed the problem-solving benefits
attached to a comparative analysis of the Northern Irish experience
when considered in light of conflict zones such as Cyprus, Lebanon
and Israel-Palestine.[45] A similar point is made by Guelke, who reminds
us that political practitioners closely immersed in peace building and
conflict management have 'often generated legitimacy when designing
and creating new institutions and constitutional relationships, as well
as mobilising popular support behind innovative or untried peace
agreements, by looking abroad'.[46] It is useful at this stage to differentiate between two important phases in the evolution of international
relations that help us to comprehend the impact of political violence on
contemporary peace processes.

Peace Processes in the post-Cold War Period
Arguably, one of the main causes of the collapse of the Soviet Union in
1989–90 can be traced to the rise of ethno-national sentiment among
sub-state groups behind the Iron Curtain. Added to already existing
pressures for self-determination – present from the onset of decoloni-
sation in the 1960s – the ending of the Cold War and the collapse of the
wider revolutionary project exploded a potent cocktail.[47] In Ireland the
ensuing reconfiguration in the international political system signalled
a major sea-change in IRA thinking.[48] Guelke has observed that one
of the 'more striking features of politics in Northern Ireland since the
start of the peace process has been the role that comparison with other
societies has played in political discourse'.[49] Indeed, analogies with
other places could be said to have encouraged the IRA to abandon its
'armed struggle'. Peace processes in South Africa and Israel-Palestine
are perhaps the most significant; after all, the IRA's move towards
ceasefire in August 1994 came in the wake of Nelson Mandela's release

from prison in 1990 and the 1993 handshake on the White House lawn between Yasser Arafat and Yitzhak Rabin. The inevitable question asked by journalists of Gerry Adams then was: 'Where is your peace process?'[50] South Africa and Northern Ireland remain the best-known examples of intra-state conflicts where peace processes have been largely successful in the post-Cold War period, while similar processes in Israel-Palestine and Spain very quickly broke down due to renewed violence, bad faith and a failure to maintain inclusive peace negotiations. The defining feature of these successful peace processes was the degree to which sovereign governments had softened their attitudes towards engaging their sworn enemies in political dialogue.

Peace Processes after 9/11
The attacks in the United States on 9/11 transformed the international political system. In many respects they were 'a symptom of trends in the international political system which primarily resulted from what was undoubtedly a watershed in world affairs, the end of the Cold War and dissolution of the Soviet Union'.[51] While one could say that the Provisional IRA and the ANC's armed wing Umkhonto we Sizwe made objective strategic decisions about their capacities in waging long wars, the same is less true of Hamas and Hezbollah despite the return to war in the Middle East in the summer of 2006. The latter groups have continued to challenge Israel's right to exist by escalating attacks at a time when, arguably, their ethno-nationalist goals are on the brink of being met.[52] Even in those conflicts where religion plays less of a role in fuelling ideological warfare – such as that in Sri Lanka – the same level of commitment to terrorist methods (including suicide attacks) remains consistent.[53]

Since 9/11 – and the wars in Afghanistan and Iraq – world leaders from Tony Blair to George W. Bush have found much purchase in drawing lessons from the Northern Ireland model of conflict resolution. Perhaps one of the most intelligent assessments on the subject was delivered by the former US special envoy to Northern Ireland, Mitchell Reiss, in a guest lecture to the University of Cambridge in 2005, in which he outlined how lessons could be learned from the local conflict.[54] He argued strongly that liberal democratic states could learn from the model and productively export the wealth of experience gained here to other parts of the globe. Reiss was certainly correct in drawing these heuristic conclusions; however, he failed to distinguish adequately between the unbridled ideas fuelling radical Islamists and the limited goals pursued by Irish republicans. This is a crucial point because it can tell us whether or not terrorists can be transformed into political practitioners.

However, it is important to draw another distinction between the types of terrorist groups that continue to pursue the incentives promised by engagement in peace processes and those groups inimical to dialogue with state actors. According to Mary Kaldor, the latter type of terrorism is 'a reaction to the insecurities generated by globalisation, as well as disillusion with the secular ideologies of the state'.[55] At the same time, jihadists make use of the opportunities created by globalisation – the new media, especially television and internet, and increased opportunities for funding from the diaspora as well as from transnational criminal groups. As a result, they differ significantly from classic terrorist groups, in ideology, tactics and organisation. One can find empirical evidence that political elites recognise the difference too. In his monthly press conference in the aftermath of the attacks on London in July 2005, Tony Blair drew a distinction between 'old' and 'new' terrorism. He contended that 'I don't think you can compare the political demands of Republicanism with the political demands of this terrorist ideology we are facing now.'[56] Blair might well have been right in flagging up the root causes of the conflict, but he was being disingenuous if he thought that a large minority of Catholics supported the methods by which the IRA prosecuted its war of attrition in Northern Ireland. Blair also neglected to mention that the international legitimacy which allowed his government to enter into negotiations was provided by the United States acting as a third party to guarantee impartiality in the process.[57] American foreign policy has since shifted from the umpire-like stance of Bill Clinton's administration, becoming more ruthlessly jingoistic with the advent of George W. Bush.[58]

The Impact of Third-Party Intervention
The role played by external third parties in 'rubber stamping' the international legitimacy accorded to political negotiations continues to preoccupy analysts of peace processes. Recent examples abound. The decision by US Secretary of State Condoleezza Rice to bring Iran and Syria in from the diplomatic wilderness on the issue of Iraq's future demonstrates the validity of third-party involvement in aiding the containment of regional violence.[59] However, it is unclear whether this will lead to a reduction in attacks on coalition forces in Iraq and Afghanistan, although it seems unlikely in the immediate future. On the other hand, there are numerous examples where there has been a failure to bring in third parties as external mediators and persuaders for peace. In March 2007 the long-awaited talks between the Ugandan government and its opponents in the Lords Resistance Army (LRA), an insurgent group seeking the eventual overthrow of President Museveni's regime, broke down amidst acrimonious dispute.[60] In this

instance, the intervention of the Southern Sudanese government was at first accepted, and then subsequently rejected, by the LRA in favour of talks being shifted from Juba to Johannesburg. Museveni's response was dismissive – as he later made clear: 'Peace in Uganda will be maintained with or without peace talks. Talks were mainly for the benefit of the terrorists. If they don't give in, that will be their problem.'[61] Other prominent examples include the US-backed Ethiopian military intervention in Somalia, Norway's involvement in mediating the Sri Lankan conflict (see Chapter 14 of this volume) and Pakistan's role as a key British and American ally in the fight against the Taliban in Afghanistan. Incidentally, it is perhaps worth noting that Pakistan's President Pervez Musharraf also pointed to the Northern Ireland peace process as a possible model for settling his country's dispute with India over Kashmir.[62] Internal conflicts with a strong regional dimension have most to lose if peace negotiations fail and violence is escalated.

However, the challenges that internationalising the conflict pose for sovereign states are vast. There is a danger that a neighbouring third party may actually be involved in fighting a war by proxy against the principal state arbitrator in an intra-state conflict, as the post-Cold War cases of Syrian involvement in Lebanon (see Chapter 13 of this volume) and the Democratic Republic of Congo's involvement in Sudan demonstrate. Robert Jackson has shown how: 'Terrorism involves sovereign states in a more direct and immediate fashion when such states provide locations or sanctuaries, financial aid, military assistance and in some cases even direct operational assistance to terrorists.'[63] The empirical evidence available to sustain this view is provided by various assessments by senior British and US defence officials, who claim that Iran has been equipping militias and insurgent groups in Iraq with the ordinance and technological expertise to carry out attacks against coalition forces, a claim denied by both.[64]

The same is true – to an extent – in relation to 'pro-state terrorism' in Northern Ireland, a term used by the sociologist Steve Bruce to describe loyalist paramilitary groups such as the Ulster Volunteer Force (UVF) and Ulster Defence Association. The military threat posed to the neighbouring state of the Republic of Ireland by loyalist paramilitaries – although limited in comparison to the IRA's bombing campaign in mainland Britain – did none the less provide the necessary impetus for the Irish government to make conciliatory overtures to the Protestant working-class community.[65] It also provided one further – yet vital – piece of the jigsaw in the peace process, that is to say, all-party involvement in inclusive negotiations. The nature of the UVF's campaign of violence meant that it sought to maintain its ceasefire insofar as the IRA remained committed to the peace process.[66] It is evident that the UVF leadership perceived the events of 9/11 as having an irreversible impact on the strategic context in which the IRA operated.[67] This is just one minor example of the influences which the international political system is currently having on a terrorist group with limited goals. Coincidentally, it is interesting to note that the IRA's September 2001 statement, announcing its re-engagement with the Independent International Commission on Decommissioning, came in the wake of 9/11. The statement began by expressing the IRA's condolences to the families of the victims of what it called 'these deplorable attacks'[68] and effectively sought to distance its separatist agenda from the deadly jihadist threat posed by Al Qaeda.

LESSONS LEARNT BY TALKING TO TERRORISTS

Despite the dogged public rhetoric adopted by governments who initially refuse to talk to terrorists, especially while the latter still pose a military threat, the opening up of (albeit secret) channels has often taken place. The election of Tony Blair's Labour government in May 1997 signalled an important step in resuscitating an ailing process in Northern Ireland. New Labour was prepared to reinstate Sinn Féin into the multi-party talks if the Provisional IRA renewed its ceasefire, which it soon did in July 1997. With the benefit of hindsight and with the aid of Peter Mandelson's revelations about his role as Secretary of State for Northern Ireland in the *Guardian*, Blair had enticed the republican movement back into the process with promises that could not be kept.[69] Nevertheless, by maintaining inclusiveness in negotiations he ensured that the British objective of neutralising the IRA's armed struggle was finally accomplished. However, the haste with which the British government sought to politicise the republican movement caused unintended consequences. As Zartman observes: 'The challenge of any peace process is to penetrate the conflict, marginalize the extremists, and co-opt the moderates into controlling their own radical fringes by offering them enough of an outcome to have them join the peace process.'[70] The moderate political leadership displayed by John Hume of the Social Democratic and Labour Party (SDLP) and David Trimble's Ulster Unionist Party (UUP) meant that political winners soon became electoral losers.[71]

CONCLUSION

From the preceding discussion it is clear that state actors have engaged in (covert and public) dialogue with terrorist groups as a means by which to neutralise armed challenges to their authority. The reason behind this diplomacy has its genesis in Cold War bipolarity, when western states, such as the US and Britain, chose to adopt unilateral approaches to fighting a common enemy in the form of the Soviet Union. Yet, this was by no means an easy task. A consequence of forging alliances along East–West lines was 'the flooding of the globe with small but highly effective weaponry', which meant that armed force could no longer be monopolised by states and their agents.[72] This has proved the interminable legacy of forty years of Cold War détente. Recognition of a transformation in the international political system is, then, the first step in any state response to terrorism.

The second step must be the sullen recognition that 'whatever the particular ideological or geographic background, no negotiations process can even get started without strong indications that the terrorists are serious about ending their armed struggle'.[73] Governments have much to lose in negotiating with terrorists, although they have also much to gain when faced by a group with limited goals wishing to enter into a peace process. For political dialogue to succeed, as Darby and MacGinty contend, there must be a willingness on the part of the protagonists to ensure that negotiations are conducted 'in good faith; that the key actors are included in the process; that the negotiations address the central issues in dispute; that force is not used to achieve objectives; and that the negotiators are committed to a sustained process'.[74] Sometimes such measures – when enacted by states – can have a detrimental effect on the strategic political environment. Conversely, as Wilkinson observes, by not pursuing a proactive policy aimed at neutralising the terrorist threat, governments can greatly exacerbate a potentially debilitating situation.[75] At this point other middle-ranging actors (such as NGOs and intellectuals) and grassroots leaders (such as community developers) are required to ensure that the 'trickle-down' benefits of peace accords are actively sold to the parties in conflict.

To ensure that governments do not lose legitimacy during negotiations with terrorist groups, a third step ought to be the involvement in the process of third parties, who may usefully serve as custodians in order to maximise international legitimacy. The Northern Ireland model demonstrates how internal actors (with external support) can reach an accord by learning from the failure of past initiatives while also imitating the success of processes elsewhere. As M.L.R. Smith has passionately argued: 'Studies which seek to illuminate the Northern Ireland conflict with reference to the wider world remain few in number and rarely connect with international relations thinking.'[76] It is not difficult to appreciate the argument that by focusing on the minutiae of a given intra-state conflict we risk losing sight of the broader and more salient features of ethno-national disputes. Yet it must also be remembered that working from a small number of empirical cases can yield comparative studies with considerable conceptual reach. This chapter has been a contribution to that ongoing debate.

NOTES

1. An earlier version of this chapter was presented to the inaugural conference of the Political Studies Association of Ireland Specialist Group on Democratization, Conflict and Peace Studies at University College Dublin on 26 May 2007. I would like to thank the organisers and the participants for useful feedback on this occasion. The chapter also benefited from the insightful criticisms offered by Stephen Bloomer, Professor Adrian Guelke, Dr Joanne McEvoy, Cillian McGrattan and Dr Roger MacGinty. The usual disclaimer applies.
2. Tony Blair speaking several weeks after the 7/7 bombings in London, 'PM's Press Conference, 26 July 2005'. Archived at: http://www.number-10.gov.uk/output/Page7999. asp. Accessed 10 March 2007.
3. Iraqi Foreign Minister Hoshyar Zebari, quoted in de Bréadún, D., 'Iraqi Politician Studying North Peace "Very Closely"', *Irish Times*, 14 November 2005.
4. Some scholars have drawn a conceptual distinction between 'old' inter-state conflicts and 'new' intra-state conflicts, particularly in light of how warfare has undergone a radical transformation over recent decades. See Kaldor, M., *New and Old Wars: Organized Violence in a Global Era*, second edition (Cambridge: Polity, 2006) and Kaldor, M., 'Iraq: the Wrong War', *Open Democracy*, 9 June 2005. Archived at: http://www.opendemocracy.net/conflict-iraq/wrong_war_2591.jsp. Accessed 9 March 2007.
5. See Ganor, B., *The Counter-Terrorism Puzzle: A Guide for Decision-Makers* (London: Transaction Publishers, 2005), pp. 25–46.
6. Wilkinson, P., *Terrorism versus Democracy: The Liberal State Response* (Abingdon: Routledge, 2006), p. 58.
7. Neumann, P., 'Negotiating with Terrorists', *Foreign Affairs*, 86, 1 (2007), p. 129; see also I.W. Zartman, 'Managing Terrorism and Insurgency through Peace Processes: Options for the Future', in L.S. Germani and D.R. Kaarthikeyan (eds), *Pathways out of Terrorism and Insurgency: The Dynamics of Terrorist Violence and Peace Processes* (Berkshire: New Dawn Press, 2005), pp. 41–9.
8. Crenshaw, M., 'Pathways out of Terrorism: A Conceptual Framework', in Germani and Kaarthikeyan, *Pathways out of Terrorism and Insurgency*, p. 4.
9. Weber, M., 'Politics as Vocation', in H.H. Gerth and C. Wright Mills (eds), *From Max Weber: Essays in Sociology* (London: K. Paul, Trench, Trubner and Co. Ltd, 1947), p. 78. One scholar has made the powerful argument that 'the territorial state has, for various reasons, lost its traditional monopoly of armed force, much of its former stability and power, and, increasingly, the fundamental sense of legitimacy'. Hobsbawm, E., *Globalization, Democracy and Terrorism* (London: Little, Brown, 2007), p. 25.
10. For a similar argument see McIntyre, A., 'Modern Irish Republicanism: The Product of British State Strategies', *Irish Political Studies*, 10 (1995), pp. 97–121.
11. Silke, A., 'The Road Less Travelled: Recent Trends in Terrorism Research', in A. Silke (ed.), *Research on Terrorism: Trends, Achievements and Failures* (London: Frank Cass, 2004), p. 207.
12. Laqueur, W., *No End to War: Terrorism in the Twenty-First Century* (London: Continuum, 2004), p. 232.
13. Kaldor, M., 'Terrorism as Regressive Globalisation', *Open Democracy*, 25 September 2003. Archived at: http://www.opendemocracy.net/democracy-americanpower/article_1501.jsp. Accessed 9 March 2007.
14. Horgan, J., *The Psychology of Terrorism* (Abingdon: Routledge, 2005), p. 22.
15. Chomsky, N., 'Who are the Global Terrorists?', in K. Booth and T. Dunne (eds), *Worlds in Collision: Terror and the Future of Global Order* (Basingstoke: Palgrave, 2002), pp. 128–37.
16. Wilkinson, P., 'Can a State be "Terrorist"?', *International Affairs*, 57, 3 (1981), p. 468.
17. Walzer, M., *Arguing about War* (New Haven, CT: Yale University Press, 2004), p. 61.
18. For more on this ongoing debate see Rolston, B., '"An Effective Mask for Terror":

Democracy, Death Squads and Northern Ireland', *Crime Law and Social Change*, 44 (2005), pp. 181–203.

19. Townshend, C., 'Terrorism: In Search of the Definite Article', *Open Democracy*, 3 July 2007. Archived at: http://www.opendemocracy.net/conflicts/democracy_terror/what_is_terrorism. Accessed 19 July 2007. Note that Townshend views it as a 'political strategy', not a 'tactic', thus further highlighting the rationality of terrorism.

20. Ibid.

21. For a similar argument see Halliday, F., 'Terrorism and Delusion', *Open Democracy*, 11 April 2006. Archived at: http://www.opendemocracy.net/globalization/delusion_3447.jsp. Accessed 22 May 2007.

22. Guelke, A., *Terrorism and Global Disorder: Political Violence in the Contemporary World* (London: I.B. Tauris, 2006), p. 272.

23. Burke, J., *On the Road to Kandahar: Travels through Conflict in the Islamic World* (London: Allen Lane, 2006), pp. 152–3.

24. Blair, T., 'A Battle for Global Values', *Foreign Affairs*, 86, 1 (2007), p. 79.

25. See 'Reid Calls for Changes to Geneva Convention', *Guardian*, 3 April 2006; see also Richardson, L., *What Terrorists Want: Understanding the Terrorist Threat* (London: John Murray, 2006), p. 219.

26. For an empirically informed discussion of the existing literature, see Horgan, *The Psychology of Terrorism*, especially Chapter 3.

27. See Guelke, A., 'The Northern Ireland Peace Process and the War against Terrorism: Conflicting Conceptions', *Government and Opposition*, 42, 3 (2007), pp. 272–91.

28. MacGinty, R., 'Irish Republicanism and the Peace Process: From Revolution to Reform', in M. Cox, A. Guelke and F. Stephen (eds), *A Farewell to Arms? Beyond the Good Friday Agreement*, second edition (Manchester: Manchester University Press, 2006), p. 125.

29. Neumann, P., 'Bringing in the Rogues: Political Violence, the British Government and Sinn Féin', *Terrorism and Political Violence*, 15, 3 (2003), p. 168.

30. McIntyre, A., 'Modern Irish Republicanism and the Belfast Agreement: Chickens Coming Home to Roost, or Turkeys Celebrating Christmas?', in R. Wilford (ed.), *Aspects of the Belfast Agreement* (Oxford: Oxford University Press, 2001), p. 205.

31. Cox, M., 'Bringing in the "International": The IRA Ceasefire and the End of the Cold War', *International Affairs*, 73, 4 (1997), pp. 671–93; see also Maloney, E., *A Secret History of the IRA*, second edition (London: Penguin, 2007).

32. Zartman, I.W., 'The Timing of Peace Initiatives: Hurting Stalemates and Ripe Moments', in J. Darby and R. MacGinty (eds), *Contemporary Peacemaking: Conflict, Violence and Peace Processes* (Basingstoke: Palgrave, 2003), p. 19.

33. Guelke, A., 'Negotiations and Peace Processes', in Darby and MacGinty, *Contemporary Peacemaking*, pp. 53–64.

34. Maloney, *A Secret History of the IRA*, pp. 246–60.

35. Lederach, J.P., 'Cultivating Peace: A Practitioner's View of Deadly Conflict and Negotiation', in Darby and MacGinty, *Contemporary Peacemaking*, pp. 30–7; O'Kane, E., 'When Can Conflicts be Resolved? A Critique of Ripeness', *Civil Wars*, 8, 3–4 (2006), pp. 268–284.

36. Patterson, H., *The Politics of Illusion: A Political History of the IRA* (London: Serif, 1997); McIntyre, 'Modern Irish Republicanism: The Product of British State Strategies', pp. 97–121; Bean, K., *The New Departure? Recent Developments in Republican Strategy and Ideology*, Occasional Papers in Irish Studies, 6 (Liverpool: Institute of Irish Studies, 1994). My thanks to Dr Bean for passing on a copy of his paper.

37. See also Patterson, *The Politics of Illusion*, p. 286.

38. O'Doherty, M. 'Talking to Terrorists', *Fortnight*, No. 448 (November 2006), pp. 24–5.

39. Taylor, P., *The Provos: The IRA and Sinn Féin* (London: Bloomsbury, 1998).

40. Margaret Thatcher, Press Conference at Vancouver Commonwealth Summit, 17 October 1987. Archived at: http://www.margaretthatcher.org/speeches/displaydocument.asp?docid=106948. Accessed 14 July 2007.

41. Maloney, *A Secret History of the IRA*, pp. 246–7; see also Brooke's comments to Peter Neumann in 'Bringing in the Rogues', pp. 162–3.

42. Stedman, S.J., 'Spoiler Problems in Peace Processes', *International Security*, 22, 2 (1997), p. 7.

43. Stedman, S.J., 'Peace Processes and the Challenges of Peace', in Darby and MacGinty, *Contemporary Peacemaking*, p. 103.

44. Ibid., p. 104.

45. Wright, F., *Northern Ireland: A Comparative Analysis* (Dublin: Gill and Macmillan, 1987).

46. Edwards, A., 'Interpreting the Conflict in Northern Ireland', *Ethnopolitics*, 6, 1 (March 2007), pp. 137–44.
47. Hoffman, B., 'Change and Continuity in Terrorism', *Studies in Conflict and Terrorism*, 24 (2001), pp. 417–28.
48. Cox, 'Bringing in the "International"', p. 677.
49. Guelke, A., 'Political Comparisons: From Johannesburg to Jerusalem', in Cox, Guelke and Stephen, *A Farewell to Arms?*, p. 367.
50. Ibid., p. 373.
51. Guelke, *Terrorism and Global Disorder*, p. 257.
52. It could be argued that these groups are currently exploring political options, particularly in light of the US embargo on the Hamas regime following its landslide victory in the Palestinian elections in early 2006. Nevertheless, there is much empirical evidence to suggest that this is tangential, owing principally to the violent confrontations between Hamas and Fatah for control over territory in the West Bank and Gaza. Furthermore, this is not to deny that Israel has sought to undermine conciliation efforts by escalating the conflict with its heavy-handed attacks on Hezbollah in southern Lebanon, as events in the summer of 2006 showed.
53. See Weinberg, L., 'Suicide Terrorism for Secular Causes', in A. Pedahzur (ed.), *Root Causes of Suicide Terrorism* (Abingdon: Routledge, 2006), pp. 108–21.
54. Reiss, Mitchell B., 'Lessons of the Northern Ireland Peace Process', speech delivered at Emmanuel College, Cambridge, 9 September 2005. Archived at http://www.state.gov/p/eur/rls/rm/54869.htm. Accessed 9 March 2007.
55. Kaldor, 'Terrorism as Regressive Globalisation'.
56. Blair, 'PM's Press Conference, 26 July 2005'.
57. Dumbrell, J., 'Working with Allies: The United States, the United Kingdom, and the War on Terror', *Politics and Policy*, 34, 2 (2006), pp. 452–72.
58. For an insightful discussion of America's changing role in the world, see Cox, M., 'Empire, Imperialism and the Bush Doctrine', *Review of International Studies*, 30 (2004), pp. 585–608.
59. DeYoung, K., 'At Meeting on Iraq, Doubt and Détente: Nations Manage to Find a Way Forward as U.S. Meets Briefly With Iran, Syria', *Washington Post*, 5 May 2007.
60. For more detailed empirical research on the LRA, see Vinci, A., 'The Strategic Use of Fear by the Lord's Resistance Army', *Small Wars and Insurgencies*, 16, 3 (2005), pp. 360–81; Vinci, A., 'The "Problems of Mobilization" and the Analysis of Armed Groups', *Parameters: The US Army War College Quarterly*, 36, 1 (2006), pp. 49–62; Vinci, A., 'Existential Motivations in the Lord's Resistance Army's Continuing Conflict', *Studies in Conflict and Terrorism*, 30, 4 (2007), pp. 337–352.
61. Reuters, 'Uganda's LRA Says it Won't Renew Expiring Truce', 28 February 2007. Archived at: http://today.reuters.com/news/CrisesArticle.aspx?storyId=L28637269. Accessed 3 March 2007.
62. Power, J., 'Interview: Pervez Musharraf', *Prospect* (March 2007), p. 32.
63. Jackson, R., 'Sovereignty and its Presuppositions: Before 9/11 and After', *Political Studies*, 55, 2 (2007), p. 313; for a similar argument see Staniland, P., 'Defeating Transnational Insurgencies: The Best Offense is a Good Fence', *Washington Quarterly*, 29, 1 (2005), pp. 21-40.
64. MacAskill, E. 'Iran and US see "Positive" Steps in First Formal Talks Since Hostage Crisis of 1980', *Guardian*, 29 May 2007; see also Milne, S., 'Insurgents Form Political Front to Plan for US Pullout', *Guardian*, 19 July 2007; Reuters, 'US Say More Accurate Green Zone Attacks Aided by Iran', 26 July 2007. Archived at: http://uk.reuters.com/article/worldNews/idUKCOL62182620070726. Accessed 26 July 2007.
65. For background on Irish government involvement, see McCaffrey, B., 'Minister Crossed the Border to Help Seal UVF Ceasefire: Interview with Chris Hudson', *Irish News*, 5 May 2007; and McDonald, H., 'Ahern Approves Grant to UVF Stronghold', *Observer*, 22 July 2007.
66. Edwards, A., 'The UVF Abandons its Campaign of Terror', *Fortnight*, No. 452 (May 2007), pp. 12–13.
67. Edwards, A. and Bloomer, S., *A Watching Brief? The Political Strategy of Progressive Loyalism since 1994*, Conflict Transformation Papers, 8 (Belfast: LINC Resource Centre, 2004), p. 15.
68. *An Phoblacht/Republican News*, 20 September 2001.
69. Watt, N., Wintour, P., and Bowcott, O., 'Blair Guilty of Capitulating to Sinn Féin – Mandelson', *Guardian*, 13 March 2007.

70. Zartman, 'Managing Terrorism and Insurgency through Peace Processes', p. 42.
71. Tonge, J., *The New Northern Irish Politics?* (Basingstoke: Palgrave, 2005).
72. Hobsbawm, *Globalisation, Democracy and Terrorism*, p. 37.
73. Neumann, 'Negotiating with Terrorists', p. 137.
74. Darby, J. and MacGinty, R., 'Conclusion: Peace Processes, Present and Future', in Darby and MacGinty, *Contemporary Peacemaking*, pp. 256–74.
75. Wilkinson, 'Can a State be "Terrorist"?', p. 467.
76. Smith, M.L.R., 'The Intellectual Internment of a Conflict: The Forgotten War in Northern Ireland', *International Affairs*, 75, 1 (1999), p. 81.

Chapter 13
Internationalising the Arms Issue: The Politics of Decommissioning in Northern Ireland and Lebanon

Michael Kerr

To decommission is to withdraw from active service, and with specific reference to arms it means to dismantle and make safe. In Northern Ireland, the symbolic importance of the act of paramilitary groups putting weapons beyond use came to greatly outweigh the military significance of illegally held arms. With reference to the recent developments in its political process, many academics have highlighted the symbolic importance of arms decommissioning as a confidence-building measure and in the establishment of trust between the Northern Ireland parties. The issue was significant in the background to the 1998 Belfast Agreement. However, decommissioning came to dominate the political agenda during intergovernmental attempts to implement it between 1998 and 2005, as the other major symbolic issues of the conflict were largely addressed. McInnes has argued that decommissioning became linked – with varying degrees of success – to political issues such as the release of paramilitary prisoners, executive formation and political exclusion.[1] MacGinty illustrates how decommissioning, possessing an intrinsic symbolic value and acting as a litmus test for the creation of political trust, became a classic 'wedge issue' in Northern Ireland's political process.[2] In a comparative context, Schulze and Smith have shown how decommissioning was achieved in 'situations of much greater complexity and in far more fractured societies than Northern Ireland'.[3] Similarly, in a more recent study, O'Kane has argued that decommissioning became a 'powerful bargaining chip that republicans used to secure political concessions from other participants in the process', suggesting that, had the British and Irish governments been less flexible on the issue, it might not have proved such a durable stumbling block to progress in the negotiations.[4]

The issue of paramilitary decommissioning also came to be used as a veto on political progress by different parties in Lebanon, as intervening powers sought to pursue their regional interests through its frail confessional system. Long after the Ta'if Accord marked the beginning of the end to Lebanon's civil war in 1989, Hezbollah, the Iranian-backed Lebanese Islamist movement, faced pressure to either disarm or be excluded from executive government. This crisis came to a head with the July war of 2006 between Israel and the militant Islamists.

The promotion of a political solution and the internationalisation of the decommissioning issue in Northern Ireland granted Sinn Féin the leeway to disarm without suffering significant political losses as a consequence. In Lebanon, however, an attempted military solution to the unresolved tensions caused by Hezbollah's military prowess became inevitable as external powers vied for influence in the strategically important but deeply fractured Lebanese state.

This chapter will examine why the decommissioning issue stalled the 1998 Belfast Agreement's implementation process for almost a decade and brought Lebanon to the brink of civil war following Syria's 2005 military withdrawal. It argues that, by internationalising the process of disarmament, the British and Irish governments under the respective leaderships of Tony Blair and Bertie Ahern allowed Sinn Féin to maximise political capital on the issue. It will then examine how the decommissioning issue and Hezbollah's political–military duality saw instability return to Lebanon in the wake of Syria's 2005 retreat. It further argues that, while the Irish Republican Army's (IRA) weapons became militarily insignificant following the 11 September attacks on the US, arms became indispensable to Iran's vanguard in Lebanon in the absence of Syrian military control.

PUTTING WEAPONS TO GOOD USE

There has been much debate about which party involved in Northern Ireland's political process breathed life into the decommissioning issue.[5] On 7 March 1995, Northern Ireland Secretary of State Sir Patrick Mayhew formally politicised the decommissioning issue in what became known as his 'Washington III' proclamation.[6] He did so under pressure from Ulster Unionist and Conservative backbenchers who harboured doubts over Sinn Féin's commitment to exclusively peaceful means, as laid out in Paragraph 10 of the Downing Street Declaration. The Irish government also publicly placed illegally held weapons on the political agenda. On 15 December 1993, Tánaiste Dick Spring stated in the Dáil that 'it was not possible' for Sinn Féin to participate in talks with the other Northern Ireland parties prior to the decommissioning of IRA weapons.[7] However, both of these statements were made long before unionists took ownership of the decommissioning issue. The IRA's arms became tactically important to the Ulster Unionist Party (UUP) only when Jeffrey Donaldson publicly split with its negotiating team, shortly before it reached agreement on Good Friday in 1998.[8] For the UUP leader David Trimble, the politics of decommissioning threatened to undermine his leadership as Sunningdale's Council of Ireland had done to Brian Faulkner's bid to share power with nationalists in 1974.[9]

British Prime Minister John Major formally linked IRA decommissioning with Sinn Féin's potential inclusion in official talks between the Northern Ireland political parties and the government, allowing disarmament to create a convenient bottleneck in the political process as his parliamentary majority dwindled. On taking office with a far more robust position at Westminster, Blair promptly dropped decommissioning as a prerequisite for Sinn Féin's political participation, before fudging the issue in the subsequent inter-party negotiations. For republicans, however, ending the IRA's campaign of politicised violence against the UK meant reaching a settlement that involved both British demilitarisation and an inclusive political framework within Northern Ireland.[10] As such, it seems unlikely that the IRA would have moved significantly on this issue prior to an agreement on executive formation. Consequently, the question of when and how decommissioning would occur remained open to future negotiation, but the ambiguities in the text of the Belfast Agreement allowed the majority of Northern Ireland's unionist and nationalist parties to accept an Anglo-Irish settlement in 1998.

Many commentators viewed the Belfast Agreement's 'constructive ambiguity' as central to creating a political atmosphere, in which most unionist and nationalist parties could accept, if not support, the accord.[11] However, Trimble required IRA disarmament to take place as a post-Agreement confidence-building measure in order to secure his continued leadership of a unionist community that remained bitterly divided over the settlement. Essentially, the Agreement's ambiguity left Trimble reliant on Blair to ensure that Sinn Féin honoured its commitment to 'use any influence they may have, to achieve the decommissioning of all paramilitary arms' by 22 May 2000, and the Prime Minister's own commitment to exclude republicans from executive office should they fail to do so.[12] Questions regarding how this 'influence' would be measured and what pressure the two governments were prepared to exert in order to achieve decommissioning remained central to the political process until Trimble lost his Westminster seat in the 2005 general election.[13]

The crux of the problem for unionists was that Blair had not made decommissioning an explicit prerequisite for inclusion in a future Northern Ireland power-sharing executive in the Belfast Agreement's final text. He did, however, commit himself to exclude parties that failed to fulfil their pledges on disarmament in an eleventh-hour 'side-bar letter' to the UUP.[14] Trimble and his senior colleagues accepted Blair's promise to bring forward legislation to strengthen exclusion mechanisms in the Agreement, should the text prove inadequate. The UUP accepted because the 'side-bar letter' constituted the Prime Minister's word but, more importantly, the majority of its negotiators believed that the constitutional settlement on offer would not be improved by any future negotiation.[15] For Trimble, the section referring to decommissioning in the text, though ambiguous, committed Sinn Féin to deliver 'total disarmament' and 'the Blair letter confirmed that interpretation'.[16] Therefore, Trimble did not believe that the Agreement committed the UUP to entering into government with Sinn Féin and, by accepting, he sought to consolidate the constitutional gains that the settlement entailed for unionism. Any ambiguities in the Agreement could be ironed out at a later date. Reflecting on the long-running 'decommissioning issue', Trimble felt the UUP had achieved a great deal 'in terms of renegotiating the agreement ... because suspension, the Independent Monitoring Commission [IMC] and exclusion' went a long way to 'repairing what we saw on 10 April 1998 as a weakness in the agreement'.[17]

Trimble was pragmatic about decommissioning. The UUP's reliance on loyalist paramilitary representatives to form a majority of elected unionists in the negotiations reinforces the view that the issue was not high on its political agenda prior to that point.[18] Therefore, Trimble did not expect to fully address the decommissioning issue during the negotiations, as the two main loyalist paramilitary organisations were not prepared to disarm.

Reneging on his 'side-bar letter' commitments, Blair pressured Trimble into making his famous 'no guns, no government' *volte-face*, as he and Northern Ireland Secretary of State Peter Mandelson saw no possibility of 'a start to decommissioning if the institutions were not up and running'.[19] To his internal critics, this move resulted in a 'loss of support, a lack of credibility and confusion in the minds of the unionist electorate'.[20] Therefore, IRA decommissioning became such an imperative for Trimble that he was prepared to go into government with Sinn Féin, not because he felt committed to do so by the agreement, but in order to achieve at least a start to the disarmament process. It remained an issue, however, over which Trimble had no direct influence and he was therefore reliant on Sinn Féin to ensure that the IRA delivered and on Blair to punish them if they failed or refused to do so.

Consequently, Trimble was always making up lost ground on the arms issue, but he did pressure Blair into suspending Northern Ireland's devolved institutions and setting up the IMC to evaluate the level of paramilitary activity at different junctures in the process. The impact of these political successes was diminished by the struggle for power within unionism itself, and the IRA's unwillingness to decommission in a manner that reinforced unionist confidence in the process. To what extent more timely, visible or substantial decommissioning would have alleviated pressure on Trimble remains unclear. But when three acts of IRA decommissioning occurred during his tenure as UUP leader, Trimble's senior adviser, David Campbell, felt that they were 'always set against a major division within the party', with critics either 'denying' disarmament had taken place or 'minimizing' its significance.[21] Anti-Agreement unionists locked in on the question of disarmament, as it became a significant issue with which they could weaken Trimble's leadership. This division within unionism enabled Sinn Féin to trade its weapons in the negotiation process with the British government for a political price that far exceeded their military value.

More than a decade after Mayhew politicised the issue, the Independent International Commission on Decommissioning (IICD) reported on 26 September 2005 that the IRA had 'met its commitment to put all its arms beyond use'.[22] The IICD head, Canadian General John de Chastelain, commented that it was satisfied that the arms destroyed represented the 'totality of the IRA's arsenal'.[23] The amount of material decommissioned, he noted, was in harmony with the inventory estimates that had been made available to the Commission by the security services of both the UK and the Republic of Ireland. Questions as to whether or not the IRA had actually decommissioned its entire arsenal, however, were promptly raised. The DUP accused the government of a 'cover-up',[24] and subsequent intelligence reports indicated that 'not all IRA weapons' had been decommissioned in September.[25] These intelligence reports were described as 'credible' by Lord Alderdice of the IMC, who did not 'share' de Chastelain's 'level of confidence' that the IRA had engaged in acts of completion.[26]

Aside from the political symbolism attached to IRA decommissioning, arms were of little practical use to the republican movement in the long-term. By the time the IRA engaged in acts of decommissioning, the British and Irish security services knew the location of its weapons dumps. More importantly, the republican movement had been penetrated at a very high level by British intelligence. Serious tensions within the IRA surfaced over this issue in May 2003, when IRA man Freddie Scappaticci denied allegations that he was the British agent codenamed 'Stakeknife'.[27] This came to a head in 2006 when a senior Sinn Féin official – Denis Donaldson – was assassinated in Donegal, following his exposure as a long-serving British Special Branch informer.[28]

When the IRA first put weapons beyond use in October 2001 under international pressure,[29] there was also speculation that the decommissioned guns and ammunition were already beyond use in terms of their operational utility. Two years later, when the IRA engaged in its third act of decommissioning,[30] it was clear from de Chastelain's demeanour that republicans had manipulated the IICD for its own political purposes. Whilst the IRA's acts of completion in 2005 were substantive in military terms, the fact that disarmament occurred after Trimble's electoral defeat that year highlighted the expendable nature of arms to Sinn Féin. Moreover, the IRA completed its decommissioning process ahead of any resumption of Northern Ireland's power-sharing institutions, preventing the DUP from gaining political credit at its expense. On Sinn Féin's part, whether by default or design, this ensured that decommissioning never became a symbolic victory for unionists.

On the loyalist side, the decommissioning issue had limited political impact. That it was not a significant issue in the process suggests that both Blair and Ahern saw paramilitary arms as a practical problem, and one that would be overcome, in time, through negotiation. For these two leaders, engaging with Sinn Féin simply did not represent the sort of moral conundrum that it had been to many British and Irish politicians before them. It seems unsurprising, then, that little weight was given to the issue of Ulster Defence Association (UDA) and Ulster Volunteer Force (UVF) weaponry until 2007, given both the reactionary nature of their paramilitary campaigns and their marginal role in unionist politics.

On 28 July 2005, the IRA officially signalled an end to its most recent 'armed campaign', ordering all units to 'dump arms' ahead of acts of completion.[31] In contrast, loyalist paramilitaries indicated that they still had cause to maintain both their paramilitary structures and their recourse to political violence. In a statement on 13 April 2006, the UVF – as opposed to its political wing, the Progressive Unionist Party – made a statement on the stalled implementation of the Belfast Agreement. The UVF affirmed its continued support for the accord or, 'Plan A', as they liked to refer to it, stating categorically that the organisation would not decommission its weapons until it became clear whether or not the power-sharing institutions would be restored.[32] The UVF also hinted that, if the DUP failed to go into government with Sinn Féin, it might reject the two governments' 'Plan B' – an intergovernmental administration that, in its view, would amount to a 'greener' version of the 1985 Anglo-Irish Agreement and – potentially – joint authority.[33]

When power-sharing between the DUP and Sinn Féin appeared imminent, the UVF marked an end to its campaign. On 3 May 2007, its representatives met with the IICD, but its position on transparent decommissioning remained ambiguous as the group claimed to have itself put weapons 'beyond reach'.[34] The UVF appeared to be satisfied that the DUP would not risk Northern Ireland's constitutional position within the UK by refusing to share power with Sinn Féin, but this may also have been a belated attempt to finally place its arms on the negotiating table in the hope that decommissioning would lead to political and economic concessions. In contrast to the IRA experience, the decommissioning of loyalist weapons did not become a significant issue in the process, largely because the UVF and the UDA lacked significant political influence.

On one level, the creation of the IICD meant that paramilitary organisations were effectively exempted from the normal procedures for dealing with illegally held arms in the UK and the Republic of Ireland. They were not expected to hand over weapons to either the British or Irish governments. Such a move might have been construed by their supporters as an act of submission. Politically, this suited Blair and Ahern as it removed any question of their administrations supervising the process of disarmament. However, internationalising the problem significantly reduced the prospect of it taking place within a defined timeframe, which suited their political agenda. Letting the IRA disarm on their own terms was a price they were willing to pay for a political settlement to the conflict.

Neither government was prepared to 'impose' decommissioning or apply excessive pressure on the IRA to deliver it. This was evident from the British government's tactics following the failed UUP–Sinn Féin sequence of 2003. Trimble conceded that he had been 'relying very much on the government' at that time in order to pressure republicans into providing certainty that there would be completion, in terms of both paramilitary weapons and, indeed, paramilitary activity. He did not get 'a terribly satisfactory response', which left him 'simply hoping that things would go right on the day'.[35] When this did not happen, Blair concentrated on the security aspects of the Belfast Agreement before attempting to again restore power-sharing, this time between the two hard-line parties – the DUP and Sinn Féin – after their respective victories in the March 2007 assembly elections.

Days after the IRA announced an end to its armed campaign, Secretary of State for Northern Ireland Peter Hain announced a two-year demilitarisation plan to reduce the British army's presence in Northern Ireland and repeal certain counter-terrorism legislation.[36] Progressing with this demilitarisation agenda when the political institutions were failing certainly helped republicans finally accept Northern Ireland, including the new policing and justice arrangements,[37] something which Sinn Féin credited to the departing prime minister.[38]

Blair and Ahern had learnt lessons from the collapse of the IRA ceasefire on 9 February 1996, and from how their predecessors had dealt with its political fallout. Major's government viewed the crisis as a sign of the IRA's lack of commitment to purely democratic means, whereas the Irish government interpreted it as an indication that republicans had been pushed too far on the decommissioning issue.[39] The creation of the IICD removed any possibility of the IRA having to enter into a decommissioning process solely at the behest of the two governments. This was something all three parties had sought to avoid for different political and historic reasons. The composition of the IICD itself became a further incentive for the IRA to acquiesce in the process of disarmament. Had it been headed by an American, rather than a Canadian general, pressure on republicans after the 11 September attacks would have been even more intense, especially when IRA men were arrested whilst training Marxist guerrillas in Columbia.[40]

By putting the weapons issue out to tender to bodies that had little political leverage in the process, the two governments, partly delegated their responsibility for ensuring that the IRA's arms were fully dealt with. Charging an international body that lacked any powers of enforcement with the task of overseeing the completion of decommissioning enabled the IRA to largely determine when, where and how its incremental decommissioning process took place. Essentially, de Chastelain was a military man faced with the task of overseeing symbolic acts of demilitarisation without the full political backing of those who ultimately had the power to enforce them.

The two governments had initially opted for a tripartite international commission, headed by former US Senator George Mitchell, de Chastelain, and former Finnish Prime Minister Henri Holkeri, which was to report on how decommissioning should be achieved by January 1996. The fact that unionists became politically hung up on the issue, preferring de Chastelain to Mitchell on account of the latter's Irish–Lebanese ancestry,[41] merely added to the advantage that silent IRA guns represented for Sinn Féin.

AUXILIARY ARMS AND THE TUG-OF-WAR FOR LEBANON

In 1989, an international agreement brokered in Ta'if, Saudi Arabia, marked the beginning of the end to Lebanon's protracted and seductive civil war.[42] The accord was a regional compromise which charged

Syria with politically reconstructing the country through a return to a lightly modified version of its old power-sharing formula. As in Northern Ireland, the key to finding a diplomatic or military solution to the dilemma posed by the residue of illegally held arms lay with the influence that external powers brought to bear on the process. The international legitimacy Syria gained from Ta'if enabled it to disarm all the militias in Lebanon, with the exception of Hezbollah (Party of God).

In stark contrast to Northern Ireland's long-drawn-out decommissioning process, disarming Lebanon's paramilitary organisations proved relatively uncontroversial, despite the political uncertainty that followed the end of its civil war. Decommissioning was partially achieved through the incorporation of approximately 20,000 militiamen into the state's security services and governmental bureaucracy.[43] A committee was set up to oversee the dissolution of the militias and ensure their structures were permanently dismantled.[44] Lebanon's major Christian, Muslim and Druze militias all decommissioned weapons and, in some cases, returned them to their suppliers. The Christian Lebanese forces discharged arms into the Israeli security zone in southern Lebanon; the Druze Progressive Socialist Party returned arms to Syria and the Shi'a Amal presented many of its weapons to the Lebanese army.[45] However, none of these groups disarmed completely. The Christian and Druze militias concealed weaponry in their mountainous retreats and Amal sent arms to the south to counter the continued Israeli occupation.[46]

Two groups opposed the concept of decommissioning – Hezbollah, the self-styled Lebanese resistance, argued that the end of the civil war did not impinge upon its ongoing struggle with Israel to free occupied Arab territories, while there was also what remained of the Palestine Liberation Organisation (PLO) in Lebanon, which made a similar case. Of the two, Hezbollah had long since become the more reliable and malleable ally of Syria in Lebanon. Furthermore, almost all Lebanese factions blamed the PLO, to varying degrees, for exacerbating the internal and external tensions that led to the outbreak of civil war in 1975. So when they refused to decommission, the PLO was forced militarily to relinquish its heavy weaponry by a re-formed Lebanese army in July 1991.[47] In what amounted to a show of national solidarity, the army took pride in reining in a foreign paramilitary organisation which had split the country by mounting attacks on Israel from Lebanese territory in the early 1970s, having consolidated its control over much of southern Lebanon through the 1969 Cairo Agreement. This accord effectively granted the PLO freedom of action against Israel from within Lebanese territory, thus yielding control over parts of southern Lebanon to a foreign non-state actor.[48]

Hezbollah, the Shi'a Islamist party created and nurtured in Lebanon by Iran as both a counter to western intervention and a vanguard against Israel after its 1982 invasion, sought special status with regard to arms. The continued strategic importance of Hezbollah to Syria and Iran following Ta'if allowed the Shi'a militia to both maintain and adjust its paramilitary capacity, whilst incrementally politicising its organisation. Hezbollah's dual political-military structure became institutionalised within Lebanon's political system under Syrian patronage, but not all the Lebanese communities accepted this. It was domestic tension arising from this duality that prompted moves by Hezbollah's opponents to reduce its influence in Lebanon. However, Israel's failure to eliminate Hezbollah's paramilitary threat in the 2006 July war actually strengthened the Islamic movement's recourse to political violence, reinforced its significance to regional and international disputes over the Middle East, and significantly reduced the prospect of decommissioning taking place in Lebanon outside the rubric of a negotiated regional settlement or another war. In contrast to Northern Ireland, where the British tactically moved away from pursuing a military solution to the conflict, Israel's aim after 2005 was exactly that. Viewing the July war as a portent of events to follow, former United Nations Interim Force in Lebanon (UNIFIL) spokesman Timur Goksel put it that 'Israel can't live in the Middle East with the impression they lost to Hezbollah, a militia.'[49]

Claiming military victory from the Israeli withdrawal of 2000, Hezbollah enhanced its legitimacy in Lebanon, its political standing within the Shi'a community and its prestige throughout the Arab world. Withdrawal was both a political and military success for the Shi'a militia, but the end of Israel's illegal occupation left it somewhat lacking its *casus belli*. Following the withdrawal, low-intensity conflict simmered over the contested Shebaa farms. The Israelis captured this small piece of land from Syria during the Six Day War of 1967, but Lebanon claimed it as part of its sovereign territory. The issue granted Hezbollah a convenient pretext for maintaining its political–military structure, as the occupation of Shebaa meant Israel's withdrawal was deemed incomplete by the Lebanese government.

During this period, Syria's political domination over Lebanon prevented Hezbollah's dual nature leading to internal conflict. This all changed when international pressure forced Syria into a military withdrawal in the aftermath of former Lebanese Prime Minister Rafic Hariri's assassination on Valentine's Day 2005.[50] Prior to this, Syria had ruthlessly controlled every aspect of Lebanon's political system.

The decommissioning problem stemmed from Syrian hegemony in Lebanon. When Syria retreated militarily, Hezbollah's special status was called into question by some of the other parties to its new government. Lebanon suddenly lacked the external referee that had forcefully regulated conflict between the different communities so efficiently since Ta'if. Hezbollah had not formed part of Lebanon's post-Ta'if government of national unity but, over the following decade, the movement underwent a process of incremental politicisation. Hezbollah publicly dropped its call for the establishment of an Islamic state in Lebanon. This pragmatic approach towards Lebanon's confessional system remained matched by an uncompromising stance towards Israel's continued occupation. After participating in national elections for the first time in 1992, Hezbollah then formed a significant opposition grouping in the Lebanese parliament.[51] This political transition continued when the Shi'a movement finally accepted two seats in a coalition government following parliamentary elections in May 2005.

Those elections saw three blocs emerge. The first was the pro-Hariri/anti-Syrian coalition, which brought together Sunni, Christian and Druze MPs. They viewed US support as a means of consolidating Lebanon's independence from Syria, minimising Hezbollah's influence in its power-sharing formula and tempering Iranian influence. They gained seventy-two of the one hundred and twenty-eight seats that they contested. The second was the Hezbollah–Amal alliance, which gained thirty- five seats on an anti-Western/pro-Syrian ticket. Finally, the third bloc formed under the populist Maronite leader Michael Aoun, who won the remaining twenty-one seats in alignment with a number of pro-Syrian Christians.

The new Christian–Muslim 'independent' coalition government lacked stability from the outset, emerging from the vacuum created by Hariri's murder and Syria's retreat. Lacking its external referee in Damascus, the Lebanese government began to implode in December 2005. A National Dialogue Committee was composed of representatives from the different Lebanese communities, convening on 2 March 2006 to address the constitutional crisis.[52] This met regularly but failed to reach agreement, with Hezbollah rejecting all calls to disarm on the basis that its weapons were necessary to defend Lebanon from Israeli aggression.[53] Hezbollah responded to this pressure with a show of strength rally in Beirut on 8 March 2006, which was attended by some 400,000 people. On 14 March, up to one million pro-government supporters responded with a counter-rally that filled the capital's streets. These figures are estimates, but the fact that huge numbers of citizens engaged in unprecedented acts of democratic protest was politically significant. Under the 'Cedar Revolution' the West had welcomed such street protests as proof of 'people power in the Middle East', when protesters had ousted the then pro-Syrian government a fortnight after Hariri's murder.[54]

The status of Hezbollah as a member of the power-sharing government which, in coordination with Iran and Syria, deployed its own private army against Israel outside the new Lebanese government's political control, could not be reconciled. Furthermore, decommissioning could not be enforced domestically as Hezbollah's paramilitary wing was the strongest armed force in the country following the Israeli and Syrian withdrawals. Seizing upon this division, the US backed the 14 March camp in moves to further isolate Syria and reduce Iran's rapidly growing influence. As has so often been the case in Lebanon, widening inter-communal divisions were synonymous with escalating international tension across the Middle East.[55]

In the absence of Syrian dominance, Iran sought to reinforce its position in Lebanon through its political, financial and military support for Hezbollah. The US, however, had a score to settle with Iran and its protégés, dating back to 1983 when Shi'a terrorists detonated suicide truck bombs in Beirut, killing hundreds of American and French marines and effectively ending US President Ronald Reagan's intervention in the Lebanese civil war. The US held Iran directly responsible for these attacks and the suicide bomb blast that had destroyed its embassy in Beirut some months earlier.[56] Prior to Hariri's death, the US had applied increased pressure both on Hezbollah to disarm and Syria to withdraw. On 2 September 2004 the UN Security Council adopted Resolution 1559, which called for 'all remaining foreign forces to withdraw from Lebanon' and 'the disbanding and disarmament of all Lebanese and non-Lebanese militias'.[57]

In January 2006, the Security Council sharply criticised Hezbollah for firing rockets into Israeli territory and urged the Lebanese government 'to assert its authority in the south ... and to prevent attacks from Lebanon'.[58] On 12 July 2006, Hezbollah attacked the Israel Defense Forces (IDF), killing three and capturing two soldiers in an operation that provided the pretext for a full-scale assault on the Islamic movement.[59] Hezbollah leader Hassan Nasrallah claimed that his party had not imagined that there was a 'one percent chance ... snatching the two Israeli soldiers' would spark such a response.[60] Had they anticipated this move, he said, Hezbollah fighters would not have gone ahead with the operation.

Israel's initial response was to bombard Lebanon's international airport, impose a sea blockade, cut off all main transport arteries and shell Hezbollah strongholds. The military operation might have been more successful had the Israeli government stopped there, as Arab and western governments had broadly condemned Hezbollah's act of aggression, despite the disproportionate response it provoked from Tel Aviv. Over the following month, however, Israel became entangled in close combat with Hezbollah in southern Lebanon, whilst maintaining its bombardment under the disapproving eye of the world's media. As civilian casualties mounted and Hezbollah proved a match for the IDF in the south, the Israeli government's tactical errors became increasingly apparent. The turning point came on 30 July, when twenty-eight civilians died during a bombing raid on the town of Qana. International support for the Israeli offensive withered as reaction to the tragedy echoed the condemnation it faced in 1996 when the IDF shelled a UN shelter in the town, killing over one hundred.

The war ended the façade of unity that still existed on paper in Lebanon's political coalition. All five pro-Syrian Shi'a ministers resigned from the Lebanese government in November 2006, depriving it of cross-community support. This followed a cabinet decision to authorise a controversial mixed Lebanese and international tribunal to investigate Hariri's assassination.[61] Opposition leader Michel Aoun then called for Prime Minister Fouad Siniora's government to resign at the start of what became a continuous protest outside Beirut's parliament buildings.[62] The opposition's demand for enough seats in Lebanon's cabinet to grant it a one-third veto mechanism on governmental decisions was also rejected.[63] In southern Lebanon, a multinational force was deployed to fill the military vacuum through the extension of UNIFIL's mandate. UN Security Council Resolution 1701 called for a permanent ceasefire between Israel and Lebanon based on the:

> ... full implementation of the relevant provisions of the Ta'if Accords, and of resolutions 1559 (2004) and 1680 (2006), that require the disarmament of all armed groups in Lebanon, so that, pursuant to the Lebanese cabinet decision of 17 July 2006, there will be no weapons or authority in Lebanon other than that of the Lebanese state.[64]

The resolution welcomed the government's pledge, on 7 August, to deploy a 15,000-strong Lebanese armed force to coordinate with the Israeli withdrawal and authorised the enhancement of UNIFIL by up to 15,000 troops. The outcome of the war coupled with Siniora's enhanced dependence on US support left no one in any doubt that disarmament was neither on Hezbollah's agenda nor in the interests of its external sponsors. Essentially, it was in Iran's interest to ensure Hezbollah remained armed and prepared for further conflict with Israel and, conversely, in the US government's interest to ensure the threat it posed to Israel was forcibly removed.

While peace was quickly restored to the country, Lebanon's National Pact had been broken. Since gaining independence in 1943, power-sharing between its various Christian and Muslim communities had been bound by the coda of 'no victor – no vanquished'.[65] During the Second World War, Maronite Christian and Sunni Muslim leaders had agreed that the Lebanese state would have an 'Arab face', but that its government would remain neutral on intra-Arab disputes. This appeased both those who favoured an independent Christian Lebanon and those harbouring pan-Arab aspirations who wanted Lebanon to become part of a united-Arab entity in the Levant or beyond. The Ta'if Accord attempted to resolve this ambiguity, stating that Lebanon was an Arab country with an Arab identity, but that the Lebanese state was its final and definitive form. In 2005, the old division concerning the existence of the Lebanese state had been replaced by a new tug-of-war over whether or not its independence from Syria would be consolidated and Iranian influence reduced. In broad terms, the Saudi-backed Lebanese government aligned itself tightly with the US in its push for regional dominance, whereas the opposition sided with revolutionary Iran as the principal challenger to American hegemony.

Like the PLO before them, Hezbollah, in line with Syrian and Iranian foreign policy goals, had brought about foreign intervention in Lebanon through its conduct of unsanctioned paramilitary operations against Israel. During this crisis, Siniora's government remained in office through the political backing of the US after it provided the diplomatic cover for Israel's invasion. Relations between the two blocs had deteriorated to such an extent that Nasrallah openly accused Siniora's government of working with Israel against the Lebanese militia.[66] Furthermore, conflict widened as an externally manufactured Palestinian group with clear links to both Syria and al-Qaeda challenged the Lebanese government. The battle, which began in May 2007 between the Lebanese army and Fatah al-Islam, a small Palestinian faction, highlighted the government's chronic inability to domestically address the decommissioning issue when its forces ran out of ammunition within the first week of hostilities.[67]

CONCLUSION

In Northern Ireland and Lebanon, the issue of illegally-held weapons became inextricably linked to the creation and maintenance of political stability, the level of confidence that different communities had in their respective political processes and the amount of influence that external actors could bring to bear upon them.

In Lebanon, inter- and intra-elite rivalry lay at the heart of the breakdown of its new government, which was accentuated by

Hezbollah's unwillingness to disarm. The end of Syria's self-serving role as political referee between the Lebanese communities and the stand-off between the US and Iran (over the latter's nuclear development programme and regional ambition) stretched Lebanon's National Pact to breaking point. For the anti-Syrian coalition, decommissioning became as intractable a political issue as it had been for unionists during the Belfast Agreement's initial implementation. Like the unionists in Northern Ireland, the Lebanese government became reliant on external powers to disarm paramilitary groups that existed outside the state's control. However, in contrast to the IRA, Hezbollah's weapons remained a significant paramilitary threat to political stability as a result of these internal and external pressures. As such, Israel held a strategic interest in launching a war in Lebanon in order to remove Hezbollah from its northern border.

Following the 11 September attacks, an IRA that engaged in political violence and terrorism against the UK could no longer expect the sort of political and financial support in the US that it had enjoyed in the past. Closer to home, the IRA could no longer point to the Republic of Ireland's constitutional claim to Northern Ireland in its justification of political violence. The context for a permanent end to IRA violence was created when the British government demonstrated that it had 'no selfish strategic or economic interest in Northern Ireland',[68] through its efforts to implement the Belfast Agreement. As a result of the differing international contexts, however, Hezbollah did not share Sinn Féin's level of domestic political comfort. In stark contrast to the two governments' approach to Northern Ireland's process, excluding Hezbollah became a key part of the Bush administration's vision for Lebanon. The 1998 Anglo-Irish settlement was fundamentally premised on the inclusive principle of 'no victor – no vanquished' that had ended Lebanon's civil war. Hezbollah's military continuity had been assured by the authority of Syria, and its absence caused tension to fester over its outlier position in Lebanon's political system. Equally, Israel enjoyed the cover of the US-led 'war on terror' and a pre-emptive self-defence doctrine, which fitted neatly with the Bush administration's regional agenda. Therefore the decommissioning issue had a completely different magnitude in the two cases.

In Northern Ireland, the British and Irish governments had fudged the issue of disarmament and diluted their responsibility for bringing it about by setting up independent bodies to do the job for them. The internationalisation of the process ensured that arms dominated the Belfast Agreement's first implementation period. In comparison to other symbolic aspects of the agreement, such as police reform and prisoner releases, IRA disarmament became an issue that the two governments could not address within a set timeframe. The republican movement benefited from the arms issue, whereas unionists divided over weapons that no longer held any military value to Sinn Féin in its quest for a more united Ireland. In contrast, the international tug-of-war over Lebanon exacerbated deep-seated fears on all sides of the political divide. During the July war, Henry Kissinger expressed those fears and the sense of *déjà vu* that pervaded the Bush administration's policy towards Lebanon. He warned that if the Islamic militants were not disarmed, Lebanon was 'likely to be taken over by Hezbollah, sooner or later, and this whole crisis will repeat itself'.[69]

NOTES

1. McInnes, C., 'A Farewell to Arms? Decommissioning and the Peace Process', in M. Cox, A. Guelke and F. Stephen (eds), *A Farewell to Arms? Beyond the Good Friday Agreement*, second edition (Manchester: Manchester University Press, 2006), pp. 154–69.
2. MacGinty, R., 'Issue Hierarchies in Peace Processes: The Decommissioning of Paramilitary Arms and the Northern Ireland Peace Process. Lessons for Ending Civil Conflicts', *Civil Wars*, 1, 3 (1998), pp. 24–45.
3. Schulze, K. and Smith, M.L.R., 'Decommissioning and Paramilitary Strategy in Northern Ireland: A Problem Compared', *Journal of Strategic Studies*, 23, 4 (2000), p. 102.
4. O'Kane, E., 'Decommissioning and the Peace Process: Where Did it Come from and Why Did it Stay so Long?', *Irish Political Studies*, 22, 1 (2007), p. 100.
5. MacGinty, 'Issue Hierarchies in Peace Processes', pp. 24–45; McInnes, 'A Farewell to Arms?', pp. 154–69; and O'Kane, 'Decommissioning and the Peace Process', pp. 81–101.
6. *Joint Declaration* (London: HMSO, 1993).
7. Dáil Éireann, Debates, 15 December 1993, Vol. 437, Col. 77.
8. Godson, D., *Himself Alone: David Trimble and the Ordeal of Unionism* (London: Harper Collins, 2004), pp. 352–5.
9. *Financial Times*, 21 November 1973.
10. Interview with Jim Gibney, 11 April 2001.
11. Dingley, J., 'Constructive Ambiguity and the Peace Process in Northern Ireland', *Low Intensity Conflict and Law Enforcement*, 13, 1 (Spring 2005), pp. 1–23; Interview with Jim Gibney, 5 April 2007.
12. *The Belfast Agreement* (London: HMSO, 1998).
13. Kerr, M., *Transforming Unionism: David Trimble and the 2005 General Election* (Dublin: Irish Academic Press, 2005).
14. Millar, F., *David Trimble: The Price of Peace* (Dublin: Liffey Press, 2004), pp. 66–70.
15. Interview with Lord Kilclooney, 15 February 2001.
16. Millar, *David Trimble*, p. 72.
17. Interview with Lord Trimble, 8 June 2005.
18. Tonge, J., *Northern Ireland* (Cambridge: Polity Press, 2006).
19. Interview with Peter Mandelson, 2 July 2001.
20. Interview with Jeffrey Donaldson, 14 August 2001.
21. Interview with David Campbell, 8 June 2005.
22. *Report of the IICD*, 26 September 2005. Archived at: http://news.bbc.co.uk/1/shared/bsp/hi/pdfs/26_09_05_decommissioning.pdf.
23. *Daily Telegraph*, 27 September 2005.
24. *Guardian*, 28 September 2005.
25. *Eighth Report of the IMC* (London: HMSO, 2006), Paragraph 3.23.
26. BBC, 1 February 2006. Archived at: http://news.bbc.co.uk/1/hi/northern_ireland/4670412.stm.
27. *Daily Telegraph*, 14 May 2003.
28. *Irish Times*, 5 April 2006.
29. BBC, 28 October 2001. Archived at: http://news.bbc.co.uk/1/hi/northern_ireland/1625061.stm.

30. *Irish Times*, 22 October 2003.
31. IRA statement, 28 July 2005.
32. UTV, Brian Rowan interview with UVF spokesman, 13 April 2006.
33. 'Showing Paisley the Way', *Magill*, May 2006, pp. 32–3.
34. *Belfast Telegraph*, 4 May 2007.
35. Interview with Lord Trimble, 8 June 2005.
36. *Irish Times*, 2 August 2005.
37. *The Times*, 29 January 2007.
28. Interview with Jim Gibney, 5 April 2007.
39. O'Kane, 'Decommissioning and the Peace Process', p. 93.
40. *Guardian*, 28 October 2001.
41. Godson, *Himself Alone*, p. 193.
42. Kerr, M., *Imposing Power-Sharing: Conflict and Coexistence in Northern Ireland and Lebanon* (Dublin: Irish Academic Press, 2005), pp. 159–78.
43. 'Plan for the Incorporation of Militiamen into the State', *Beirut Review*, Lebanon Documents (1991), p. 119.
44. Schulze and Smith, 'Decommissioning and Paramilitary Strategy in Northern Ireland', p. 84.
45. Schulze, K., 'Taking the Gun out of Politics: Conflict Transformation in Northern Ireland and Lebanon', in J. McGarry (ed.), *Northern Ireland and the Divided World: Post-Agreement Northern Ireland in Comparative Perspective* (Oxford: Oxford University Press, 2001), pp. 254–8.
46. Ibid., p. 257.
47. Hanf, T., *Coexistence in Wartime Lebanon: Decline of a State and Rise of a Nation* (London: The Centre for Lebanese Studies, 1993), pp. 619–21.
48. Khazen, F., *The Breakdown of the State in Lebanon, 1967–1976* (London: I.B. Tauris, 2000), pp. 140–75.
49. *Daily Star* (Beirut), 28 June 2007.
50. Kerr, M., 'Approaches to Power-Sharing in Northern Ireland and Lebanon', in R. Miller (ed.), *Ireland in the Middle East: Trade, Society and Peace* (Dublin: Irish Academic Press, 2007), pp. 138–50.
51. Norton, A.R., *Hezbollah: A Short History* (Princeton, NJ: Princeton University Press, 2007), pp. 98-103.
52. *Daily Star* (Beirut), 3 March 2005.
53. *International Herald Tribune*, 9 June 2006.
54. *Daily Telegraph*, 24 January 2007.
55. Kerr, M., 'The Philosophy of Lebanese Power-Sharing', in Y. Choueiri (ed.), *Breaking the Cycle: Civil Wars in Lebanon* (London: Centre for Lebanese Studies, 2007), pp. 237–54.
56. Norton, *Hezbollah*, pp. 71–2.
57. UN Security Council Resolution 1559, 2 September 2004.
58. UN Security Council Resolution 1655, 31 January 2006.
59. *Washington Post*, 13 July 2006.
60. BBC, 27 August 2006. Archived at: http://news.bbc.co.uk/player/nol/newsid_5290000/newsid_5291500/5291580.stm?bw=bb&mp=wm.
61. *Daily Star* (Beirut), 13 November 2006.
62. *Guardian*, 2 December 2006.
63. *Irish Times*, 4 December 2006.
64. UN Security Council Resolution 1701, 11 August 2006.
65. Kerr, *Imposing Power-Sharing*, pp. 112–40.
66. *Haaretz*, 8 December 2006.
67. *Daily Telegraph*, 28 May 2007.
68. *Joint Declaration* (London: HMSO, 1993).
69. FOX News, 9 August 2006. Archived at: http://www.foxnews.com/story/0,2933,207539,00.html.

The author is grateful to Dr Paul Keenan and Dr Rory Miller for their comments.

Chapter 14
The Impact of Third-Party Intervention on Peace Processes: Northern Ireland and Sri Lanka

Eamonn O'Kane

INTRODUCTION

There has been an increasing interest in a comparative approach to the examination of peace processes and attempts at conflict resolution in recent years. Whilst it is important to acknowledge that each conflict is unique, comparisons between conflicts may help to ascertain whether lessons can be learnt from one that may be useful in resolving others. This chapter seeks to examine the role that third parties have played in the attempts to resolve the conflicts in Northern Ireland and Sri Lanka. Similarities can be drawn between the two conflicts. Both can be classed as inter-ethnic conflicts over identity/secession;[1] issues of civil rights and discrimination against the minority communities were instrumental in the development of the conflicts and both have had peace processes in recent years (with markedly different outcomes). In terms of intensity at one level there is little comparison between them. In Northern Ireland around 3,600 people have been killed since 1969 and in Sri Lanka estimates range from 60,000–70,000 deaths since the early 1980s. Yet the difference is not as stark when taken as a proportion of population, as Northern Ireland has approximately 1.5 million inhabitants compared to Sri Lanka's 20 million. Indeed, on a visit to Sri Lanka in 2006 the former Northern Ireland Secretary of State, Paul Murphy, claimed that there were 'striking similarities between the Northern Ireland and Sri Lanka conflict'.[2] Yet there are of course far more differences than similarities. Unlike the Liberation Tigers of Tamil Eelam (LTTE) in Sri Lanka, the IRA never ran a *de facto* state in parts of Northern Ireland. The level of fighting between the IRA and the British government was never comparable to that between the Government of Sri Lanka (GOSL) and the LTTE. Although on occasions the human rights record of Britain and the IRA have been questioned, the situation in this regard also bears no resemblance to the tragic situation in Sri Lanka, where issues such as the use of child soldiers, indiscriminate suicide bombings and oppression of rival groups by the LTTE, and torture and unlawful killing by government forces, have been consistent features of the conflict.[3]

Yet these differences do not negate the worth of examining the role of third parties in the two conflicts comparatively. Both conflicts have at times attracted the attention of the international community, and external third parties have sought to play a role in resolving (or containing) the conflict. But there have been marked differences both in the form these attempts have taken and in the results that have been achieved. Given the identified similarities and differences between the conflicts they provide an opportunity to discuss some key questions regarding the role that third parties can play in conflict resolution attempts. The chapter will look at what is meant by third-party intervention; which third parties have (and have not) become involved in the two conflicts and why; what tools they have sought to employ; and how important such intervention has been in the case of Northern Ireland and Sri Lanka.

WHO ARE THIRD PARTIES?

Getting an accurate, all-encompassing definition of third parties in conflict resolution terms is difficult. In essence third parties are state or non-state actors who are not directly parties to the conflict but seek to play a role in its resolution (or in some cases its continuation). Problems arise, however, with the question of what constitutes being a party to the conflict? In the Northern Ireland case, for example, the British government has often sought to portray itself as having a mediating role rather than being a party to the conflict itself, a stance that has been questioned by the (other) parties to the conflict. This also links to the problem over whether it is necessary for third parties to be impartial. Academic opinion is divided over this issue (and indeed what impartiality means).[4] Third parties are rarely universally seen as impartial and, even when they are, they are unlikely to retain this designation once they have been involved in facilitation or mediation for any length of time.

THE ROLE OF THIRD PARTIES

Third-party intervention can take many forms. The most common one is that of mediation. Mediation is, however, a wide term under which many different roles can be placed. (Chris Mitchell, for example, lists a total of fourteen roles for a mediator, which span the three periods he identifies as pre-negotiation, talks or negotiations and post agreement).[5] Mediation is also often portrayed in a somewhat benign and unthreatening light. Jacob Bercovitch claims that mediation

> ...is a voluntary process in which a third party offers nonbinding assistance (in various forms) to the disputants to help them move toward a mutually acceptable agreement. Given the voluntary, noncoercive nature of mediation, and the polarized and entrenched nature of internationalized ethnic conflict, mediation provides, on the face of it, a non-threatening form of transforming, de-escalating, or settling such conflicts.[6]

However, this is too benign a view of the process and suggests a level of autonomy on the part of the conflict participants and benevolence on the part of the mediators that may not always be the case.

The question of where the power of a mediator stems from also needs to be considered. Jeffrey Rubin argues there are six bases of power for a mediator, some of which would not fit under Barcovitch's characterisation of mediation. The six are: reward power; coercive power; expert power; legitimate power (based on legal authority or international law); referent power (result of the relationship between the mediator and the parties to the dispute) and informational power (mediator acts as a message carrier between the disputants).[7] Given the complexities of attempts at conflict resolution and the long timescales involved, most conflicts see a combination of several such sources of mediation power used (as well as several potential third parties seeking to play a role).

WHY DO THIRD PARTIES GET INVOLVED?

Third parties can, then, take the form of states, regional or transnational organisations, groups or individuals. A link can be drawn between the type of third-party actor under discussion, the source of their power and why they get involved. It is abundantly clear that not all conflicts receive equal attention from potential third parties, and that the propensity of actors, particularly states and regional organisations, to get involved in a particular dispute is a result of the interaction of myriad factors and considerations. These may alter over time and increase or decrease the likelihood of future or continued intervention. One such factor is the intensity of the conflict in question. Logically a case can be made for a correlation between the level of violence and the necessity of attempts to resolve it. In reality, though, the link between intensity and intervention is far from clear. Several factors account for this, notably the argument that there is little point in intervening until conditions are ripe, usually indicated by parties perceiving themselves to be in a hurting stalemate.[8] The lack of a direct correlation between a conflict's intensity and the likelihood of third-party intervention is also (perhaps more so) the result of considerations by potential third parties of the possible costs of intervening in an intense and active conflict. These, however, need to be compared to the potential costs to a state or region of not intervening. States may be unwilling to intervene in a conflict if there is a high likelihood that such intervention will result in a loss of life for their armed forces. A marked feature of an escalating conflict is often the emergence of a related refugee problem, which may have implications for the economic prosperity and stability of surrounding states. Intra-state, inter-ethnic conflicts might spread beyond the state's borders and destabilise surrounding states (contagion). Such considerations may increase the likelihood of third-party intervention.

The question of who intervenes is also closely related to how (and why) they intervene. Rubin's observations regarding the sources of power are useful in this regard. One stumbling-block to third-party intervention has traditionally been the potential conflict with issues of sovereignty and perceived incompatibility between uninvited intervention by external third parties and the convention that states do not interfere in the domestic concerns of other sovereign states. In the past this led to the belief in some quarters that mediation had to be at the behest, or at least with the agreement, of the parties to the conflict. This convention has been challenged in recent years and claims made that new international norms have been created in this regard.[9] Cases of third-party intervention against the wishes of the sovereign governments of states have occurred (for example, Kosovo, Iraq, Afghanistan) and are justified in relation to international law and humanitarian considerations (although such assertions are on occasion contested and problematic).

The issue of reward power and coercive power is also related to issues of the resources and inclination of the third parties in question. Questions as to whether power mediators who can use leverage (mediation with muscle) are more likely to be successful in interventions than those who have no leverage and have to rely on other attributes, such as referent and informational power, abound in the literature. The general view is that power mediators are more likely to be effective.

NORTHERN IRELAND AND SRI LANKA

What, then, has been the experience of Northern Ireland and Sri Lanka in terms of third-party intervention? The first question that perhaps needs to be examined is who are the third parties that have sought to intervene in the two cases, and what were their reasons for doing so?

The role of third parties in the Northern Ireland case has been the subject of a lively and useful debate in the academic literature in recent years. A strong case has been made for the important role played by the 'international dimension' in advancing the peace process and seeking to resolve the conflict.[10] The main focus of the debate has been the role of the US[11] (and to a lesser extent the EU[12]). The US played a more visible, and at times it was argued a more critical, role in the Northern Ireland conflict with the advent of Clinton's presidency in 1993. The increased US interest in Northern Ireland seemed to coincide with the emergence of the peace process. A case has been made that the two were not unrelated, and a variety of explanations have been offered as to why the US role appeared to change in the early 1990s. Several of these are tied to the end of the Cold War, which, it was claimed, altered both how the world saw conflicts such as Northern Ireland's and how the participants (in particular the IRA) saw their 'struggle' in relation to wider ideological struggles. The relationship between the US and Britain was also believed to have changed, with the 'special relationship' being perceived by some as less special than before. Mick Cox has argued that the fact that 'it was only in the 1990s, once the Cold War had actually come to an end, that the process reached a successful conclusion' was not a coincidence.[13] The personality of Bill Clinton, his interest in the problem and his determination to play a role in seeking to help resolve it, have also been suggested as important factors.

These interpretations and their importance in explaining the peace process have, however, been challenged. Richard English has questioned the impact of the international dimension on the grounds that factors which were instrumental to the peace process (such as the reconsideration by the IRA of the effectiveness of the 'armed struggle'; the existence of a military stalemate between the IRA and the British; and an increasing awareness by republicans of the importance of addressing the issue of unionists) were a result of 'internal' rather than 'external' forces. According to English, the IRA's strategy was not largely altered by factors related to the ending of the Cold War. English also argues that, given the power imbalance between the US and Britain, the Americans could have intervened over the issue during the Cold War if they had chosen to do so.[14] Paul Dixon has also questioned the importance of the international dimension in the peace process and argued that 'the developments which resulted in the peace process were already underway well before the ending of the Cold War' and that there were marked continuities in British policy which are evident both during and after the Cold War.[15]

It is clear, though, that Clinton played a more active and visible role on the issue than did his predecessors. Under Clinton the issue of Northern Ireland 'entered the US political mainstream'.[16] However, there is an element of 'chicken and egg' over why this was the case. Did this increased interest on the part of the Americans help create a peace process, or did the signs of the emerging peace process lead to an increased interest on the part of the Americans? The US got involved for a variety of reasons: because of Clinton's personal interest and commitments he had made when wooing the Irish vote in 1992; as a chance to develop a new foreign policy in the emerging post-Cold War era[17] and, perhaps most importantly, because he was encouraged to do so, first by Dublin, but increasingly by London. A case can therefore be made that the US was more active on the issue during Clinton's time in office because this coincided with major changes within the political arena in Northern Ireland and that, despite some reluctance on the British side at the start, both London and Dublin came to see the advantages of playing the American 'card', particularly during the Good Friday/Belfast Agreement negotiations. The emergence of an American president who was interested in the issue at the same time as developments within Northern Ireland made progress on the issue possible was fortuitous. Without the latter, though, the former would have had limited impact.

At a more fundamental level, however, it could be argued that whatever the reason the US became more involved in the early 1990s, if its involvement was instrumental in the development and achievements of the peace process, then the case illustrates the potential for successful third-party intervention. An interesting aspect of the intervention that was evident in Northern Ireland is the form it took. Although the US was very much equipped to use both coercive and reward power, it largely limited itself to reward power (or carrots rather than sticks). In general the role played by America was what Will Hazelton has called 'encouragement from the sidelines'.[18] The approach was far closer to the benign one traditionally ascribed to mediators than to the more evident mediation with muscle employed by the American Richard Holbrooke over the Bosnian talks that led to the Dayton Accord. The most visible and perhaps important contribution by the Americans was the role of Senator George Mitchell in chairing the negotiations that led to the Agreement in 1998. Mitchell's approach was the exact opposite of the one adopted by Holbrooke in Bosnia.[19] This raises important question regarding not only the capacity of the third party but also its inclinations and restraints. There was never any suggestion that the US would employ coercive power against Britain in relation to Northern Ireland, and the coercive power that it did employ was primarily directed at the republicans (over issues such as visas and fund-raising activities).

Traditionally the British government has been keen to limit the role of third parties in Northern Ireland, and has taken a firm line against any suggestion that the UN or EU should become involved. The reason for such a stance was the issue of sovereignty and the belief that what was happening in Northern Ireland was not something for the wider international community to adjudicate or mediate upon. The Irish government at times attempted to internationalise the issue when faced with what it saw as Britain's reluctance to grant Dublin a role or consult with it on the conflict.[20] Dublin sought to involve itself in the issue not only because of the professed desire to see Ireland united, but, more importantly, because of the fear that, if unresolved, the situation in Northern Ireland could undermine the stability of the South. To this end the South was more concerned with creating stability within Northern Ireland than with the creation of a united Ireland. London's attitude towards Dublin altered and a formal consultative role was acceded to the Republic of Ireland by Britain with the signing of the Anglo-Irish Agreement (AIA) in 1985. The change of attitude towards the Irish government was a pragmatic one on the part of the British government. Since 1985 and increasingly during the peace process period the British have not only seen themselves as playing a mediating role between the conflicting parties in Northern Ireland but have also acceded a role to the Dublin government in this regard. As a result the British and Irish governments could be characterised as behaving as third-party mediators, albeit internal (and partial) ones in relation to the conflict. At times they acted in a manner which could be fitted into all of the sources of power in Rubin's typology: reward power, entry into the peace process for Sinn Féin after the ceasefire; coercive power, both governments sought to pressurise both republicans and unionists at different times; expert power, the role of British and Irish civil servants in negotiations; legitimate power, as sovereign states Britain and Ireland can legislate for change; referent power, each state's relationship with their co-nationals in Northern Ireland; and informational power, both governments having at times served as a conduit for communication between the conflicting parties. But as noted above, the problem in this regard is in the depiction of Britain and Ireland as third parties to the conflict.

There has also been an economic dimension with the periodic attempt by third parties over the years to offer financial inducements to the sides in conflict. The most obvious example of this was the International Fund for Ireland that was created after the AIA was signed and that received contributions from the US, EU, Canada, Australia and New Zealand. Similarly, at times during the peace process the British and Irish governments used the promise of further financial assistance to try to encourage the restoration of sustainable devolved government (with some apparent success). What is clear, though, is that whilst economic incentives can be useful tools in seeking to entice parties out of conflict, they are unlikely to be adequate tools on their own (as is the case with their related 'stick' of sanctions in conflict situations).

In terms of who the third parties were, the role they played and tools they sought to employ, the situation in Sri Lanka is somewhat different from that of Northern Ireland. In recent years the most high-profile third party seeking to intervene in the conflict has been the Norwegian government. Norway's involvement dates back to 2000, when it was invited by the then President, Chandrika Kumaratunga, to mediate between the government and the LTTE. Why did Norway become involved? Several reasons have been offered. Norway had a track record in third-party intervention, notably with its role in brokering the Oslo Accord. Its lack of a major historical or colonial involvement in Sri Lanka was believed to be an asset. Norway's involvement in development projects in Sri Lanka and the existence of an expatriate community of Tamil refugees in Norway have also been seen as factors that made Norway willing to become involved, and be viewed as an acceptable mediator to both the GOSL and the LTTE.[21] The role of Norway offers examples of both the opportunities and limitations of non power-based mediation. Norway was credited with being instrumental in the brokering of a ceasefire agreement between the GOSL, led by Prime Minister Ranil Wikremesignhe, and the LTTE in 2002. Yet Norway soon suffered from the intense ethnic outbidding that has long been a feature of Sri Lankan politics over the Tamil question[22] and was accused of bias towards the LTTE (illustrating the difficulties for impartial mediators to retain that status). Accusations of bias are a common feature of third-party intervention and relate to the wider debate regarding whether it is better to have partial or impartial mediators (and indeed whether an impartial mediator is possible). In Sri Lanka, however, given the lack of leverage available to the Norwegians, their ability to pressurise either side to alter their position, and indeed their ability to criticise either side, was limited. This, when combined with the intense inter-party and inter-personal rivalry that developed between President Kumaratunga of the Sri Lankan Freedom Party (SLFP) and Prime Minister Wikremesignhe of the United National

Party (UNP), led to Norway's ability to act as a mediator becoming increasingly limited. The President claimed that Norway's actions were undermining the sovereignty of the country, and an aide publicly denounced the Norwegians as 'salmon-eating busybodies'. The power struggle which resulted in November 2003 between the PM and President caused real problems for the peace process and Norway's role as a mediator.[23]

The allegations of bias levied against the Norwegians stemmed in part from Norway's lack of muscle. The Norwegian peace envoy to Sri Lanka, Erik Solheim, noted, 'Remember, Norway has no way of imposing peace in Sri Lanka, we have no marines to send, we are not a military power, we do not even have any meaningful way of putting diplomatic pressure on them. We can only assist them if they so wish.'[24] Norway therefore saw its role as accepting that which was acceptable to the parties to the conflict. Norway, conscious of its lack of leverage, was keen not to take action that was overly critical of either side and which might alienate them from the process. As a result the Norwegians treated the LTTE as the sole spokespersons for Tamils and failed to condemn them for alleged human rights abuses. In some respects, though, they were not remarkable in this regard. The GOSL has periodically appeared to concede a similar status to the LTTE, and there has long been a tradition of not tackling conflict parties on difficult issues in pursuit of the believed greater goal of conflict resolution (including in Northern Ireland). Ultimately this lack of leverage meant that when relations between the parties broke down and violence began again to escalate, Norway's ability to act as a mediator also declined. Although Norway was instrumental in brokering the ceasefire, once it appeared that the parties no longer wished to be assisted, there was little the Norwegians could do but encourage the parties to reconsider, seek to employ moral pressure, and wait.

A very different model of mediation was applied in Sri Lanka by India in the late 1980s. The Indian approach was very much of the mediation with muscle/leverage variety, which ultimately had disastrous consequences for the third party. The role of India in the Sri Lankan conflict is problematic. India, as the dominant regional power, perceived itself as being the regional hegemon and was uneasy about states within what they saw as their sphere of influence taking actions that could be perceived as contrary to India's interests. This view was intensified when Indira Gandhi returned to power in the early 1980s. The opportunity to assert its role as regional hegemon presented itself with the outbreak of the anti-Tamil riots in Sri Lanka in 1983.[25] India's interest in Sri Lanka is not of course simply a reflection of its regional status, but is complicated by the issue of Tamil Nadu and Indian support for the plight of Sri Lankan Tamils in the north and east of the country and the Indian/Estate Tamils, who are largely based in the hill country, tea-producing region. The proximity of some sixty million Tamils in the South of India has led to the majority Sinhalese community in Sri Lanka being described as a majority with a minority complex. As a result the issue of Indian involvement in the conflict has long been problematic for the Sinhalese and the Sri Lankan government. However, the 1983 riots led to pressure from the regional government of Tamil Nadu on Indira Gandhi to intervene and, given the influx of refugees from Sri Lanka to India (eventually totalling 1,250,000), a case could be made that India had a legitimate interest in the issue.

Whilst there is sympathy in Indian government circles with the plight of the Tamils, and Tamil rebel groups have historically used southern India for training purposes, there is no support for the stated objective of Tamil nationalism in Sri Lanka, the creation of the independent state of Tamil Eelam. India has consistently asserted its wishes to see the territorial integrity of the Sri Lankan state maintained. The main reason for this lies in fears that the creation of a Tamil nation in Sri Lanka may increase demands from Tamil separatists within India itself. This has led India to seek to act as a supporter and protector of Tamil interests but to prevent them achieving their objective. This resulted in the disastrous Indian intervention in the north and east of Sri Lanka in 1987. When the LTTE escalation of violence in 1987 led to an increased military push by Sri Lankan forces into the Jaffna peninsula in the north of Sri Lanka, India acted in support of the LTTE in Jaffna. The Indo-Sri Lankan accord of 1987 led to the deployment of Indian troops (the Indian Peace Keeping Force, IPKF). At its height the IPKF had around 100,000 troops in Sri Lanka (more than the British contingent in India under the Raj).[26] There was a fundamental misreading by India of the likely attitude of the LTTE to their intervention. India found itself in a disastrous conflict with the LTTE and lost over 1,000 soldiers before withdrawing in 1990 (with some arguing the LTTE was actually stronger than before the IPKF arrived[27]). Perhaps somewhat unsurprisingly since these events, and the assassination of Rajiv Gandhi in 1991, widely believed to have been the work of the LTTE, India has been reluctant to play a major role in the conflict.

The Indian intervention was also disastrous for the GOSL given the violent backlash that the Indian presence in Sri Lanka provoked amongst elements of Sinhalese nationalism, led by the Janatha Vimukthi Peramuna (JVP). A further 1,000 people were killed during the insurrection. (UNP politicians were targeted, resulting in the death of a cabinet minister, district minister, party chairman and secretary. President Jayewardene himself narrowly escaped assassination.)[28]

A further potential third-party in the case is the British government. In April 1997 Foreign Secretary Malcolm Rifkind and his deputy, Liam Fox, urged the Sri Lankan parties to adopt a bipartisan approach to the problem, citing the British experience in Northern Ireland.[29] This approach came to little, but interestingly in the most recent period there has been renewed input from Britain. During his trip to Sri Lanka in November 2006 Britain's 'special envoy', Paul Murphy, argued: 'Ten years ago, people didn't think that the Northern Ireland conflict could be resolved. But it has happened through political negotiations. There are similar hopes and prayers for a political solution in Sri Lanka.' Murphy claimed that Tony Blair had sent him 'to give our experiences in Northern Ireland where I was Secretary of State for many years to see if people in Sri Lanka can learn from our experiences'.[30] In February 2007 Foreign Office Minister Kim Howells went to Sri Lanka and again drew parallels with Northern Ireland. (Interestingly, Howells was accompanied by the head of the British–Irish Intergovernmental Council.) Howells indicated that Britain was willing to play a larger role in the conflict, and some suggested that it should effectively replace Norway as the mediator.[31] (Sinn Féin's Martin McGuinness also visited Sri Lanka twice in 2006 to meet GOSL and LTTE representatives, drew parallels with the situation in Northern Ireland, and offered to play a continuing role in its peace process.[32])

EVALUATING THE EFFECTIVENESS AND LIMITATIONS OF THIRD PARTIES

What, if any, lessons can we draw from the two cases regarding third-party intervention and its role in conflict resolution? As noted above, there are more differences than similarities between the conflicts and these can illustrate the factors that limit the scope for, and inclination of, third parties to become involved.

One major difference is the role that ethnic outbidding plays in the conflicts. Britain and Ireland have been freer in this regard than the Sri Lankan parties. Given the lack of electoral saliency that Northern Ireland has, particularly in UK elections outside Northern Ireland, British governments have had greater autonomy in acting over Northern Ireland than Sri Lankan governments have had in seeking to resolve their conflict. Bipartisanship in Britain towards the issue of Northern Ireland has meant that governments have generally received wide support in Westminster for initiatives (or at least little opposition). As Neil de Votta has shown, ethnic outbidding has long been a feature of Sinhalese politics, and this severely limits the opportunities for Sri

Lankan governments to make the types of concessions that are necessary to have a functioning peace process.[33] Every attempt by Sri Lankan
governments to reach an accommodation with the Tamils has led to
accusations from the other major parties that they are embarked upon
a path that will undermine the unity and stability of the state. Whilst
this remains the case it is likely to be a severe limitation for both third-
parties and Sri Lankan governments attempts to resolve the conflict.

In the Northern Ireland case, although the conflict did attract some
attention from the major powers, notably the US, the international
community as reluctant to get overly involved or to criticise or pressurise Britain to any great extent. Several reasons account for this.
There was generally an acceptance by the international community of
the legitimacy of British sovereignty over Northern Ireland and a belief
that the form of government being exercised in Northern Ireland was
acceptable (if not perfect). Importantly, Britain also appeared to be taking steps to resolve the issue. Such international criticism as there was
towards Britain was somewhat reduced once Dublin was conceded a
consultative role in 1985. Britain was also a key ally of the US and a
member of the European Community for the period of the conflict in
Northern Ireland, which may also have served as a check on overt and
(from a British perspective) unwelcome third-party intervention. It is
interesting that external third parties played a greater role in the conflict not when it was at its height but when it appeared to be moving
towards resolution. Issues such as the status of the sovereign power in
a conflict, its relationship to possible intervening third powers and the
stage that the conflict is at in the conflict cycle may impact on the likelihood of intervention.

The Sri Lankan experience, by contrast, offers a different case study.
It demonstrates that even comparatively bloody conflicts can fail to
attract concerted international attention. Why has the situation not
attracted a greater and more proactive interest from major potential
third parties? In part this may be because 'the norm of territorial
integrity makes the international community generally hostile to the
political division of islands'.[34] But the lack of third-party intervention is
also a reflection of the comparative insularity of the Sri Lankan situation and its lack of wider geo-strategic significance (a factor it shares
with Northern Ireland). The major powers such as the US and indeed
the UN[35] have been happy to leave the conflict to mediators such as
Norway and the regional hegemon, India. Former US ambassador to
Sri Lanka, Teresita C. Schafer, told a conference on the international
dimension of the Sri Lankan conflict in Colombo in 2005 that, given the
US's commitments in Iraq, the US was unwilling to become involved in
any more intractable conflicts, but would play a supporting role.[36]

This is not to suggest that the international community has completely ignored the Sri Lankan conflict. As we have seen, Norway has played an active role in recent years in seeking to mediate, and India was directly involved militarily in the 1980s. These interventions aside, the major tools that have been invoked by the international community have been financial. There has been a good deal of financial assistance given to Sri Lanka, primarily by the four main donors – Japan, Norway, the US and the EU. However, attempts to link aid to advances in the peace process have not so far been successful. Concerns in the US and UK over actions taken by the GOSL against the LTTE and wider Tamil community led the two governments to suspend part of their aid package in 2007. The international community appears to be growing frustrated with both the Sri Lankan government of President Rajapaksa, elected in 2005, which is accused of seeking to pursue a hard-line, militaristic approach to the conflict, and with the conflict itself. As one foreign diplomat reportedly said, 'At a certain point in time, you give up on Sri Lanka.'[37] Yet such international pressure and criticism does not appear likely to force a change in approach in Colombo. The Sri Lankan Defence Secretary (and president's brother), Gotabaya Rajapaksa, claimed: 'This is discrimination and bullying by the international community... Without understanding the problem, they are trying to bully us, and we won't be isolated. We have all the SAARC countries, the Asian countries ... Britain or Western countries, EU countries, they can do whatever. We don't depend on them.'[38]

The Sri Lankan case also illustrates that neither mediators with leverage/muscle nor those without will necessarily achieve success. Both approaches when employed in Sri Lanka appeared, in the early stages, to offer hope of a breakthrough, but both failed to achieve a resolution or transformation of the conflict.

CONCLUSION

Whilst it is clear that third parties can perform a useful role in conflict resolution initiatives, as evidenced by the support offered by the US in Northern Ireland since the early 1990s and the successes of the Norwegians in the early period of their involvement in Sri Lanka, we must be careful not to overstate their importance or likely impact. Northern Ireland's peace process has been more successful than Sri Lanka's not because of more intensive or better third-party intervention but because of a number of (primarily domestic) developments in the 1990s. Sri Lanka's conflict appears to remain intractable, not because of the failure of third parties to intervene to a greater degree, but because of mistrust, the continuing quest for a military victory on both sides and the pursuit of incompatible objectives over which the main protagonists in Sri Lanka will not compromise.

Both cases suggest that the role third parties play in conflicts is influenced by the attitudes and objectives of the third parties themselves, whether they believe that conditions are conducive to such intervention, and issues such as the intensity and geo-strategic importance of the area in question. Similarly, what tools third parties seek to employ, and how successful they will be, will differ from conflict to conflict. Coercive power may work in one situation but worsen another; the difficulty is in knowing which sources of power to utilise and when. In both the Northern Ireland and Sri Lankan conflicts domestic factors hold the key to the solution. The wider international community can play an important role in attempting to facilitate change but cannot itself resolve such conflicts.

NOTES

1. Ramsbotham, O., Woodhouse, T. and Miall, H., *Contemporary Conflict Resolution*, second edition (Cambridge: Polity Press, 2006), p. 64.
2. *The Hindu*, 17 November 2006. Archived at: http://www.thehindu.com/2006/11/17/stories/2006111718961400.htm.
3. See, for example, Amnesty International's report of 2007. Archived at: http://thereport.amnesty.org/eng/Regions/Asia-Pacific/Sri-Lanka.
4. Ramsbotham et al., *Contemporary Conflict Resolution*, p. 279.
5. Mitchell, C., 'Mediation and Ending Conflicts', in J. Darby and R. MacGinty (eds), *Contemporary Peace Making* (Basingstoke: Palgrave Macmillan, 2003), pp. 77–86.
6. Bercovitch, J., 'Managing Internationalized Ethnic Conflict: Evaluating the Role and Relevance of Mediation', *World Affairs*, 166 (2003), p. 61.
7. Discussed in Siniver, A., 'Power, Impartiality and Timing: Three Hypotheses on Third Party Mediation in the Middle East', *Political Studies*, 54, 4 (2006), pp. 806–26.
8. Zartman, I.W.,'The Timing of Peace Initiatives: Hurting Stalemates and Ripe Moments', in Darby and MacGinty, *Contemporary Peace Making*, pp. 19–29; and O'Kane, E., 'When Can Conflicts be Resolved? A Critique of Ripeness', *Civil Wars* 18, 2–3 (2006), pp. 268–84.
9. Wheeler, N.J. and Bellamy, A.J., 'Humanitarian Intervention and World Politics', in J. Baylis and S. Smith, *The Globalization of World Politics*, third edition (Oxford: Oxford University Press, 2004), pp. 391–408.
10. See Cox, M., 'Bringing in the "International": The IRA Ceasefire and the End of the Cold War', *International Affairs*, 73, 4 (1997), pp. 671–93; Cox, M.,'Rethinking the International and Northern Ireland: A Defence', in M. Cox, A. Guelke and F. Stephen (eds), *A Farewell to Arms? Beyond the Good Friday Agreement*, second edition (Manchester: Manchester University Press, 2006), pp. 427–42; Guelke, A., *Northern Ireland: The International Perspective* (Dublin: Gill and Macmillan, 1988).
11. See O'Clery, C., *The Greening of the White House* (Dublin: Gill and Macmillan, 1996) and Holland, J. *The American Connection*, second edition (Maryland: Roberts Rinehart Publishers, 2001).
12. Meehan, E., 'Europe and the Europeanisation of the Irish Question', in Cox et al., *A Farewell to* Arms, pp. 338–56.
13. Cox, 'Rethinking the International and Northern Ireland: A Defence', p. 430.
14. English, R., *Armed Struggle: A History of the IRA* (London: Pan Macmillan, 2004), pp. 303–12.
15. Dixon, P., 'Rethinking the International in Northern Ireland: A Critique', in Cox et al, *A Farewell to Arms*, pp. 415-16.

16. Holland, *The American Connection*, p. 237.
17. Hazelton, W., 'Encouragement from the Sideline: Clinton's Role in the Good Friday Agreement', *Irish Studies in International Affairs*, 11 (2000), pp. 104–17.
18. Ibid.
19. See Wallensteen, P., *Understanding Conflict Resolution*, second edition (London: Sage, 2007), pp. 269–72.
20. See O'Kane, E., 'The Republic of Ireland's Policy towards Northern Ireland: The International dimension as a policy tool', *Irish Studies in International Affairs*, 13 (2002), pp.121–133.
21. Moolakkattu, J.S., 'Peace Facilitation by Small States: Norway in Sri Lanka', *Cooperation and Conflict*, 40, 4 (2005), pp. 385–402.
22. de Votta, N., 'From Ethnic Outbidding to Ethnic Conflict: The Institutional Bases for Sri Lanka's Separatist War', *Nations and Nationalism*, 11, 1 (2005), pp. 141–59.
23. Martin, H., *Kings of Peace, Pawns of War* (London: Continuum, 2006), pp. 116–17.
24. Ibid., p. 104.
25. de Silva, K.M., *Regional Powers and Small State Security: India and Sri Lanka* (New Delhi: Vikas, 1996), p. 99.
26. de Silva, K.M., *Reaping the Whirlwind* (London: Penguin Books, 1998), p. 244.
27. Wickramasinghe, N., *Sri Lanka in the Modern Age* (London: Hurst, 2006), p. 292.
28. de Silva, *Reaping the Whirlwind*, p. 238.
29. Dixon, P., 'Sri Lanka and Bipartisanship: Lessons from Northern Ireland?' *Association for the Study of Ethnicity and Nationalism Bulletin*, 16 (1999), pp. 26–8.
30. *International Herald Tribune*, 16 November 2006; *Tamilnet*, 16 November 2006. Archived at: http://www.tamilnet.com/art.html?catid=13&artid=20299.
31. *Tamil Guardian*, 24 February 2007. Archived at: http://www.tamilguardian.com/article.asp?articleid=1119.
32. See *Irish Times*, 26 January 2006 and *Belfast Telegraph* 5 July 2006.
33. de Votta, 'From Ethnic Outbidding to Ethnic Conflict'.
34. Guelke, A., 'Northern Ireland and Island Status', in J. McGarry (ed.), *Northern Ireland and the Divided World* (Oxford: Oxford University Press, 2001), p. 228.
35. Sri Lanka is characterised by Wallensteen as one of the UN's 'most forgotten conflicts'. Wallensteen, *Understanding Conflict Resolution*, p. 232.
36. Centre For Policy Alternatives. Report archived at: http://www.cpalanka.org/research_papers/International_Community_Final_Report.doc.
37. Reuters, 3 June 2007. Archived at: http://www.reuters.com/article/latestCrisis/idUSCOL242540.
38. Reuters, 12 June 2007. Archived at: http://www.reuters.com/article/featuredCrisis/id USCOL58218.

Index